CHANNEL REVOLUTION
Stefan Utzinger

CHANNEL REVOLUTION

A pragmatic guide to building and maintaining a profitable channel

Stefan Utzinger

Editorial Team
Tatjana Dems, Christine Frank, Elena Stieben, Wendy Wilkins

Second edition: January 2011

ISBN 978-1-4467-2350-0

Contents

Introduction

If the following situation sounds familiar, then this book is for you: You've started building a partner network ("the channel") and things seem to be going really well. Lots of partners have signed up and you've presented your product in numerous workshops. And then … NOTHING happens. Hardly any of the partners are achieving the promised revenues, you're getting negative feedback from end users and the number of partners promoting your product is shrinking day by day. Luckily, this isn't the end of the world and there is a solution to this fairly typical problem. This book should help you find it.

I've been in the IT industry for nearly 20 years now and I thought it might be worthwhile to share my experience and lessons learned (more often than not the hard way). The industry has undergone tremendous change, especially in the last few years, but there is more to come. Just think about the impact of Software as a Service business models. This book should help you (and here I'm referring to software manufacturers mainly) avoid some disappointments, fallbacks and fruitless investments. If you are working with the channel or want to start building a partner network, this guide will help you define the right strategy, select the right partners and motivate them to sell your products. If you're actually a reseller, this book may be useful to gain insight into the thinking of an independent software vendor and help you understand what you can expect from them.

Of course this book isn't a blueprint for successfully establishing an indirect sales channel. But I'm convinced that if you follow some of my recommendations, it'll pay off. By the way, the book is full of examples and calculations. These can be downloaded at www.channel-revolution.com. You're welcome to use the spreadsheets to come up with your own models.

Part I and II of the book take stock of the channel business and provide insight into the different business models of channel partners and how these affect an independent software vendor's revenue calculations. You'll soon get the idea that things are changing rapidly and the world is becoming much more complex. That's why I think it's time to take a "revolutionary" channel approach, as described in part III. Finally, part IV focuses on execution, how to actually get it done.

One of my favorite sayings is: "You get what you PLAN for." Being successful is about analyzing situations, making decisions, developing clear strategies and executing them. It's not about making things up as you go along.

I hope you'll enjoy reading this book and come across a few new ideas, helpful recommendations and useful tools. I'm very interested in getting your feedback, so please don't hesitate to get in touch with me through LinkedIn or XING.

Stefan Utzinger

Part I: Channel Evolution

My father said: "You must never try to make all the money that's in a deal. Let the other fellow make some money too, because if you have a reputation for always making all the money, you won't have many deals."

Jean Paul Getty

The World Trade Organization estimates that 75% of all goods sold worldwide flow through various indirect channels.[1] Up to 50 million businesses worldwide resell goods. Without the existence of trade between individuals and nations it would not be possible for the development of personal wealth to be where it is today, nor the cultural development of human society.

Surprisingly, most literature ignores the fact that trade is mostly carried out through middlemen and that for almost every product there exists a specific channel. You'll find thousands of books about sales methods, but only very few talk about the channel. Therefore, it's hardly surprising that there are still many senior managers in organizations who think that their company can grow without building a reliable channel. These executives are reluctant to give margins to the channel or support their channel partners, since that would mean sharing the wealth created. Whenever possible, they'll push their sales teams to deal directly and compete with their own channel partners. Something these executives have failed to understand is that there isn't a single major international IT company left that sells its products without using a network of resellers.

Even companies like Dell, who for many years were very successful without using the channel, were forced to change their strategy drastically and started building a channel. It became imperative for Dell to make this dramatic change after losing market leadership to competitors with strong channels. An important lesson from this

---

[1] World Trade Organization www.wto.org

example is that it's not the best product that wins, but in the long run, the company with the best channel comes out ahead. There is a second lesson here as well. Dell also lost its market leadership because they simply lost track of innovation. Because of their sales strategy, they didn't understand their need for innovation. Without channel partners and their feedback, Dell had become disconnected from the market.

Working with the channel can provide you with valuable feedback on market trends and requirements. The channel is not only necessary for selling products, but often more importantly, the channel is the only way to generate ideas about what the consumers, end users and companies really need.

A (Brief) History of Trade

Trade, which defines the process of manufacturers selling their products through different middlemen to the end customer, is an essential driver for innovation.

The history of trade begins with the establishment of the earliest human societies. The first long distance commerce is dated as far back as 150,000 years ago, proving that trade took place throughout all of recorded human history.[2] Long-range trade routes began to appear in the 3rd millennium BC in Mesopotamia. Later on, the Phoenicians, who were noted sea traders, traded across the entire span of the Mediterranean Sea. They established colonies and created an unbelievable wealth from their trading activities. They acquired not only money from their ventures but new ideas, and eventually political systems, also became established because of trade.

The development of nations can be measured by the availability of technology. One of the first important technological developments for humans was the process of iron smelting. This technology first

[2] Peter Watson, "Ideas: A History of Thought and Invention, from Fire to Freud", Harper Collins (2005)

emerged in Asia around 1500 BC and began spreading around the world no more than one hundred years later. The ability to smelt iron enabled people to build weapons and agricultural tools - it represented an enormous step in the development of mankind. The improvement of agricultural tools resulted in an increase of productivity which then led to a surplus of food. The surplus created a flow-on effect which generated additional demand for other goods such as clothing, jewelry and better housing. The result of all of this was that it led to stronger economic development in general. The impact of iron smelting can be seen in relation to Maslow's famous "hierarchy of needs" which states that food comes first. If people's bellies aren't full, they won't start thinking about making innovations.[3]

With the innovation of iron smelting, people were also able to build better ships and sail longer distances to source what they needed (including new partners to work with). The increase of trade and colonization also led to a reorganization of political systems. Political stability and clear rules were required to make long-distance trading more secure. The growing demand for new materials, different foods and tools, along with the development of long-distance trade routes such as the Silk Route and the shipping lanes of the Mediterranean seas, motivated people to begin travelling the known world.

The fall of the Roman Empire had a horrible impact on the trading networks. Trading suddenly became too dangerous and too difficult and most of the established networks collapsed. This led to a period of instability, plagued with death, disease and poverty. The Dark Ages represented a huge step backward in the development of human society. It took hundreds of years to regain the wealth and knowledge lost at the fall of the Roman Empire and to reach a similar level of culture and civilization.

Of course, I could provide a lot more details on the history of trade, but this brief overview already makes it very clear that the success-

---

[3] http://en.wikipedia.org/wiki/Maslow's_hierarchy_of_needs (2010)

ful expansion of trade was inextricably linked to the existence of brave middlemen who travelled the world and served as the link between buyer and seller.

Readers who are interested in exploring this topic further should take a look at Peter Watson's insightful book titled "A History of Thought and Invention, from Fire to Freud".[4]

I made this short diversion into the history of trade to reinforce the view that channels have existed as long as people have traded goods. The cost of making sales directly from a manufacturer to an end user has always been too high or the process itself has simply been virtually impossible. Very often, the best way to reach the end user is to utilize a variety of vendors to play different roles in the process.

The Global IT Market

The worldwide Information and Communication Technology (ICT) market is worth approximately €2 trillion (almost US$2.6 trillion, that's US$2,600,000 million). Even though more than half of this is related to telecommunications, the software and IT service market makes up a very substantial portion. Software accounts for approximately 11% (US$290 billion) of the market share and IT services for approximately 21% (US$550 billion).[5]

From a regional perspective, Europe, the US and Japan are by far the biggest markets. Within Europe, however, Germany represents approximately 21% of the market, closely followed by the UK.

---

[4] Peter Watson, "Ideas: A History of Thought and Invention, from Fire to Freud", Harper Collins (2005)
[5] Based on research from EITO (European Information Technology Observatory) (2007)

Worldwide Information and Communication Technology Market (2007)

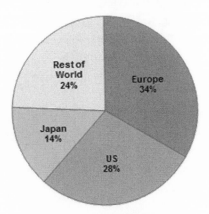

Total Value = € 2,033 billion

For many software vendors, especially smaller companies and startups, it's nearly impossible to access even a small piece of this market without the support of established market players. But most independent software vendors (ISVs) need to address a larger and international market so they can cover their R&D, sales and marketing costs. As you will see in the next chapter, hundreds of thousands of potential channels exist to help you sell to a much larger share of the market than you could cover on your own.

	2006 Value*	2005 %	2006 %	2007 %
Europe**	680	33.9	33.4	33.1
US	574	28.1	28.3	28.4
Japan	286	14.5	14.1	13.7
RoW***	492	23.5	24.4	24.8
Total	2,033	100.0	100.0	100.0

Note: * Value in € billion
    ** Europe includes the EU, Norway and Switzerland
    *** RoW = Rest of World
Source: EITO (European Information Technology Observatory), 2007

The Structure of the IT Channel

I know from experience that the general structure of the global IT channel is very similar to the specific structure of the German channel. This is also confirmed by research from leading analysts in other countries. I've therefore based many of the following global projections on the latest research data from the German market.

International Data Group (IDG), the world's leading technology media and research company, has published studies of the IT channel in Germany that support my claim that it is virtually impossible to become highly successful without a working channel or strategic partnerships with other vendors.[6]

Studies show that 65% of the decisions made by end users concerning technology purchases are influenced by resellers' recommendations.[7] This number rises when it comes to deciding upon more complex solutions such as when software must be configured to the special needs of the customer or implemented in a more complex environment. End users also tend to work with their preferred local channel partners such as resellers or system integrators. There exists a large variety of different types of channel partners in the current market. I'll define their respective roles in the IT channel later.

If you observe the real global players closely, you'll see that every major software vendor has a large reseller base and invests great effort in maintaining this base. Microsoft has around 415,000 partners worldwide and collectively they represent more than 80% of Microsoft's business which amounts to over US$60 billion. Symantec uses around 60,000 resellers in order to gain access to a broader audience for their products.[8] Each of these channel partners knows

---

[6] IDG Business Media GmbH, Munich, "ITK-Fachhandel" study (2009)
[7] www.channeltracks.de (Computer Reseller News, Germany)
[8] Maxine Cheung, "Symantec encourages partners to look at services," *Computerworld* (2007)

the mindset of the customers in their region, giving them a big advantage when it comes to the end user's decision making process.

The combined number of IT resellers that are registered with leading German distributors such as Ingram Micro, TechData or Actebis Peacock approximates 40,000. Since Germany represents approximately 6.5% of the worldwide IT market, we can make the rough assumption that there are an estimated total of 600,000 IT resellers worldwide.

In addition to this large number of registered resellers there are also many individuals who resell software or provide IT services as a side business or on a freelance basis. IT resellers, registered and unregistered, represent around 40% of the total number of technology companies in the market. System integrators, consulting partners and value added resellers (VARs) together represent about 50% of the market (approximately 750,000 companies). The remaining 10% are hardware and software vendors, distributors and other IT related companies.

All of the above mentioned groups represent the pool of potential channel partners for a software manufacturer. If you consider these numbers, there are about 1.5 million technology companies that serve the worldwide market (assuming the roles of various reseller types). Microsoft's soaring number of resellers has given them an extraordinary presence in the market and has created an almost automatic demand for their software while providing them with a steady stream of helpful feedback.

It's interesting to note that more than 60% of the resellers in the above categories employ less than 10 employees. Around 40% of them make less than US$0.5 million in revenue per year. Another 20% employ less than 50 employees and have annual revenues under US$2.5million. You'll also notice a high turnover in this market segment - companies tend to come and go a lot.

To succeed in this market, you have to decide which types of re-sellers you want to target. Ask yourself these questions: How can you build up a group of successful channel partners, and how can you maintain them? Does your enterprise generate enough revenue to create a sustainable business for you and your resellers? Keep in mind that there's a potential pool of around 420,000 partners in the US and 500,000 partners in Europe. There are close to 100,000 partners each in Germany and the UK alone. Which of these re-sellers will bring you the revenue and not just cost you time and money? In order to answer these questions, it's important to under-stand the different roles of the resellers and how the channel really works. That's what Part II of this book will focus on.

Part II: Channel Reach and Revenue

The important thing is not to stop questioning.

Albert Einstein

"Build it and they will come," worked well in the movie "Field Of Dreams". Kevin Costner turned a cornfield into a ballpark and they (the players) came. But hey, we're talking about a Hollywood movie here. In the real world, it's just not that easy.

The IT industry is defined by a fairly unique cost structure. This applies particularly to manufacturers of standard software (ISVs). In almost every industry, it's necessary to make an initial investment to develop a product. In the ISV's case, this initial investment is mainly made up of labor costs and is relatively high; while the product life cycle is often very short.

In addition to these initial costs, a significant portion of recurring expenses for each time period does not depend on the number of products manufactured or sold, so these costs are independent of scope. In order to finance such fixed periodic expenses, the company needs to achieve a certain minimum level of sales. The variable costs for each additional unit sold are very low, especially now in the "online era" where software and documentation are "shipped" over the internet. The level of sales where the total contribution margin from the company's operations equals its fixed costs is known as the famous and much referred to break-even point. Most companies that produce software or other information goods (e.g. downloadable music or movies) are characterized by similarly low marginal production cost structures.[9]

---

[9] Jennifer A. Rivers, "Cost Structure Analysis and Forecasting," www.earticles.info (2007)

To understand why the channel is so important in the IT industry, especially for ISVs, we need to understand the relationship between the various costs associated with building, maintaining and selling the product and the company's business volume. Every sophisticated software product requires a certain amount of manpower in order to be developed and maintained. These resources are required regardless if there are sales being made in the early stages or if the product is still in the development stage where only tests can be conducted with dedicated customers. During this phase, the ISV must also make further investment into its marketing and sales in order to prepare for market entry and place itself in the right position for generating future sales.

Before we dive deeper into the math I want to make it crystal clear that I firmly believe that the channel is THE ONLY WAY to achieve global market penetration. But (yes there's always a but) I'll also tell you that there's no better way to burn a lot of money in a very short time than by using the channel incorrectly. It's absolutely critical to develop a solid strategy.

I'd like to use a practical example[10] to illustrate how using the channel impacts the revenues and the number of products an ISV has to sell. A software company, let's call it "StartUp3000" has a development team of 10 engineers. They also have 10 people in support, professional services, marketing, administration and sales. The average cost for the staff is US$100,000 p.a. and labor represents 80% of the total business costs. This all adds up to total operations cost of US$2.5 million per year.

StartUp 3000's product is sold for US$20 per unit. Each additional unit does not incur further expense since the product is delivered via the internet and all documentation is made available in digital form only. In other words, the company earns revenue of US$2 million for every 100,000 units. Therefore the company needs to sell products to the value of US$7.5 million just to reach the break-

---

[10] This simple example ignores the fact that the company has a history or any other income sources.

even point in three years. So in a direct sales approach, based on the price of US$20 per copy, StartUp 3000 would have to sell and support 375,000 copies in the first three years.

Management realizes this is unrealistic, so, in order to sell the necessary number of licenses, the company decides to implement a channel. One of the main challenges that they will face though is that the channel can reduce the profit margin per sale dramatically. Depending on which channel the company uses, the number of licenses the company needs to distribute could grow by 50% or more. Let's assume they choose two channel partners that both receive US$8 per copy sold (so StartUp 3000 earns US$12 per unit). This means, in order to recover costs of US$7.5 million in three years, StartUp 3000 would now have to sell 625,000 units, an increase of 66% versus the direct sales approach.

So the channel clearly has its costs. That's why it's so important to think about when to start working with the channel and which business model to use. The next chapters will focus on topics such as product life cycle, the economic framework of the channel, and various channel models. The key question we'll have to answer is: How do I select the right channel partners and work with them efficiently?

Don't lose sight of the fact that both you AND your channel partners need to profit from the partnership. Don't view the channel as a one way street!

The Product Life Cycle

It's absolutely critical for your channel approach to understand where your product is in the "product life cycle". I've seen many companies develop a new product and then fail miserably when they tried to sell it using the channel. The main reason for their failure was that their product wasn't actually ready. In addition to this, they didn't have a strong brand or customer following. So let's see where your product should be in the life cycle when you want to introduce it to the channel.

The original concept of the product life cycle (PLC) is based on the biological life cycle. For example, a seed is planted (introduction); it begins to sprout (growth); it shoots leaves and grows roots as it becomes an adult (maturity); and after a period as an adult the plant begins to shrink and dies (decline).[11]

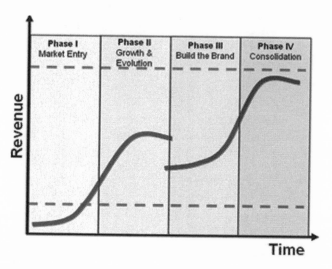

In order to apply the PLC to a technology product, I've modified the concept to address a "technology life cycle." The graph shows that a technology product passes through four specific phases: market entry, growth & evolution, build the brand, and consolidation. Each phase is described in more detail below. Please note that I'm talking about a new product, not a new company. So imagine you're an existing ISV and just finished developing a new product.

The drama of the (too) early market entry

Phase I is defined as "market entry." After a period of development, the product is introduced or launched into the market. In the beginning, the sales are low and the costs are high. There is also a

---

[11] See www.marketingteacher.com/Lessons/lesson_plc.htm (2009)

lot of investment associated with launching the product successfully. The main goal during this phase is to make customers aware of your company, your product and its benefits. You also want to prove that you can attract customers and generate reference cases. Companies have to act fast here because in this phase more and more market players will take note of the innovation, competitors become alerted to the benefits and may start to develop competitive products.

It's important to note that during this phase a product can usually only be sold by its developer - which is you. As long as the solution has not been proven in the market and components such as documentation, functionality, use cases and references are missing, introduction to the channel will be counterproductive. Even experienced companies have been known to ignore this important fact.

Introducing new, not yet finalized products while they are still in this early phase and have no prior market experience will burn the ISV's most successful existing channel partners.

I recommend a different way of working with the channel during this vulnerable phase. Why not build a beta group with some loyal channel partners, thus enabling you to start some first projects with reference customers? If the channel partner and the end user are both aware that the product is in an early stage you can learn a lot from them and even give them the chance to add necessary functionalities to the product. At the same time, you prevent disappointment and loss of credibility, because you're not claiming that the product is final.

How to work with partners on product growth & evolution

Before you enter the next phase, you need to have your marketing, sales and support teams in place. You'll also need to be sure that your R&D team has the resources to fix bugs quickly and deal with missing functionalities. During the "growth & evolution" phase, your product will become more mature and hopefully win more and more customers. Revenues achieved with the product should grow rapidly as more customers and channel partners become aware of the product and its benefits. Using customer feedback, you will be able to improve the product. During this stage, you should establish a web presence for the product and ensure the availability of documentation, use cases and first customer references. Once you've reached this state, you can begin to target new market segments.

As mentioned earlier, it's possible that during this stage some competitors - having heard about your new product - will start to develop similar products. Even if these competitors are bigger than you and have a stronger market presence, it's actually possible to transform their market entry into a competitive advantage - as long as you act smart and fast. It can even help you build the channel because you won't be the only one talking about the benefits of your product. So don't panic when there's competition.

During the growth & evolution phase, the product will ideally prove its success as a solution and public awareness will increase. This means that customers should start asking for the product.

While until now you've only involved the channel as beta group or in other non-sales related roles, now is the time to shift from a purely direct sales model to broader distribution including channel partners. The smartest approach is to begin working with your best channel partners and give them the necessary support to ensure their success.

At the end of this phase, you may see even more competitors introducing similar products to the market. Make sure you have dedicated resources in place for disarming these competitors. For example, you can counter their actions by introducing a new, more mature, version of the product and expanding its distribution through the channel.

A key success factor during this phase is to work together with your channel partners to generate market feedback. Find out how the channel partners and end users use your product. Then you can begin the next stage of development that is based on "real world" use cases. It's also important that you learn how your channel partners make money with the product. Are they just reselling it or are they also implementing the software? You should also find out if they are combining your product with other products. If they are, then try to work with these other manufacturers to add more value to your combined channel partner base.

Let the channel help you build a brand

"Build the brand" is about using your experience to position yourself as THE market leader in defined market segments as well as introducing the product to a broad range of channel partners. During this phase of the broad channel roll-out, which is normally significantly longer than the other phases, costs per unit can be reduced in many ways. Not only can R&D costs be divided among a larger number of products sold, but you'll benefit from moving up the learning curve effects as the whole sales and implementation process becomes more mature and thus faster.[12] The larger the number of successful installations, the better your marketing material will be, and you will have great product documentation and technical support.

Engaging a variety of channel partners, you should now begin creating solutions for different market segments and differentiate your pricing so it's relevant to these specific segments. There are a number of ways you can approach this; you can build solutions with your channel partners as joint developments of vertical modules, combine your solutions with existing products or use their special implementation skills to create more value for the end user.

In this phase you might need to react to a drop of pricing due to the emergence of competing products that have similar functionalities. By working together with your channel partners, you should be able

---

[12] Michael E. McGrath, Product strategy for high technology companies: accelerating your business, McGraw-Hill (2000)

to create value so that end customers will still accept a higher price for your brand. This is when you can begin selling business solutions and not just software products alone. The progress from software product to business solution will not only increase the value of your product but will also increase the market entry barrier for other "cheap" ISVs who often just copy ideas from innovative vendors.

Be prepared for consolidation

The last phase in the PLC is "consolidation." No technology company can avoid this phase which entails market saturation and an ultimately declining market interest in the core product. If you want to be clever, you should anticipate this development and prepare for it in the prior phases by positioning your product as a complete solution. Successful companies with long product life cycles such as Microsoft with their Office product line, Oracle with their database products or SAP with their ERP solutions all utilize the early phases of the product life cycle in order to position their product not only as a product, but as a part of the customer's complete solution.

As a technology company you can successfully prepare for this phase of consolidation. You have to use the first three phases of the product life cycle to build your brand, the channel network and to position your product as a valuable solution. If you demonstrate how you've added features requested by channel partners and end users and how you've reengineered the product over time, your customers and channel partners will respond with brand loyalty. They will help you to find new uses for the product.

So now you know when to integrate channel partners into the product lifecycle. But how do ISVs integrate themselves into the channel landscape? That's what I'll be looking at next. The first step is to find out how a channel works and how various types of channel partners differ.

The Channel Value Chain

Often, when I'm talking to people in the IT industry, questions about the channel come up. People want to know how it really works and what kinds of distribution models exist and how the channel value chain works. It's important to understand the specific advantages, disadvantages and challenges of the channel in general and different partner types in particular. So let's first take a look at the "standard" ways of using the channel as intermediary. Then I'll group channel partner types according to their focus either on selling software and hardware products from another manufacturer or on selling their own products.

A distribution channel to the market is a method for getting your product into the customer's or end user's hand. You can either use a direct sales method or different forms of resellers. Direct sales can occur face-to-face, over the phone, on the web or by email order. Indirect or channel sales typically refer to sales that occur through a reseller. A reseller can order directly from the manufacturer (forming one tier between you and the end user), or from a wholesale distributor. In the later case, the manufacturer sells the product to a wholesale distributor who then sells it on to multiple resellers. This scenario creates two tiers between you and the end user and it is commonly termed "two tier" distribution.

Two Tier Distribution Model

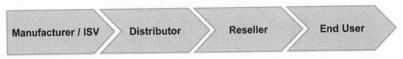

Manufacturer / ISV | Distributor | Reseller | End User

The typical value chain used today for the distribution of packaged software and services is the two tier distribution model.[13] When using this model, the main challenges the manufacturer faces are the

[13] Packaged software refers to a commercial application program or collection of programs developed to meet the needs of a variety of users, rather than being custom designed for a specific user or company. Packaged software is normally put on a CD (or disks), packaged in a box and sold to the general public.

huge discounts to the channel and limited access to the end user. Often the manufacturers don't know their customers, making it very difficult for them to build a relationship with the end user. The relationship with the end user is, however, essential for the manufacturer's growth and survival. It's only from the end user that they can learn how to improve their products and services. It's impossible to secure recurring business or build a steady revenue stream (e.g. selling updates or maintenance) unless you have a good relationship with the end user.

Other challenges will also present themselves in the day-to-day business. For example, how can you ensure that the end user has access to purchasing maintenance or upgrades for the product? How can you validate the end user's rights for the newest release of the software?

The internet has offered solutions to this problem. The web has forever changed the entire process of buying software and services and its impact will continue to evolve. This huge shift must ultimately result in a revolution of channel practices. The revolution has in fact already begun and small vendors, in particular, can benefit from this. I will provide more details about this exciting development in the e-commerce chapter later in the book. You'll find out how to use an e-commerce platform to sell products to the channel and how to start a self service channel business. Once these structures are in place, ISVs may exploit them to build a relationship not only with the reseller, but also with the reseller's customer who is using the software product.

Types of Channel Partners

Before an ISV can start to build an effective channel structure, it needs to define and understand the different types of resellers and channel partners.[14] Even though the definitions of channel partner

---

[14] You can find descriptions of different reseller types on various ISV websites. For example, see www.ca.com/us/partners.aspx (2009)

types can vary from vendor to vendor (every "partner program" from the various ISVs will use different terms), the categories listed below describe typical channel partners.

There are two main channel partner categories. In order to work successfully with them you will need to take a different approach for each. There is a big difference between the needs of the two channel partner groups. One wants to maximize margins, the other wants to increase sales of their own products.

Product oriented resellers

Product oriented resellers are channel partners with a focus on re-selling software or hardware. This means that they require a wide range of products from many different vendors.

Partner Type	Definition
Distributor (Broadliner)	Distributors or broadliners are wholesale dealers who sell to other resellers. Companies like Ingram Micro, TechData or Actebis Peacock are defined as broadline distributors. In the past, broadline distributors have been able to operate very effectively by providing local stockholding of IT products which are supported by logistics and credit facilities. They are focused on providing commercial solutions for small and medium businesses. Many resellers still buy through broadline distributors – up to 80% of all resellers place orders with them.[15] But the majority of today's resellers also buy online from e-tailers or directly from an ISV. Advantages for ISVs • Easy to find (there are only a few well-known broadline distributors in each country). • Reach out to a vast reseller/channel partner base. • Make it easy for resellers to order different products without doing a lot of research. • Offer financing options for resellers. • Inventory balancing (if some resellers need to return stock).

---

[15] CMP-Weka Research and Consulting, Channeltracks, www.channeltracks.de

Partner Type	Definition
	▪ Offer promotional programs to reach specific types of resellers. Disadvantages for ISVs ▪ Expensive to work with (especially for smaller and unknown vendors). ▪ Nearly impossible to get mindshare of their sales team. ▪ Manufacturers often don't know who is buying their products, so they can't establish a direct relationship and create a recurring revenue channel. ▪ Stock rotation can kill small vendors.[16] ▪ Long payment terms. ▪ Resellers do not receive technical support from distributors. This can be a big problem, especially for more complex products. ▪ Price transparency in the internet makes it more difficult to work with this type of channel because they will always want the best price. It can restrict the ISV's ability to sell through different channels using different pricings.
Value Added Distributors (VAD)	Typical value added distributors focus on specific market segments. The main difference between a broadliner and a VAD is that a VAD doesn't have the wide range of products and is viewed by their resellers as more of a consulting partner who helps them make the right decisions. Some typical value added distributors are Bell Micro, Avnet or Azlan. Advantages for ISVs ▪ Highly skilled in their area. ▪ Very good network of resellers. ▪ Easier to do business with and gain mindshare of their sales group. ▪ Offer training and often also technical support to the resellers. ▪ Good market-overview in a specific niche (e.g. storage or security). ▪ Limited number of vendors in one area. Disadvantages for ISVs ▪ Harder to win as partner because they already offer similar products. ▪ Long payment terms.

[16] Stock rotation in this context does not mean that the reseller (distributor/retailer/reseller) will place the product in a more prominent position or do more marketing to sell it. It means that the reseller will send the products back to the ISV in order to get the newest release of the software.

Partner Type	Definition
	▪ Often also sell to end-users, which can create channel conflicts.
Direct Market Reseller (DMR) (B2B)	A direct market reseller, also known as a B2B e-tailer, is a company that sells directly to consumers online without running storefront operations of any kind. On the business to business (B2B) level some examples of DMRs are companies such as PCMall, CDW and TigerDirect. Advantages for ISVs ▪ Very good market presence. ▪ Can make a vendor extremely visible to the public and help to establish a brand. ▪ Make active call-outs to resellers and end-users. Disadvantages for ISVs ▪ Difficult to get mindshare of their sales and marketing team. ▪ Expensive to work with (most of them ask for a lot of marketing funding). ▪ Sell to resellers and end users (especially corporate end-users), which can result in a channel conflict.
e-tailer (B2C)	E-tailers are a sub-form of direct market resellers. We describe e-tailers as the business to consumer (B2C) counterparts of the DMRs. These B2C e-tailers often have a very good web presence, an easy buying process and very aggressive pricing. Typical e-tailers include companies such as Amazon, NewEgg and Zip-ZoomFly. Advantages for ISVs ▪ Very good mailing lists can be used to increase ISV's market presence. ▪ Faster cash-flow than "brick and mortar" partners. ▪ Easy to work with for the resellers. ▪ Accept many different payment terms, which is popular with customers. Disadvantages for ISVs ▪ Sell only what the customers are asking for – no free of charge active product promotion. ▪ No specific product knowledge (no human interface). ▪ Price pressure for the vendor – they aim to undercut everybody's pricing by far, which can kill the ISV's pricing strategy.
Value Added Resellers (VAR)	Value Added Resellers are resellers that normally buy their products from distributors, combine them with their own services and sell the solution to the end user. Most of the VARs operate in a

Partner Type	Definition
	specific niche. Their niche can be geographical or they might be specialists for one vertical. VARs can often be positioned in a grey zone between product oriented and project oriented resellers.

Advantages for ISVs
- VARs are local heroes (can be used to try a product in a test market).[17]
- Active lead development possible.
- Offer support and training to the end users.
- Can sell more complex products.
- Promote "your" product if they really like it.
- Easy to work with.

Disadvantages for ISVs
- Difficult to find and to select.
- Only a regional or vertical experience – difficult to scale.
- Some of them are not very active in sales and marketing.
- Need a long "ramp-up" time and then the 80/20 rule applies, which means that only 20% of all acquired resellers will actually work out and start selling your product.

Project oriented resellers

The main difference between channel partners who resell software and hardware and channel partners who complement their own solution with third party products is their focus.

The channel partners who focus on their own products and services will have a different motivation for working with you than a reseller who is just looking for a good margin. Project oriented resellers want to use your product to increase sales of their own product.

Partner Type	Definition
Education Partner	Education partners are industry experts or institutions trained to offer professional education services on behalf of the software vendor. Normally education partners must demonstrate exceptional technical and delivery skills regarding the vendor's technology.

---

[17] A "local hero" is a partner who has established himself, with success cases, in a particular geographical area as a specialist.

Partner Type	Definition
	Advantages for ISVs • Can educate a large group of resellers. • Act as vertical experts where the product is relevant (e.g. government). Disadvantages for ISVs • Reselling the software is not the focus of their business. • ISVs need their own experience and reference cases in this vertical.
Technology Partners	Technology partners are hardware and/or software companies who offer solutions that complement their own products or solutions. Normally a technology partner needs to hold certification indicating that their integrated solution has been tested and certified by the manufacturer. Certification enhances the capability of a standalone solution. It assures customers that the complete solution will work and that the technology partner has support from the manufacturer. Advantages for ISVs • Large volumes. • Serve different markets and different channels. Disadvantages for ISVs • Long evaluation cycles. • Low average price point per copy. • Requires a lot of technical and marketing support.
OEM Partners	OEM partners are original equipment manufacturers / system builders. They offer devices, components, appliances, white label PCs, servers and laptops. They add value to their solutions by embedding another vendor's technology in their products. Advantages for ISVs • Can open new markets – especially if they serve a special industry or vertical market. • Can increase branding of the ISV and the solution. • High volume. • Create access to new VARs and other channel partners. • Generate lots of input for your own product development. Disadvantages for ISVs • Low average price point. • Long sales cycles.

Partner Type	Definition
	<ul><li>Total sales volume and revenue often unclear.</li><li>Often ask for 100% white label[18] solution.</li></ul>
System Integrators (SI)	System integrators or service partners are service companies that can scale and complement the ISV's skills. They provide services to support the ISV's product line. Most system integrators require a lot of training and support from the ISV. Advantages for ISVs <ul><li>Easy to find, mostly easy to work with.</li><li>Serve a specific local area and most of them have specific industry knowledge.</li><li>Customers trust their advice.</li><li>Together with an SI the ISV can create solutions for specific customer groups based on the standard product.</li></ul> Disadvantages for ISVs <ul><li>Most of them sell what the customer is asking for instead of recommending your solution.</li><li>Difficult to get mindshare of the sales organization.</li><li>Low volumes in term of projects (they only buy when they need a product).</li><li>Must select the right one, the 80/20 rule applies.</li><li>Slow processes – it takes time from the first contact to first revenue.</li></ul>
Global Alliance Partners (GAP), Global System Integrators (GSI)	Global alliance partners are global companies that provide IT offerings, business solutions and/or regulatory solutions that can add value to the vendor's offering. Typical global alliance partners are industry leading ISVs such as IBM, Microsoft or SAP. Examples of global system integrators (GSI's) are Accenture, Cap Gemini or HP. A sub-type of GSI are Global Outsourcers including companies like T-Systems or Wipro. Advantages for ISVs <ul><li>Global reach and a vast customer base.</li><li>Ability to implement large projects with complex products.</li><li>Increases brand recognition.</li></ul> Disadvantages for ISVs <ul><li>Difficult to gain access to the "right" level of contacts in the customer's organization.</li><li>Difficult sales process – often has very long sales cycles and requires huge investments of time and resources to reach</li></ul>

---

[18] A "white label" product or service is produced by one company (the producer) which other companies (the marketers) then rebrand to make it appear as if they produced it.

Partner Type	Definition
	the goal. • Difficult to work with – long contracts, hierarchies, uncertainty if you are talking to the right people. • They own the customer – very often the vendors have no access to the end users, even in bigger projects.
Software as a Service (SaaS) Resellers	The business model of SaaS resellers differs from any other business model in the channel. Instead of stocking the products and reselling them, the main goal of a SaaS reseller is to build a long lasting recurring revenue stream with their customers. SaaS partners deploy the systems, usually build their own brand and deliver ongoing services to their customers. Advantages for ISVs • Recurring revenue. • Actively sells the solution as part of a comprehensive offering. Disadvantages for ISVs • Monthly payments versus large upfront payments can lead to cash flow problems • Very few active SaaS resellers exist today.

Selling Through the Channel

In today's market environment, vendors will typically work with various different channel partners. This is necessary to achieve good market coverage. Today, approximately 80% of all resellers buy from broadliners, but many also work with at least six different types of distribution partners. Roughly 20% of the resellers buy from e-tailers and the number is growing.[19] The majority of resellers do their market research via the internet, searching for the best price. For more complex products they look at where they can get the best service.

Due to market pressure, the loyalty between channel partners and manufacturers is generally not very high. Partners switch suppliers very fast nowadays and as a vendor you can't rely on only one single reseller.

---

[19] CRN "Channeltracks", www.channeltracks.de (2009)

A typical model for selling a product through different channel partners is shown in the graph. The ISV offers all or selected products through his own online store (OLS). The shop is used to sell products directly to channel partners and end users offering a standard discount to partners only. The ISV also partners with a VAD and a broadliner offering partners to buy from these sources. End users may also buy the product from an e-tailer. In addition to these sales channels, broadliners may sell to e-tailers who may sell products not only to end users, but also to the partners. This may sound confusing, but don't worry, I'll explain in more detail how to choose and combine different channels.

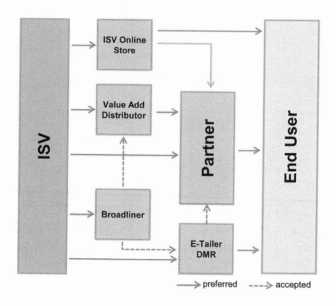

As a manufacturer you can choose whether to sell your product directly to the end user or to sell it through the channel. Both methods can also be carried out with an online store. Here's an example of direct selling: a sales representative contacts the end user directly and sells him/her the product, avoiding any interaction with the channel or any type of reseller in between. Another way to sell directly is through your own online store. The most direct way to sell whilst still using the channel is to sell your product via a partner (VAR or system integrator) to the end user. This is described as a one tier channel where the vendor works directly with their channel partners to sell to the end user.

In order to reach a broader audience and ramp up sales even faster, the manufacturer can build a two tier distribution model instead. This entails the manufacturer selling to a broadliner, VAR or DMR/e-tailer who then sells the product either to another VAR or directly to the end user. In a typical market place, the DMR/e-tailer sources their product from a broadliner or VAR instead of buying directly from the vendor. This is especially the case when the vendors are smaller and their products don't create a large enough revenue stream.

Many combinations of different channels are possible. To make the best selection, ISVs need to understand the thinking of the channel partner. All channel partners will attempt to optimize their sourcing process. If they see that it's more economical to buy directly from the vendor they will (if the vendor lets them). If the product is just a small part of their business or is seen as "complementary", they will continue to use distributers. You need to be very realistic when choosing your channel partner.

The next chapter will help you identify the right channel partner. I'll also provide some calculations for the different distribution models.

Identifying the Right Channel

When selecting a distribution channel, ISVs need to analyze which factors lead to successful sales processes and deliver real value to the end user. Quite often a product cannot offer a big value purely on its own, but its real value is created when it's bundled together with other products and services. For example, many Enterprise Resource Planning solutions from vendors such as SAP, Oracle or Microsoft must be tailored to the specific needs of the end user (by the channel partner) in order to achieve their full potential.

Thus, ISVs need to view the products from the end user's perspective and need to then select the right partners from the end user's point of view. Remember to keep in mind that end users don't look for "products," they look for "solutions" to their problems. It's very important that you analyze why the end user needs the solution. Find out where the logical point of sales should be and who will deliver your solution in the best manner. This is where you'll find the right channel partner.

For example, in order to sell an enterprise software solution you must provide some additional services other than just the software product itself. This might include providing analyses of customer's business processes upon request; ensuring proper implementation of the product; providing training for the customer's employees and follow up product support. In fact, the entire sales process of an enterprise project relies heavily on trust between the end user and the vendor/reseller - proving that the "pure" software solution itself can actually become less important than the development of a broader solution to fit the end user's needs.

It is typical for many different types of channel partners to be involved in larger enterprise projects. Very often the end user will start the project with an analysis of business processes and ROI that is carried out by a consultant. Then they define an internal or external team to search for the best business solutions. At this point in time, they may not even be thinking about a specific software solution. However, it's common for end users to hire a system integrator to short-list potential software solutions and speak to some vendors on their behalf. Once they have selected a vendor, very often another system integrator will be engaged to implement and run the solution.

This scenario shows just how many partners can be involved in the process. It's important that manufacturers ask themselves: Where do I want to be in the food chain? In the above example, the manufacturer (ISV) isn't in a very strong position because they don't know enough about the business processes and the real goals of the end user. That's why many of the bigger software and hardware vendors have large consulting divisions that let them form much better relationships with their corporate end users. The consultants can also educate and help the ISV's channel partners during the implementation stage. Bigger software and hardware vendors have large channels that involve many different partners from all over the world.

Even when some areas of competition exist, the evidence shows that in most situations both parties will benefit as long as the channel model is executed in the right way. However, if clear rules are not put in place and the consultants go after end users directly then frustration arises in the channel. This can result in an unproductive situation for all parties involved; the channel partners, the ISV and the end user.

Channel Business Models

The involvement of many different players in enterprise projects - from system integrator to consultant to manufacturer - as described above shows how much caution ISVs must take when deciding which channel to use to introduce a product to the market. This chapter analyzes the following four channel types in more detail:

- Direct sales
- Reselling channel (VARs/system integrators)
- Distribution channel (distributors/broadline distribution)
- Original equipment manufacturers (OEMs)

The following table explains the channel's different business models, highlights their advantages and disadvantages from an ISV's point of view and outlines success factors, potential risks and necessary action items.

Though OEMs rarely play a role in enterprise projects (which I will use as an example later on), I've included them here since they are an effective option for distributing a product widely and establishing a brand.

When choosing how to engage the channel, ISVs need to be aware that the structure of the channel and the appropriate action items are directly related to the kind of product, the complexity, the resources and existing sales processes of the manufacturer. The main question I want to answer here is how the different sales channels can be combined to create an efficient "multi-channel strategy".

I'll show you how you can reach as many potential customers as possible without incurring excess expenditure on marketing and margins, or losing touch with your partners and end users.

	Direct Sales	VAR	Distribution	OEM
Definition	Sales process is directly between the manufacturer and the end user.	Sales via authorized partners, who combine the product with their own products and services.	Sales via resellers, who actively market and resell different products.	Embedding or bundling of the product with the products of the OEM partner, who sells these products through their own channels.
Advantages	Direct involvement and understanding of the end user's needs. Control over the sales cycle. Creation of reference projects. Direct market feedback for the products and services. Allows proximity to market trends and enables manufacturer to become an expert in this market.	Potential access to partner's customer base. Local presence is possible. Larger market presence and better scalability if the channel distribution works well. Input for product development from the partner. Access to resources (technical, sales, marketing). Partner can provide first or second level support.	In most cases highly effective marketing by channel partner (distributor). Increase of market awareness for product and manufacturer, brand building. Manufacturer avoids long-term investments (building a sales team etc.).	Effective product marketing within the catalogue. Reaching new target and customer groups. Cost-effective opportunity for internationalization (accessing new markets).

	Direct Sales	VAR	Distribution	OEM
Disadvantages	Having your own sales team is expensive. Requires a high level of technical support. Often the relationship between customer/key accounts is more important than the relationship to the manufacturer. National or global set-up is very difficult.	Building and managing the partner network requires a great effort. Partners request a margin of up to 30%, depending on the services offered. Access to market information is more difficult (partner communicates with customer). Difficult to steer the sales pipeline.	Positioning and strategy must be clear. Responsibility for customer support and contracting must be clear. Channel partners demand high margins of roughly 45%. Small manufacturers often need to sign exclusive distribution contracts with partners.	Product is secondary to OEM product. Mostly anonymous customers. Complex and extensive negotiations (contracts etc.). Branding can only be achieved long-term.
Success factors	Clear customer segmentation. High customer satisfaction. Creation of active customer relationship management. Good control of distribution and projects. Efficient methodology for conducting projects and scaling resources.	Development of clear partner typology. Critical VAR selection. Definition of an enterprise message for indirect communication and for marketing and sales material. Transparent task definition to avoid channel conflicts.	Product must be suitable for channel distribution. Define clear targets with partners (so your product receives proper attention). Provisions for specific employees in the partner organization. Second and third level support.	Selecting the employee suited to push the project. OEM distribution strategy (regional/national coverage). Definition of clear benefit scenarios. Track and trace management.
Goals	Maximize revenues per client. Create strong reference projects. Build vertical solutions. Reference selling in vertical customer networks.	Build a critical mass of active distribution partners. Maximize revenues per partner. Train external resources. Build a partner community.	Maximum number of licenses. Conquering a market segment (brand building).	Move a greater number of licenses and earn by selling updates. Build the brand. Opportunity to create a new market segment (white label).

	Direct Sales	VAR	Distribution	OEM
Risks	Losing focus and uneconomical projects. Product development often directed by individual customer needs. Lack of license revenue, meaning no focus on product character and readiness for the channel.	Channel conflicts hard to avoid, must be managed. Too little and low quality sales and marketing material result in inefficient partners. "Dead" partners and partners that move on damage manufacturer and product image.	Product, documentation etc. must be ready for the channel. If channel distribution fails, investment and image are wasted. Time gap between channel entrance and revenue.	Significant amount of resources required to prepare the distribution process. Development and support must take partner requests into account.
Action items	Build a lead database. Clear definition of benefit oriented customer scenarios for different target groups and business classes. Build and manage a sales team.	Organize partner workshops. Develop a clear partner strategy. Define partner's rights and responsibilities. Finalize communication material (website, fact sheets, success stories, sales guidelines etc.).	Adopt marketing message to the channel. Define simple use cases. Define the customer benefit in a manner that is easy to communicate. Develop clear product road map.	Select OEM partners from an end user perspective, answering the question: Which products complement each other? Install a service and update hotline.

Please keep in mind that I'm trying to provide an easy to understand overview here. The above groupings may not be 100% accurate and obviously there are partners that fall somewhere in between groups.

So how do the different channels impact a manufacturer's bottom line? That's what the next chapter will focus on.

Channel Impact on Revenues and Margins

I find that using examples and real calculations helps understand different business models. In this chapter, I'll look at the revenues that can be achieved by using the different sales channels. My example refers to an enterprise project which is why, for now, I'll ignore the OEM channel.

I'll keep the example simple, as I really want to focus on the key economic differences between the various channel approaches. I will take into consideration the different discount levels that are associated with each channel type, but I will ignore any other associated costs involved in building the channel.

Basic Example

An ISV develops and sells different enterprise solutions. On average, revenues per project are US$20,000 for licenses and US$80,000 for implementation or "professional services" (PS). For simplicity I've calculated the license portion using a gross margin of 100% and the PS portion using 30% (which also includes potential project risks). Let's imagine the company's goal is to generate a gross margin of approximately US$1 million in the first year so they compare the various sales channels.

Channel	Gross Margin per Project		Projects Required	Market Volume	Gross Margin Channel Partner
Direct incl. PS	100%	$44,000	23	$2,300,000	$0
Direct excl. PS	100%	$20,000	50	$5,000,000	$1,200,000
VAR Partner	70%	$14,000	72	$7,200,000	$1,728,000
Distributor	55%	$11,000	91	$9,100,000	$2,184,000

The table above demonstrates that if you act like a "one stop shop" (creating the software, winning the customer and carrying out the implementation) you only need 23 projects in order to reach a gross margin of US$1 million. From these 23 projects, the manufacturer gains US$460,000 (23 x US$20,000) in revenue from software and US$1,840,000 (23 x US$80,000) from services. The gross margin will actually be slightly higher than US$1 million, with the combined gross margin of US$460,000 from software and US$552,000 (30% of the revenue) from services.

In order to achieve the same results without being responsible for the implementation, 50 projects are necessary. You will need reliable partners to take care of the implementation process (but not the sales process). The service revenue of the channel partners will be 4 times higher than the software revenue. In this case you as the manufacturer of the software only make US$1 million in revenue. The implementation partners make US$4 million in revenue which results in a gross margin of US$1.2 million (30%).

If the manufacturer decides to sell the product through the channel they need 72 to 91 customers in order to produce the target gross margin of US$1 million. The chart clearly demonstrates that if sales are made via a channel partner (which lowers the gross margin) the number of projects needed increases significantly. What's not shown in this chart is how important and challenging it is to find the right partner to present and sell your product. In any case, the manufacturer needs to evaluate if it's possible and realistic to create and manage a channel that requires a minimum of 3 times more projects in the same time as if the product was sold direct.

Don't misunderstand my message though; I must reiterate here that I am a big fan of the channel. I believe it's the only possible way to create and maintain market leadership and generate exponential growth. There are many reasons for this but here are just two: First of all, in order to find more than 20 customers (using my previous example), build trust and implement the project, it will very often require much more time than using channel partners with existing customer relationships would. The second and even more important reason is that ISVs very often don't have the resources to implement their projects within an acceptable time frame. Building and maintaining an in-house professional service team to implement this number of projects will present a big challenge for any ISV. It makes much more sense to use a PS partner.

Now that we've taken a look at this simple calculation, I want to go into more detail. This is important because many ISVs become frustrated if they don't reach their targets when using the channel. As a result, they start selling directly which puts them in competition with their newly implemented channel partners. This causes the whole channel strategy to collapse and all their previous investment into the channel is lost. My goal in providing these calculations is to give ISVs the information they need to develop their own channel strategy. They need to know how many partners they will need, what their expectations should be and so on. Later in the book I'll provide information about how to recruit these channel partners and how to build a "lead pipeline" together with them. Simply carrying out some calculations such as these at the beginning of designing your channel strategy will help to create a clearer picture of the time needed to reach your goals.

Direct sales calculation

Let's assume an ISV just provides software licenses and the only revenue stream is from the sales of these licenses. We'll compare the different sales methods and the necessary number of projects required to generate a certain level of revenues. In the following examples, the goal is always to generate US$1 million in software license revenue. I'll compare a direct sales method with one tier and two tier channel sales. These calculations will also be helpful for setting the right price point for the software and the solution.

No. of Projects	License Revenue per Project (Direct Sales)			
	$5,000	$10,000	$100,000	$1,000,000
1	$5,000	$10,000	$100,000	$1,000,000
10	$20,000	$50,000	$1,000,000	
100	$500,000	$1,000,000		
200	$1,000,000			

This is how to read the charts: The left side shows the "number of projects", across the top you'll find "license revenues per project" and in the middle you'll find total revenues for the respective number of projects. In the one and two tier calculations, the discount is also taken into account (25% vs. 45%). The number of projects grows with the percentage discount that is given to the channel partners. If the average license revenues per project are US$5,000 you will need 200 projects to reach the US$1 million target. As the revenue per project grows, the number of projects required shrinks. If you plan on selling direct, you as an ISV need to ask yourself the following questions:

- Will we generate enough revenues if we only sell direct?
- Where could a channel add value?
- Do we have the resources to address the number of projects?
- Can we provide the necessary PS capacity?
- Does our solution sell alone or do we also need additional products or services?
- Do we have the knowledge to serve the target customers (e.g. for vertical industries)?

One tier calculation

The next scenario is the one tier channel. A one tier channel means that there is only one "middleman" between you and the end user. In a typical example, the vendor sells to a VAR or a system integrator (SI) and the VAR/SI provides the solution to the end user.

In this scenario, the required margin to give to the VAR/SI is 25% minimum. This means that you and the VAR/SI need to win approximately 30% more projects so that your license revenue reaches the US$1 million gross profit target.

No. of Projects	ISV License Revenue per Project (Indirect Sales/One Tier)			
25%	$3,750	$7,500	$75,000	$750,000
1	$5,000	$10,000	$100,000	$750,000
10	$20,000	$50,000	$750,000	
100	$500,000	$750,000		
200	$750,000			

In this example, the partner receives a discount of 25% on each license. Thus, the revenue of the ISV reduced by 25% and more projects are needed to achieve the same revenue as in direct sales. The table shows that where using the direct approach, the ISV made US$1 million with 200 projects, now US$ 250,000 are "missing".

A typical VAR/SI makes 20-30% of their revenue from the reselling of software and the rest from providing professional services to the end user. This model will change in the future as more and more VARs/SIs will also provide software as a service to their end users.

The important questions in this model are:

- What additional value does the VAR/SI provide?
- Can you win the necessary amount of additional projects together with the resellers?
- How many and what type of resellers do you need?
- What specific knowledge must you provide to the partners?
- Will the reseller sell and implement the solution?
- Is the solution attractive enough to create mindshare at the customer site?

Two tier calculation

The two tier calculation involves the vendor selling to a distributor who sells to a reseller who then sells to the end user. As you might imagine, this means that there will be higher margins to the distributor (45% or more) along with additional costs for providing product training to the distributor's sales force, marketing funding and creating market demand. The following model will use the simplest scenario. A discount of 45% will be used to make the calculations - exposing the obvious challenges.

If almost half of the revenues go to a distributor, then the ISV will need double the number of projects in order to generate US$1 million gross profit in software licenses.

No. of Projects	45%	ISV License Revenue per Project (Indirect Sales/Two Tier)				License Rev.
		$2,750	$5,500	$55,000	$550,000	
1		$5,000	$10,000	$100,000	$550,000	
10		$20,000	$50,000	$550,000		
100		$500,000	$550,000			
200		$550,000				

The important questions to ask here are:

- Can we create more projects with the two tier model?
- What are the necessary resources and costs involved?
- How can you, as the ISV, help sell the projects in such an indirect model?
- Is there enough market demand within the defined timeline?
- What is the specific knowledge you must provide to the partners?
- Does the distributor have the knowledge to educate the VARs?
- What motivates the distributor to push your products to the VARs?
- What motivates the VAR to promote your product as part of a solution to the end user?

It's obvious that if an ISV gives more margins to the channel, then more projects must be sold in order to achieve the same gross profit. At the same time, profit alone is no sufficient single criteria to define your strategy. You also need to take into account the questions I've listed after each calculation.

Also, it's worth thinking more about professional services. It's an important component in the way your product benefits your partners' revenues. That's why the next chapter takes a closer look at "professional services" as one of the biggest motivators for the channel partners to sell solutions based on your product.

Professional Services (PS) as Part of the Solution

Even in the online era and SaaS times, the complexity of IT operations continues to grow. In addition, there's a growing trend of end users maintaining just a basic IT department and outsourcing the rest of their IT related work. This is creating more and more opportunities in the PS market.

ISVs may be increasing the functionality of their applications so that they can address more and more business needs but this increase in complexity results in an even greater need for good planning, customization and training. Over the last couple of years, most of the end user business has become increasingly complex. These days, selling and sourcing globally, working with multiple partners and the need of continually becoming more specialized are only but a few of the challenges in the business.

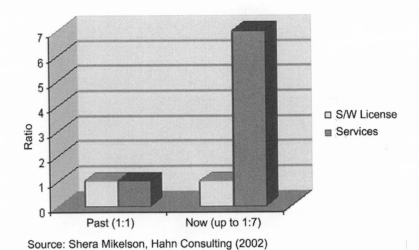

Source: Shera Mikelson, Hahn Consulting (2002)

A very interesting study carried out by Hahn Consulting shows that the budget portion which customers set aside for software projects has been increasing significantly over the years.[20] In a breakdown of

---

[20] Shera Mikelson, "Should Professional Services Be In Your Company's Services Portfolio?", www.hahnconsulting.com (2002)

customer's IT spending habits there are some attention grabbing figures. The statistics show that the current ratio of customer spending on services ranges from 2 to 7 times the amount of the product license, which is a big shift from the 1:1 "license to service" ratios we saw just a short time ago. Many other surveys also show that the average ratio today is 1:6. This means that for every dollar spent on software, the customer spends six dollars on PS. For most channel partners this devalues the process of reselling software and significantly increases the value of providing PS.

As a software vendor, one important question that you must ask yourself is: Are you going to offer PS to your end user customer base? PS, in this case, does not include presales, training or creating specifications. Even though those services are important for supporting your partners, it is a very different story if you create a PS department since this should contribute a major revenue stream. In many cases however, this also means that you will start going into direct competition with your partners.

Most big software vendors answer "yes" to the question of PS and have either built or bought a large group. IBM has their own large PS group, HP bought EDS in 2008 and even hardware manufacturers such as Dell have invested in PS, buying Perot Systems in 2009. If you're not as large as IBM however, and perhaps don't have billions to invest in a PS group, you might find the following sections not only interesting but also very useful for increasing the margin on your core business: the development of software.

Professional Services calculation

Using the following calculation I would like to answer two questions:

- Why should you offer PS projects to your partners?
- Why should you give margins on the software to your partners?

I will continue using the parameters from the previous example. So the question is, how many software licenses do you need to sell to generate US$1 million gross profit? Various studies show that along with the "cost per license" the ratio of licenses to PS is also growing. For software licenses up to the value of US$50,000 I used a ratio of 1:5. For a higher cost per license value I used 1:7. This means that for every dollar spent on software licensing in a project, 5 or 7 dollars will be spent on PS.

	Total Professional Service (PS) Revenue for Channel				
	Cost per License				
	$5,000	$10,000	$100,000	$1,000,000	RRP
25%	$3,750	$7,500	$75,000	$750,000	VAR
1	$25,000	$50,000	$700,000	$7,000,000	
10	$250,000	$500,000	$7,000,000		
100	$2,500,000	$5,000,000			
200	$5,000,000				
	License / Service Rev. 1:5		License / Service Rev. 1:7		

No. of Projects (left axis). PS Revenue (right axis).

In the above table, the first line (RRP, recommended retail price) represents the cost per license, which ranges from US$5,000 to US$1 million. The reseller buys the software at a 25% discount (VAR, value added reseller price). If software licenses to the value of US$1,000,000 are sold to the end user (e.g. 200 x US$ 5,000), the partner will make between US$5 million and US$7 million in professional service revenues plus the margin on reselling the software, while the ISV generates US$ 750,000 (200 x US$3,750).

Before I begin to compare the ISV's situation with that of the reseller, it's necessary to calculate the gross margin from PS. The next table does this using the same number of projects, including PS. How do you calculate the gross margin in PS projects? There are many different ways but since this book is not really about PS, I'll just give a brief overview.

The term "gross margin" describes the difference between revenues and costs of goods. For example, if you make US$1,000 in revenues and the costs associated with this revenue are US$700 then your gross margin is US$300 or 30%. If a reseller buys a license from you for US$700 and sells this license to the end user for US$1,000 then their gross margin is again 30%.

When working out the gross margin in PS, the calculation becomes a little different. The following examples should give a good rule of thumb however. The major cost factor to take into account when making this calculation is the cost of the consultant providing the PS. This is the only factor that really matters in the calculation.

Let's say the average salary for a consultant is US$80,000 and their non-wage labor costs add another 20% to this which makes their total cost to you US$96,000.[21]

If the consultant works a maximum of 225 days per year, the average cost per man day is US$430 (rounded up). If the channel partner charges US$1,000 per man day, the maximum revenue per consultant is US$225,000. The two major factors that can lower this figure are the number of days a consultant is booked and the risk factor. Examples of risk are a fixed price project that takes longer than expected or a customer who won't pay for certain services. If the consultant's maximum capacity utilization is 80% and the risk factor is 25%, then the maximum revenue is reduced to US$135,000 (US$225,000 x 0.8 x 0.75).

US$135,000 less US$96,000 (costs) is US$39,000 which is the gross margin (roughly 30%). This calculation explains why I use a standard gross margin of 30% in PS calculations.

The chart below shows that, based on these numbers, the partner will make at least double the gross margin that the ISV will make.

---

[21] Non-wage labor costs include fringe benefits, health insurance, social security etc.

Total Professional Service (PS) Gross Margin for Channel Partners				
Cost per License				
30%	$5,000	$10,000	$100,000	$1,000,000
1	$7,500	$15,000	$210,000	$2,100,000
10	$75,000	$150,000	$2,100,000	
100	$750,000	$1,500,000		
200	$1,500,000			
License / Service Rev. 1:5		License / Service Rev. 1:7		

No. of Projects (row axis label) — PS Gross Margin (right axis label)

Remember: If you sell your licenses over the channel with a 25% discount, then your revenue will be only US$ 750,000. The gross margin for your channel partner will be between US$1,500,000 and US$2,100,000. They will also make the 25% margin on the license, which is another US$250,000.

For you as an ISV it's difficult to increase the price of your software because you can only charge as much as the market is willing to pay. Your channel partner however, can increase their gross margin in many ways. One way is to increase the number of man days charged per consultant and to improve the project management which reduces their risk factor. If the workload rises to 90% and the risk factor decreases to 10%, your channel partner's gross margin nearly triples!

So what can we learn from these calculations? That every ISV should start building a PS group and offer complete solutions to their customers? I don't believe in this. From my point of view an ISV should:

- Analyze the market situation for their product carefully. How much PS is needed? How much risk is involved? What kind of help does the channel partner and the end user need?

- Use this analysis to decide upon your discounting structure and what kinds of discounts you are willing to give. (I will talk more about discounting later in the book.)
- Start to offer training, consulting and PS to your channel partners also. On the one hand, this helps to increase their knowledge and reduce their risk factor (bringing more profit to the channel partner) and on the other hand, it provides you with some extra revenue. You can also join forces with your channel partners in the specific areas where they are specialized.

The Truth about Discounts

You will have gathered by now, that this book is about calculations. I really do believe in the importance of numbers. If you can't or don't do the math then you'll never be able to set goals and measure your success against these goals. Having no numbers available can also result in bad management of your organization and the channel.

One major error that many ISVs make when it comes to working with channel partners is giving them discounts that are too high. If an ISV lowers their price too fast every time a channel partner cries out for a higher discount or a special deal, they will begin to ruin their own business. In this chapter I'll discuss the tremendous influence that discounts can have on the success of software companies, especially plain vanilla ISVs.[22]

The economics of software vendors

The typical cost structure of a software company involves high costs for creating, selling and marketing the software. These fixed costs are normally between 60% - 75% of total costs. The cost for (re)pro-ducing the software is often close to zero even though there are always the costs of goods sold (COGS) involved. Typical COGS are things such as packaging, credit card costs, sales commission

---

[22] "Plain vanilla" ISVs only deal with software and nothing else.

and OEM software (if the software includes a product from another vendor).

McKinsey analyzed the typical pricing and discount structure of the software industry. They came up with some very interesting results, showing that the average software vendor doesn't expend much effort on their pricing strategy and doesn't really think about how the discounts they give can affect their business.[23]

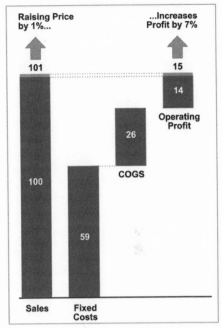

One of the main reasons I want to bring this up is that additional discounting in the channel has now become a widespread phenomenon.

Have you ever thought about why you give your channel partner a minimum of 25% discount but the distribution partner gets 40%? I think the main reason is simply to keep in line with industry standards. I hope that by the end of this book you'll have all the tools and arguments available to find the discount level that matches your strategy as well as your channel partner's strategy.

Even with an existing discount structure in place, the partner may request some "special deals" on top. Every one of us has received these types of requests - a VAR will only buy a package if they're given an additional 10% discount or they will only close the deal this quarter if the partner can offer them an additional 15% discount. These margins go against the operating profit of your company however. The chart above shows that if you are able to raise

---

[23] McKinsey & Co. Presentation, "Software License and Maintenance Pricing Principles - Best Practices and Case Studies," *SoftSummit Conference* (October 18, 2004).

the price by 1% (or avoid any additional discount) then the operating profit increases by 7%. Smart software vendors and channel sales managers know this and therefore put a lot of effort into their pricing structure.

But how can you avoid giving additional margins? Saying "no" is one way but it's not exactly helpful when you're trying to close a deal. The following pages will provide some ideas how to avoid unnecessarily high or "hasty" discounting and how to handle communication.

Educate your team

One of the most important things to do is educate your team on the significance of discounts. Your team must understand why the price of a product can be so important for your results. Most channel managers tend to try and sell a higher quantity, so they lower the price in order to achieve this.

Pricing is even more important for your results when working with the channel. If you force the channel to reach aggressive monthly or quarterly results, they will probably start "playing chicken" with you - sending their orders in at the eleventh hour and only in return for bigger discounts. Your aggressive goals will also result in management yielding to these higher discount requests. Granting higher discounts for larger quantities actually doesn't help anyone - neither you nor your committed partners. If you yield to these discount requests it will inevitably mean that your product becomes available at a lower price. This makes it impossible for even your best channel partners to create price competitive packages for the end user. Another issue to consider is that the PS budget is very often related to the price of the software. This means that if you give 50% discount on your software price, it will become very difficult to achieve the same amount of PS revenues as with the non discounted version. Remember the 1:5 or 1:7 ratio in the previous section!

It's really important to make this simple statement to your channel team: Don't clog the channel and don't give too many discounts! If you don't make this clear, it will destroy your next quarterly figures along with the relationship to your partners.

Find out where the pressure to give discounts is coming from

The next step is initiating a methodology to locate where the pressure for discounts is coming from. Phase out the partners that aren't generating extra revenue for your company. One of the most common areas this pressure can become apparent is within the sales team - particularly the individual sales people that are pressured to reach monthly, quarterly or annual quotas.

In many software companies, a substantial portion of all deals are closed within the last business days of the month. Sales reps simply do this in order to reach their quotas. The problem with this is that customers know about the pressure to meet quotas and therefore expect larger discounts for their signature. The sales rep will usually be more than willing to go along with this.[24]

But how do these monthly goals or quotas benefit the company? The standard answer is because managing sales teams on a quarterly basis only is very difficult. Management becomes much easier when there is some pressure applied to the sales people to show a monthly result. However, achieving these monthly goals by granting higher discount requests should ALWAYS be discouraged because it costs the company enormous amounts of money (real cash!) and also means melting the pipeline down to a much smaller number.

Some simple ways to avoid this dilemma:

- Make sure that your quotas don't end on the last business day of the month. Incorporate a general rule that your quotas end on the 15th day of every month.

---

[24] Sergio G. Non, "Quarter's End Bedevils Software Business," http://news.cnet.com (2001)

- Change your monthly reporting dates - make your monthly period from the 5th to the 5th. Train your sales reps how to take advantage of this "secret" when dealing with the customers - clients won't feel so confident about asking for discounts if the sales team seems relaxed at month end.
- Create a "no discount" or "maximum X% discount" rule for the last business days.
- Shorten the availability of your product and solution. If there is any customization involved then it's easy to argue: If you dear client want to have this product by this date, then you need to sign now!

This approach only works for monthly quotas however. Customers can wait for their orders until the end of a month but they can't normally wait until the end of a quarter and definitely not until the end of a year.

Smart discounting - how maintenance can solve the discount dilemma

Another way to avoid granting large discounts is to optimize your discount structure. Using a simple example I'd like to show how an ISV can reduce their discounts without seeming to be taking something away from the channel partners.

In the next table you'll see that the average price per unit is US$100 and the cost for maintenance is 25% of the listed price. This amounts to total revenues of US$200 over five years. Usually, in the channel, the unit discount also applies to maintenance. If the discount for the resellers is 25% and the discount for the distributors is 45% then the total revenue for the product over 5 years is US$150 for the ISV (as long as the ISV sells directly to the reseller). If the ISV sells through distributors, the revenue will be US$110.

Many VARs and distribution partners don't care about maintenance. If the value is too low, they won't put a system in place that lets them monitor and manage maintenance. This is especially true for typical volume products which they sell in a "fire-and-forget" mode and for which they prefer to receive the discounts upfront - meaning that only the discount on the product matters.

If the ISV decides to give a discount only on the product and not on the maintenance, then the average discount over five years can be reduced dramatically. This also creates other advantages for the ISV and the channel partner. The end user must register their product with the ISV who then provides technical support for the product and ensures that the end user receives information about new releases. New releases and high quality technical support are both necessary to hold on to the end user as a customer in the long term - both for the ISV and the channel partner.

The channel partner also has cross-selling and up-selling opportunities in this model. If the end user is known then the ISV and the channel partner have the opportunity to sell other products to them.

Price/Unit	$100
Maintenance p.a.	25%

	ISV Revenue					
Discount	Year 1	Year 2	Year 3	Year 4	Year 5	Total
0%	$100	$25	$25	$25	$25	$200
25%	$75	$19	$19	$19	$19	$150
45%	$55	$14	$14	$14	$14	$110

Scenario without Discount on Maintenance							Avg. Discount
25%	$75	$25	$25	$25	$25	$175	13%
45%	$55	$25	$25	$25	$25	$155	23%

In the above table, the price for the product (price/unit) is US$100 and the yearly maintenance is 25% or US$25 per year. In the top section of the table you can see the discounts the manufacturer gives to their channel partners, which range from 0% to 45%. The discount is valid for the product and the yearly maintenance. In the direct sales scenario, without any discounts, the total revenue over a five year period is US$200. If the product is sold using distribution with a 45% discount then the total revenue is only US$110. The bottom section of the table shows a scenario without a discount on maintenance - meaning that the manufacturer gives a discount on the product but sells the maintenance directly to the customer. In this case the average discount over five years shrinks dramatically (it's virtually cut in half!).

A different model applies, if the product value is much higher and the end user is paying for a solution instead of "only" software. Then there is a closer relationship between the end user and the channel partner who implemented the solution and will also take care of maintenance. But even in this case it's possible that the end user receives maintenance directly from the ISV. The channel partner can get a "kick back" or another form of reward for their effort.

Channel partners should finance the end user discounts

Another interesting idea is that the channel partner should partly finance the discount when a price reduction is requested by the end user. Normally the end user will be buying a complete solution from the channel partner and not only your product. This solution very often includes software, hardware, professional services, hosting and other components. For the channel partners, the highest profits are usually achieved with professional services - the lowest margins come from selling hardware. This is especially true for larger projects.

Before you accept any request for an additional discount, you should ask your channel partner what they are selling and to whom they are selling it. Using this information you can then estimate the total margin of the project, which will help you decide how you can finance the additional discount.

Don't ever lose sight of the fact that your product enables the channel partner to offer the solution - the quality of your software is therefore one of the important risk factors for the project. If you want your software to be stable and easy to implement, it must include high quality documentation and you should offer premium support. When this is the case the partner can make a much higher margin.

If the discount request is only being caused by pressure from the channel or if the channel partner won't give you more information about the project, then you shouldn't give a discount at all.

Adding value instead of giving discounts

There are several different ways of adding value to the sales of your product and this is usually better for both sides than just a price reduction.

- Create white label marketing material. You can help your channel partner to market and sell your product more easily by providing white label or dedicated marketing material.
- Run a mailing or lead generation campaign with your channel partner. There are many ways to do this; either by using your own database, buying new addresses or hiring a telesales company. Use whatever campaign works best for you. Even if you have to finance these campaigns you can be assured that they're an investment into the sales of your product which can eventually lead to new and more sales.
- Offer training for the end user. Product training for the end user can have many positive effects. Firstly, the channel partner can sell more and increase their revenues; secondly it's an easy way to create better educated end users and lastly, you get a better insight into the business of the end users. If you give your channel partner a large discount on training then they can increase the margin on the entire deal.
- Add professional services. Include an onsite installation service, project planning or other services in the total package.
- Include maintenance. Ask your channel partner for a longer commitment and include another year of maintenance.

- Increase the order volume. If your channel partner wants to get an additional 10% discount then they should increase the number of products ordered.

There are many other ways of adding value to your solution. The best way to identify them is by communicating with your channel partners. Every channel partner needs to understand that the ISV also has to make a profit in order to make further investments into the product.

Channel Trends: SaaS and Cloud Computing

It's important for every ISV to analyze trends in the market. They should make sure that they are building the right products to meet end user's needs. They also need to enable their channel partners to sell the products successfully. For example, "cloud computing" is going to have dramatic consequences for the traditional model of selling products through the channel. Existing partnerships will be challenged as new competitors start entering the market with different approaches.[25] Low margins and the booming managed services segment are not only threatening the existence of standard IT dealers, but also, increasingly, the existence of VARs. This chapter will outline the challenges the IT channel now faces and show resellers how they can transform the growing demand for managed services from a pitfall into a key enabler for future business success.

The IT market is in upheaval

There are numerous developments that are threatening the existence of IT resellers. The margins related to the sale of licenses and hardware have dropped to a "life-threatening" level, but demand from SMBs is fuelling the development of software as a service (SaaS), managed services and cloud computing. The outsourcing of IT activities should provide companies with increased scope for

---

[25] "Der Channel und die wolkige Opportunity", www.inside-channels.ch (2009)

action while allowing them to deal with increasingly complex IT environments. The impact of new technologies, changing demand from SMBs and the generally difficult situation facing the IT channel is damaging existing customer relationships and causing upheaval in the market.

Studies have shown that a turnover of around €500 million is already being generated from SaaS solutions and around €3 billion from the accompanying services and support. Specialist dealers, VARs, even system integrators and other IT service providers are confronted with the need to actively engage with managed services, not only in order to survive in this market upheaval, but also to exploit the potential of higher margins and new customers that SaaS and managed service solutions provide.

This chapter will describe the current situation and provide a review of the positive starting conditions for dealers accessing the SaaS market such as local integration or vertical specialization in specific sectors. An analysis of the practical challenges which dealers will face when setting up their own services will follow.

One thing that is required however, is a rethink of the situation. I'll illustrate this using the most significant differences between the classic hardware and software trade and the managed services sector. I'll also use a cloud backup/storage as a service example to show which criteria a service should fulfill in order to enable a dealer to gain entry to the managed services sector.

Changes in the channel through managed services, SaaS and cloud computing

Now that product advertising and sales have become increasingly common on the internet, many manufactures and internationally active dealers are using this platform to sell their products directly to the end user. In return, end users are using the resulting transparency to push the prices as low as possible with their local providers.

Product focused IT dealers, above all, are affected by this because unlike VARs or system integrators they are unable to counteract this drop in hardware and software sales through the provision of fee based services. As a result of this lower sales volume, many product focused dealers are paying higher prices than the end users - who have searched the internet to find the lowest possible price. In order to avoid this price war, many dealers have started to offer additional services for their products such as the installation of software or the assembly of diverse hardware components.

This core business area of the **value added resellers (VAR)** often has a higher customer retention level and, what's more important, much higher margins, since the overall price can be increased by adding additional services. Whereas making the move from being a specialist dealer to a VAR is often relatively simple, becoming a **system integrator** or "systems house" often involves overcoming an overwhelming amount of obstacles (especially for smaller dealers or sellers). However, the effort is well worthwhile. System integrators enjoy a much higher customer retention level than specialist dealers and VARs. They offer a much wider range of services and can often position themselves as fully vertical or horizontal service providers in the market.

System integrators can offer everything from the provision of process neutral infrastructures to the development, implementation and operation of applications and to the customization of third party systems (such as ERP/CRM) in line with individual customer requirements. Some SIs, especially the very large ones, even offer the management and outsourcing of entire processes. Many systems houses already operate their own data centers and therefore operate as **managed service providers**.

Cloud computing and SaaS as a means of accessing the managed services market

The managed services market offers a new niche in the area of cloud computing and software as a service - both of which represent ideal entry possibilities for dealers. The challenges should not be underestimated however, as globally active players such as Amazon or Google are pushing their way into this market. Standard applications such as hosting, e-mail or anti-virus software are also being offered directly by telecommunications service providers as well as international hosting companies and numerous manufacturers. However, dealers can prevail here by developing their own profiles with a local focus and vertical specialization. One of the key advantages for the dealers is their existing local business relationships.

The next graph highlights the correlation between business model, customer retention and margins. Customer retention is the key factor that enables the channel to enter the managed service market. The change from specialist retailer to managed service provider is one of the most important ways to ensure that existing dealers remain profitable in the future.

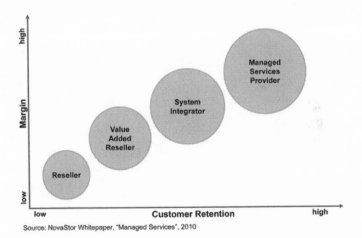

Source: NovaStor Whitepaper, "Managed Services", 2010

Market definition and size

In terms of cloud IT, the usual differentiation is made between infrastructure as a service (IaaS), platform as a service (PaaS) and software as a service (SaaS). SaaS represents the largest market segment and, according to various sources, is also the strongest growing market in absolute figures.

A study by IDC states that the SaaS market will have achieved a volume of around US$25.6 billion as early as 2013, which would represent a twofold increase in volume vis-à-vis 2009.

The following graph which is taken from the IDC study, illustrates this dynamic growth. After reaching critical mass at the end of 2007, this brand new market, which first appeared in 2005 thanks to the availability of faster internet connections and more powerful applications, has gained enormous growth momentum.

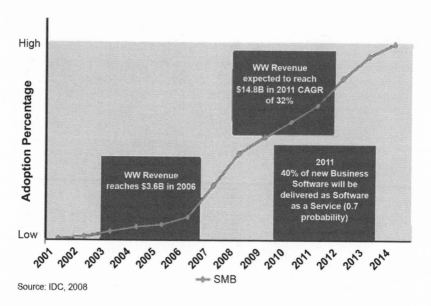

Source: IDC, 2008

The growth in the number of services being provided via the internet has also been substantiated in numerous other studies, a summary of which is provided in the next graph. All of these studies have proven that the largest part of the turnover is already being achieved by services and/or SaaS solutions. The studies also show that turnover achieved via services has increased enormously over the past few years. This is due mostly because of the increasing complexity of the applications, which need to be adjusted in line with the customers' requirements. Many of the services required by customers can often only be provided locally which provides the first real competitive advantage for local dealers.

22% Growth	**Worldwide:** 22% sales growth per year Source: IDC and Experton Group, 2009
25% Market Share	**Worldwide:** 25% of all installations in 2011 will be SaaS applications Source: Gartner, 2009
Euro 418 million in Germany	**Germany:** Euro 418 million are generated in 2009 with SaaS solutions Source: Experton Group, 2010
6 x Service Revenue	Per 1 Euro investment for a SaaS solution you create 6 Euro revenue potential Source: IPED, 2009

SaaS – German market potential

The challenges many companies face have increased significantly over the past few years, partly due to the recent financial crisis. Many companies have had to focus on their core business and reduce costs. In many cases this means that IT is no longer viewed as a core competence. However, it is not only the increasing complexity of the applications, the global threat of viruses or the rising legal requirements regarding data security and availability that demand a high level of expertise, but also the business requirements placed on information technology.

In order to be able to keep up with international competition, numerous companies are forming "virtual" units (mobile employees, outsourcing of sub-divisions, joint ventures with other companies, etc.) in order to achieve a competitive advantage. A prerequisite for the development of a virtual unit is the availability of an IT infrastructure that supports the specific requirements of virtual cooperation. Although IT is becoming a fundamental requirement for gaining competitive advantages and reducing costs, companies are still cutting IT budgets and keeping their IT departments small.

This is the case, despite the increasing demands being placed on them.

The idea of cloud computing is therefore very appealing to many companies, especially SMBs. This is particularly obvious in companies with up to 50 PC workplaces, as more than 40% of these say they want to introduce SaaS applications over the next few years. This percentage drops off somewhat as the size of the company increases, however, a significant market potential still exists.

Company Size	Firms	Employees
1 to 5	1,402,442	3,031,445
6 to 9	236,517	1,720,845
10 to 19	187,441	2,511,537
20 to 49	119,101	3,608,795
50 to 99	44,358	3,064,424
100 to 199	22,176	3,049,218
200 to 499	11,934	3,600,869
500 and more	4,543	5,591,133
TOTAL	**2,028,712**	**26,178,266**
Source: Bundesagentur für Arbeit, 2005		

The table on the right shows this potential clearly. Only a negligibly small number of German companies has more than 500 employees. Approximately 2 million companies in Germany alone face the same IT challenge: To remain competitive in an increasingly global environment with an appropriate IT infrastructure that they themselves cannot support or maintain. This trend can also be observed on an international level, since all industrial nations with similar infrastructures show the same characteristics.

Customer expectations – advantages for providers

The expectations placed on managed services are nearly as high as the interest being shown. Luckily, these expectations are usually quite realistic. Customers expect to benefit from the following advantages when they implement SaaS and cloud computing as managed services:

Introduction with no financial risks	Try first, pay later. "Pay as you go" models – no or low initial investments. Availability of the latest software versions at all times.
Strategic financial benefits	Permanent cost efficiency. Should not be carried as an asset. Cost control.

The graph clearly illustrates what customers expect - including the benefits. For SMBs costs, personnel expenditure, security and service level agreements (SLAs) are critical.

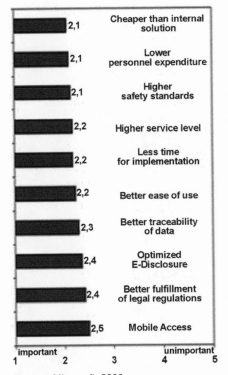

Source: Microsoft, 2008

As various studies have shown, customers expect real cost savings of up to 20%. With regard to personnel expenditure, the demands have more to do with reducing the burden on the IT department than reducing its size. IT administrators working in SMBs often have a wide variety of responsibilities and duties. These often require more time to complete than is actually available.

Security and SLAs form the basis of every IT outsourcing project. Customers want to work with serious providers who are capable of handling all activities while ensuring a maximum level of availability. The failure of important systems can be catastrophic for companies and must be avoided at all costs. Expectations regarding price reductions are therefore generally moderate, since companies are still willing to pay for quality and service.

How customers select managed service providers

As previously explained, cloud based solutions are of particular interest to SMBs. Many specialist dealers, VARs and system integrators are therefore worried that customers may start purchasing their products directly from manufacturers or global providers.

	Overall Channel & Managed Services				
	2 Years Ago	Last Year	Current	Next Year	In 2 Years
Dollar in Billions of Total Channel	$354	$373	$392	$411	$432
% Managed Services	10.4%	11.0%	13,8%	15.0%	16,2%
Managed Services	$36.85	$44.24	$54.05	$61.68	$69.95
Source: Everything Channel, 2010					

According to recent studies however, this fear is unjustified. Only approximately 16 % of all SMBs questioned said they were thinking about purchasing their products or services directly via the manufacturers. A large majority wants to maintain their business relationships with local providers. A whopping 50% even want to purchase via local VARs and remain loyal to their previous suppliers.

However, it should be mentioned once again here that large changes are to be expected in this area. Even if customers want to continue purchasing via local partners, the cards are being re-dealt. Only those VARs and system houses that expand their business in the area of managed services will be rewarded. This is irrespective of whether they want to reap the rewards for early innovations (such as higher margins) or retain their customers. A study performed by Everything Channel illustrates just how large the business potential is. According to this study, managed services already generate around 14% of the global channel turnover. And the growth perspectives for the channel are enormous, as the market is expected to grow dynamically to around US$70 billion over the next few years. However, only those dealers who offer managed services will be able to survive in the long term.[26]

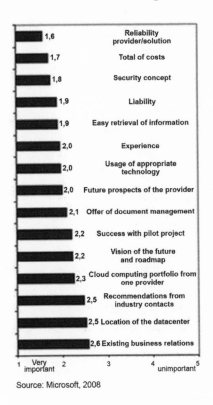

	Value	Criterion
	1,6	Reliability provider/solution
	1,7	Total of costs
	1,8	Security concept
	1,9	Liability
	1,9	Easy retrieval of information
	2,0	Experience
	2,0	Usage of appropriate technology
	2,0	Future prospects of the provider
	2,1	Offer of document management
	2,2	Success with pilot project
	2,2	Vision of the future and roadmap
	2,3	Cloud computing portfolio from one provider
	2,5	Recommendations from industry contacts
	2,5	Location of the datacenter
	2,6	Existing business relations

1 Very important   2   3   4   5 unimportant

Source: Microsoft, 2008

[26] http://www.everythingchannel.com/crn-media/index.htm (2010)

As previously stated, both the managed services and SaaS markets will continue to grow. It goes without saying that everybody wants to benefit from the upheavals in the market. However, in order to gain entry to this market or remain competitive in the future, certain requirements, such as investments in IT as well as know-how, need to be fulfilled. Customers perform precise evaluations when choosing a new partner. The table above highlights the key decision criteria of customers. Provider and solution reliability are at the top of the list of selection criteria.

The reliability of a managed service provider can be verified via certification of the data center, transparent service descriptions or customer references. Customers also place importance on the actual solution behind the services being provided. Functionality, stability and flexibility of the services and support are all critical here, as well as the specialization of the provider - not the brand name of the provider.

Small and medium sized companies, above all, prefer to use local managed service providers. Ideally, these providers themselves will utilize standard solutions from medium sized local software providers whenever possible during the implementation of the cloud platform. The reason for this is that end users know from experience that local software providers are faster when it comes to providing support services or technical adjustments for the solution in question. They can also react to changing requirements with a greater degree of flexibility.

Providers should not underestimate the importance of successful pilot installations. Good cooperation between the service provider and the manufacturer/operator of the cloud platform often plays an important role here. This is because having to make individual adjustments to the standard solution in order to be in line with customer requirements is often unavoidable, especially when vertical solutions are implemented.

End users are fully aware that outsourcing to a managed service provider is a long-term decision, and that it will only cause improvements in efficiency after the start up phase is over. For this reason, many end users want to know more about a manufacturer's vision for the future or roadmap before they reach their final decision. It is therefore advisable to prepare a presentation together with the manufacturer. This should contain appropriate information that can be presented to the customer during a webinar or personal meeting for example. Providing customers with the option of being included in beta programs or inviting them to important roadmap or steering committee meetings can also be beneficial.

The cash flow challenge

Another challenge facing the channel, in addition to the provision of appropriate services, relates to financing. In contrast to the classic model where the customer pays for everything up front (after delivery) and generates turnover immediately, the turnover generated by this new model is spread over a longer period of time. This can lead to significant cash flow problems.

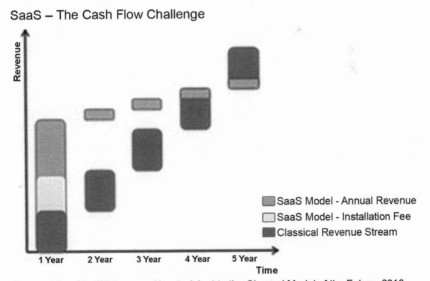

Source: NovaStor Whitepaper, How to Adapt to the Channel Model of the Future, 2010

The graph illustrates this situation well. In contrast to the classic model where the entire amount due is billed during the first year (with only a small amount of maintenance fees being generated on an ongoing basis), the billing amount for the managed services model is generally the same for every time period and is only altered when the customer requests fewer or more services. However, it's fairly normal to charge a flat fee for installation and set up during the first year.

The graph also shows that the managed service model offers many advantages for providers. Regular, unchanging payments over a longer period of time (minimum of 3-5 years generally) facilitate long-term planning along with the successive expansion of services offered by the provider. Studies have also shown that although the overall percentage of managed services will continue to rise successively, a large part of the services will continue to be provided via the traditional model over the next few years. This "hybrid model" is also something that end users will expect from their suppliers. The standard billing method will therefore continue to apply in many areas, as it will be impossible to charge for all services on a monthly basis over a longer period time. This will, in turn, help many companies to tackle the cash flow problem.

One reward for the initial risks related to reduced cash flow and additional investments in the development of managed services business is the so called "long tail" effect. The long tail effect refers to the possibility to access new customer groups. In such a case, services can also be offered to a wide variety of additional customers, not only those who are prepared to pay high initial sums up front (after delivery).

Furthermore, partial services can be provided at greatly reduced prices to customers who are not so financially strong. The ability to open up new customer groups and the continuing trend towards outsourcing can create a significant increase in new business.

The "long tail" effect: reaching new customers

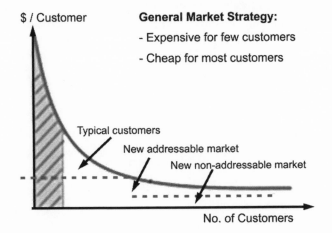

In the next chapter, a number of examples will be highlighted using storage as a service or cloud backups in order to show which services are suitable for gaining entry to the SaaS/managed service market.

Using Cloud Backups to enter the Managed Services Market

A number of reasons exist as to why cloud backups or storage as a service are suitable for gaining entry to the managed service market. One of the most significant reasons is the forecasted growth rate. According to IDC[27], an explosive growth in data volumes will help increase turnover in the cloud backup segment to around US$5.5 billion by 2012. This represents a fivefold increase in just 4 years. This growth clearly highlights the importance of this subject for IT managers.

Other reasons why the backup/storage segment is ideal for gaining access to the SaaS/cloud computing area include:

---

[27] International Data Corporation (IDC) is a global provider of market intelligence, advisory services, and events for the information technology, telecommunications, and consumer technology markets (www.idc.com).

- Data backup/protection is vitally important for companies, but it's not a part of their core business.
- Explosive growth in data volumes and the distribution of data will lead to rising complexity.
- Storage as a service is easier for customers to understand. It is therefore easier for the dealers to sell than more complex solutions such as CRM systems.

From the perspective of the companies offering storage as a service solutions, the segment provides the following advantages:

- The outsourcing of data protection/backups also generates a high customer retention level.
- Long-term contracts guarantee regular earnings that grow along with the data volumes.
- Very low initial investments in comparison with managed services/SaaS offers.
- Storage as a service represents additional value for existing customers, thereby enabling additional turnover to be generated from this group.
- Integration into existing infrastructures is relatively simple in general.
- A short learning curve means reduced training requirements for technical and sales staff.

Sharpen your profile: possibilities for differentiation

If you research the segment, you'll notice that there are countless different storage as a service and cloud backup offers available. It's therefore extremely important for companies to differentiate themselves from their competitors while providing local customers with added benefits.

The easiest way to achieve this is by offering appropriate service level agreements. Providers can (and should) exploit their proximity to customers in order to gain an advantage. However, customers won't base their decisions on a single criteria, because benefits, services and prices are also decisive factors.

In the B2B area for example, companies could decide whether or not to charge an installation fee and, further to this, which services (e.g. onsite consulting and installation) are going to be covered by this fee. Transparent billing models are also important for the customers (e.g. fixed monthly charge with a specific price for each additional GB when a fixed data volume is exceeded). Contract terms and conditions for software maintenance also play an important role.

Calculation: A medium sized systems house as a provider of cloud backup solutions

The following example will highlight the business opportunities for a medium sized systems house. We will assume that this systems house has an existing customer base in a specific region and that it now wants to start offering backup as a service. The customer base includes private users (who have purchased PCs, services and standard software in the past), as well as smaller companies whose IT systems are already being managed by the systems house. The systems house also has a few larger customers, for whom it has handled smaller activities in the past.

By offering solutions that cover online backups for private users and the outsourcing of backup infrastructures (in full or in part) for medium sized and larger companies, the systems house is not starting completely from scratch. It will however, need to invest in new technologies, sales activities and marketing in order to turn these into profitable business activities.

The table below provides an analysis for a 3 year period. For want of simplicity, some of the data included is somewhat "fuzzy," but the table does highlight real business opportunities using realistic (and market relevant) figures.

Period of Time	Home Users			SMB			Enterprise			Summary		
	1st Year	2nd Year	3rd Year	1st Year	2nd Year	3rd Year	1st Year	2nd Year	3rd Year	1st Year	2nd Year	3rd Year
Customers	100	300	500	20	50	100	5	10	20	125	360	620
Storage Req./Customers	8 GB	10 GB	12 GB	50 GB	70 GB	100 GB	250 GB	350 GB	500 GB	24 GB	28 GB	42 GB
Amount of Data TOTAL	0.8 TB	2.9 TB	5.9 TB	1.0 TB	3.4 TB	9.8 TB	1.2 TB	3.4 TB	9.8 TB	3.0 TB	9.8 TB	25.4 TB
General Offer	$10/Month incl. 10GB			$100/Month incl. 50GB			$1000/Month incl. 250GB					
Additional Storage	$1/GB/Month			$2/GB/Month			$2/GB/Month					
Local Backup/DR	$5/Month			$20/Month			$500/Month					
Services	$20/Customer/Month			$600/Customer/Year			$2400/Customer/Year					
Revenue Storage	$12,000	$36,000	$72,000	$24,000	$84,000	$240,000	$60,000	$144,000	$360,000	$96,000	$264,000	$672,000
Revenue Local/DR	$6,000	$18,000	$30,000	$4,800	$12,000	$24,000	$30,000	$60,000	$120,000	$40,800	$90,000	$174,000
Revenue Services	$2,000	$6,000	$10,000	$12,000	$30,000	$60,000	$12,000	$24,000	$48,000	$26,000	$60,000	$118,000
Revenue TOTAL	$20,000	$60,000	$112,000	$40,800	$126,000	$324,000	$102,000	$228,000	$528,000	$162,800	$414,000	$964,000
Storage (0,3$/GB/Month)	$2,880	$10,800	$21,600	$3,600	$12,600	$36,000	$4,500	$12,600	$36,000	$10,980	$36,000	$93,600

As you can see, thanks to clever marketing and good services, the number of customers grows each year in all areas (home users, SMBs, enterprises). Due to the growth in data volumes, the storage requirements of the customers also increase. The figures provided here represent the lower end of the growth scale which is being forecast by current studies.

Even with a relatively small amount of customers, a very worthwhile amount of business can be generated. A turnover of approximately €162,000 is already attained in the first year, and this increases to nearly €1 million in the third year. A price of 30 cents/GB per month has been used for storage space, which includes all associated costs such as energy, hardware, bandwidth etc. Costs for marketing, sales and operations have not been included since this would exceed the scope of this book. However, if you are interested in more details about this sample calculation, you'll want to read my white paper "Cloud Backup. Getting started" which can be downloaded at www.channel-revolution.com.

Successful entry into the SaaS market

The SaaS market provides huge opportunities. The ability to access the managed services market will be a decisive factor with regard to the future of dealers, VARs, systems houses and integrators. It will be very important not to miss the boat here. There are a few core factors that help ensuring a successful entry into the managed service/SaaS market. Before making any investments, providers must be clear about the customer groups they want to address. If this relates to the existing customer base or local or vertical groups, a market analysis regarding requirements and added benefits should be completed from the customers' perspective. Pricing models need to be simple and transparent – complexity is something that unsettles customers. Winning new customers is also important. Appropriate costs for marketing and sales must therefore be taken into account.

One factor of particular importance is clear positioning as a managed service provider with an appropriate range of offers. These offers must be aligned with the requirements of the specific market segment. For example, demand must exist and customers must be willing to pay the price. When analyzing the market, it's better to use a conservative gross profit calculation while taking a realistic sales life cycle into consideration. It may take longer for business to take off than you think.

Companies that are leaders in a vertical or horizontal market segment are most likely to succeed. If a company decides to utilize its domain knowledge in a specific vertical market segment (e.g. all doctors in a region), this must be highlighted accordingly and backed up by an appropriate level of solid expertise. With regard to horizontal market segments (e.g. all home users/private users in a region), market positioning, approach and establishment are more difficult to achieve. The decisive factor in this area is how well the provider is known.

Providers need to make sure that software and hardware partners provide them with a good level of marketing support, because they generally have a great deal of know-how in this area as well as a significant customer base. Other critical success factors include realistic financial planning as well as the selection of an appropriate software provider for the cloud computing and cloud backup infrastructures.

I believe most channel partners will work with a hybrid model for the next several years, meaning they'll start offering SaaS solutions but continue selling and generating the lion share of their revenues through conventional software sales and implementation.

Attracting Channel Partners

There are plenty of options and different approaches to choose from when building a reseller network. Some might be very suitable for your individual business and others might not work at all.[28] The good news is that it's actually quite easy to find new channel partners. The hard part comes after the channel partners have signed up with your program. Now you have to get them working, which means selling and implementing your product.

Build a solid foundation

When you begin the process of recruiting channel partners, it is very important that you build a solid foundation from the start. Don't begin the process without first defining a strategy. It's also critical that you put in place or have in place a reliable team who will provide support to your channel partners once they join you. If you start recruiting without these basic aspects in place you will run the risk of burning your partners further down the track.

Take the time to sit down and write a marketing plan. This document should detail the actions required to achieve one or more marketing objectives. Marketing plans can cover between one and five years. In any case, the plan will entail building and maintaining a professional website for partners and defining a partner program. You'll find more details about all of this in the Execution part of this book.

Promotion strategies to attract resellers

Once you have the foundation of your strategy in place, the next step is attracting a reseller base. This section will give an overview - including some useful tips - of promotions or activities that work best.

---

[28] See also www.chanimal.com – a great website to learn about different reseller programs.

It's a good idea to start early with this stage of (re)building the reseller base. That way you can see what kind of resellers respond and optimize the programs to attract the type of resellers you want to work with. Another idea is to first start working with a small group of your target reseller segment. Find out what they like and what works best for them, and then work on improving those aspects.

Blogs: Blogs are a great communication platform and can really work for you, but they require a large commitment.

White papers: White papers can be used effectively to promote your expertise and to attract the attention of resellers. They're a good marketing tool and demonstrate your thought leadership.

Press releases: Always lead with PR – it's cost-effective and believable. Resellers sell what they know and what gets good reviews. So invest in PR and make sure you publish press releases, send products to journalists for review and keep the press well informed.

Newsletter advertising: Publications like "VAR Business" have one of the largest reseller databases and send out weekly email newsletters that each have their sponsor listed at the top. This type of advertising can work if you have enough budget to maintain a high frequency and visibility.

Advertising: One of the big advantages of PR is that the publication of press releases can be very inexpensive. There is also a disadvantage however; journalists have a loyalty to their readership and they sometimes won't consider your news worthy for publishing. Even if they do, they won't necessarily say exactly what you would like them to say. Print or online ads allow you to position your products and run reseller promotions. They can also be used to announce promotions to local and regional resellers who already sell your product but are not registered with you yet.

Direct response: Direct response or "mailings" can be sent via postal mail, fax or email. This can be especially effective if you have a reliable list of prospective resellers (don't hesitate to go to competitor websites to look for resellers). The main problem is that resellers are bombarded with direct response mailings and your information can simply get lost in the pile. This means mailings need to be creative and eye-catching.

Reseller store-by-store visits and tours with seed copies: If you have your own sales force, you can mobilize them to ask local VARs to review the product and help recruit the resellers. You could also hire one of the national rep companies such as Channel Sources or The Distribution Network, or training firms such as MarketStar, Channel Force or Channel Partners. These training firms cycle through most of the nation's top VARs on a quarterly basis - sometimes in the form of tours with other complementary vendors.

Road shows: Get together with some other vendors and organize half or full-day presentations in a number of cities. If you organize the road shows and ask the other vendors to pay to participate, this is a very inexpensive marketing tool.

Trade show attendance: Although many trade shows today are attended by end user and reseller, they're still a good way to recruit resellers.

Promotions via distributors: All distributors have the contact details of their resellers. These can be used to do promotions. You'll have to check with the distributors what they offer.

Telemarketing: Professional telemarketing companies utilize a massive database for contacting end users and resellers and providing them with NFR (not for resale) copies, product information etc. You could engage a telemarketing company to get connected to your reseller base, or you could use your own team to do this type of recruiting.

Alliance cross marketing: Your alliance network of complementary products is always an excellent source for recruiting resellers. You can contact their authorized VARs and offer bundles and promotions, knowing that their resellers are already familiar with the market area.

Building the Partner Network

If you carry out all the appropriate promotions successfully, you'll attract many resellers that will want to become a partner and profit from your business. The main question you'll now face is how to build the right channel structure and work with the right number of channel partners? The next pages will provide some answers.

Reaching quota with the right channel partners

Before you begin the selection process, it's very important that you have clear objectives and a clear strategy - regardless if you are the CEO of an ISV or an individual channel manager. Your strategy should be defined in a "channel marketing plan" and be based upon real world feedback. The results of your campaigns to attract resellers should give you a clear indication of what kinds of partners are within your reach.

Let me illustrate this by using an example. Let's say you as a channel manager need to reach a quota of US$1 million or you as an ISV want to sell products to the value of US$1 million over the channel. If your product portfolio ranges from typical distribution products with an average sale price of US$25 to enterprise products with an average price of US$25,000 then you will require a wide range of different partners to reach your goal. (In reality, most ISVs only carry a specific range of products or their products are divided into different sales departments with different go-to-market strategies.)

The quota describes the revenue goal you have set within a defined period of time. The average price (avg. price) is what the ISV receives from the channel partner. The percentages at the top of the chart represent the share each product has in your overall budget. If you want to reach 10% of the US$1 million quota using your consumer product line then you will have to move 4,000 products. In order to reach 20% of this goal with a "small business product," you have to move 2,000 products; another 30% using a "network product" requires moving 300 copies; another 20% using a "corporate product" requires 40 copies. If you want to reach 20% of your target revenue using an "enterprise product," then your channel partners will need to win 8 projects.

Quota	$1,000,000					
Product	Average Price	10%	20%	30%	50%	100%
Consumer	$25	4,000	8,000	12,000	20,000	40,000
Small business	$100	1,000	2,000	3,000	5,000	10,000
Network	$1,000	100	200	300	500	1,000
Corporate	$5,000	20	40	60	100	200
Enterprise	$25,000	4	8	12	20	40

This calculation gives you an easy overview of how you can reach your goal. It is up to you however, to determine what the best combination of products should be.

Using different partners to reach your goal

There are various ways to determine the combination you should use to reach your goal of US$1 million in channel revenue. Some very important points to take into consideration are the market potential, what types of channel partners you already have, the history of these types of products and the average sales cycle. Your research, market experience and history of software installations might make you something of an expert in this field but don't become overly optimistic. It often takes some time before a channel partner will start moving your product.

Your goal when entering the channel might be to reach US$1 million in the first year, but it will be unlikely that a large number of enterprise partners will move to your technology and close deals within this first year. Normally it takes a while (up to a year) to get enterprise partners up and running. The distribution channel is not that different. Moving 10,000 or more copies from one product line within a certain period of time (within the first year) normally requires a very strong channel, good branding and a sizable marketing budget.

One of the biggest mistakes companies make when building their partner network is letting everybody sell their products instead of being more selective. ISVs often make the mistake of acquiring many unqualified partners when they begin building their partner program, giving them all the same treatment and discounts instead of dividing them into different groups.

Many decision makers I've talked to are not aware that there are significant hidden costs associated with building and maintaining channel distribution. These costs are caused by the channel manager, marketing support and marketing material, partner trainings and education etc.

The situation can also become frustrating for your existing partners if you take on too many new channel partners. Their profit margin will shrink if there are too many resellers that offer your product. If the situation becomes critical and new or existing competitors begin offering the same kind of product, then the existing resellers will start selling your competitor's products. Often, the resellers who are first to leave are unfortunately those that offer real value to your partner network.

To ensure that your product doesn't become "over-distributed" and that you select the right number of partners, it's very important that you use a well informed selection process.

The Partner Selection Funnel

Once you've defined your strategy, business goals and what types of partners you need to reach these goals, you should design a custom-made "funnel" for your channel partner selection process. I recommend creating different funnels for different groups of channel partners.

To illustrate a typical selection process, I've designed a generic funnel. I'll use it to explain the necessary steps when selecting the right partners. These "right" partners will eventually form the "peer group". Then you can develop action plans together with this peer group for achieving your goals.

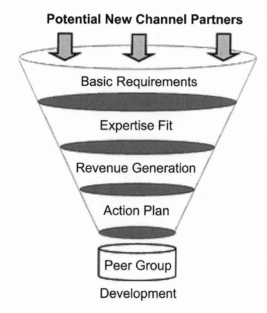

The "potential new channel partners" (who appear as a result of the different marketing methods described earlier in the book) must go through a screening process. Don't forget to store information about all the potential partners in a database for easy access in the future. I'll write more about this in the Execution part of this book

Basic requirements

The first screening phase involves asking the question: Does the partner meet my basic requirements? It's crucial that you understand the importance of this phase. You must answer the question clearly, as each step thereafter costs more time and effort. If you spend too much time with partners that are not worth it, your partner acquisition costs will be too high. It can also be frustrating for the resellers. If a reseller spends time on the project initially, but doesn't end up becoming your partner (and making revenue), then it would have been better to know this right from the beginning or very early on in the process.

Following is a list of typical basic requirements for potential partners.

Does the potential partner fit into one of your target channels? In the beginning it's important that you only focus on a limited number of channels (e.g. VAD, VAR). If you start working with every kind of channel partner you can't meet high quality standards or deliver the necessary material.

Does the potential partner have a business focus that is related to your business? If you are selling e-commerce software, then the partner should have experience in implementation of these kinds of solutions. Or they should have access to the markets that require or resell e-commerce solutions.

How big is the revenue potential? The effort that you expend on a partner must always be in proportion to the potential revenue. If the partner's core business is distribution, and you want to use them to sell your US$50 solution, then you must check that they have the distribution power to do this. This is one of the first checks you should make. Then you can carry out more detailed analysis using the "partner funnel" later.

Can you win mindshare? Winning mindshare means that your partner will give your products the proper attention they require to become successful. You can only become successful if your partner starts thinking about the product and it becomes important to them.

Do you have access to the right people in the company? It's important that you have access to the management level of the company, especially when you are the smaller partner.

How does your partner generate profits? If your first contact from the potential channel partner is with a marketing person then it's wise to be skeptical. Very often, partners such as broadliner distributors and e-tailers make more money from the marketing funding they request than with the actual gross margin on your product.

Expertise fit

The "expertise fit" tells you whether or not the potential partner has the ability to resell your products in the way you think is best. Typical expertise fit criteria are:

Access to specific market segments
- For example, a broadliner may service a wide range of resellers that you don't have access to or that cannot be served directly by you in an efficient way.
- Regional or international presence. If your solution requires onsite consulting or heavy interaction with the end user then a local partner is necessary to sell the product into this region.
- Vertical market knowledge. Many products demand that the partner has specific knowledge and "speaks the language" of the end user.

Technology fit
- Does the company have the technical ability to explain or implement the product?

- Does your product complement other products in the portfolio of the channel partner from a technical perspective?
- Can the channel partner's technical and sales team invest the time necessary to learn about the products?

Complementary products

- Does your partner sell the same kind of products to a specific customer group? Do they have the ability to add complementary products to enhance the final solution?

Revenue generation

If the first screening of your potential partner reveals that they meet the basic requirements and technology expertise fit is positive, then you should start taking a closer look at their revenue potential. Let's use an example where the partner currently generates US$5 million p.a. in revenue, of which US$1 million is license revenue and US$4 million is revenue from professional services. The partner's total staff is 40 people, of which 25 work in professional services. You hope to carry out 4 enterprise projects with them that will require approximately 100 man days each. First you must ask yourself: Does this partner have the potential to sell and implement 4 projects within my time frame? My recommendation is that you assign each potential partner a goal. Then you can work through the list, establishing what each partner is capable of (what ability do they have to reach this goal?). If you can't answer this question positively then you need to look for other partners.

Please try to be realistic here. Don't make the mistake of investing a lot of time and resources just because you like a partner. The following points are important when evaluating how much revenue is possible:

Access to (existing) sales force

- Does the potential partner have an existing sales force that can also sell your products? How many products do they currently sell?

- Can you educate the sales force and work with some of their existing clients to sell your product?
- Will the sales force receive a specific quota or commission on your product? What motivates the sales force to sell your product?

Marketing capabilities and budget

- Does the partner have product managers who can influence others and speak about your product?
- Do they have a database of customers to whom you can promote your product?

Existing clients/references

- Do their clients need your product?

Compelling event

- What is the main reason the partner wants to start doing business with you? Have they sold products from your competitors before?

Action plan

If you've evaluated your potential partner and the results are positive, the next step is to build an "action plan" together with your partner. In the good old days, the action plan was called a "business plan". Usually, these business plans required a huge amount of time and involved many people from both companies. It was also very common that during the process of creating the plan, no business was being done.

My experience has taught me that it's much better to create a short and simple action plan instead, which clearly outlines the partner's commitment and responsibilities. Once this is in place, you can begin making money together straight away. If you and your channel partner start being successful together then you can work on developing a more detailed business plan. This way you are only outlaying the necessary time and effort with the most successful partners. Another advantage of this approach is that there is no better way to build a strong partnership than being successful together. When creating an action plan (even a simple one), you should evaluate the following points:

Sponsorship from management

- Make sure that you have a sponsor on management level. You must ensure that your new partnership gets a high priority and is visible in your partner's company.
- Update their management about the agreed tasks and make sure that your management is involved too.

Training and education

- The channel partner's sales force and technical team must know your product in detail. They must understand the product positioning, who the target customers are, what the competitive advantage is and what the value to the end user is.
- Offer technical support to the technical team. They will only recommend what they know and what they are comfortable with.
- Help your partner's sales force by accompanying them on sales calls and holding joint customer meetings.

Short-term revenue potential

- How much revenue is possible within the next 6 months? Who are the first clients or markets that the partner will address with your products?
- Make sure that you target existing customers and generate early success cases. Even if you don't earn money from these first deals, this will inspire commitment from your partner that can potentially be of bigger value.

Marketing and sales initiatives

- Define the first marketing initiatives and make someone in your team directly responsible.
- Create some specials to promote your product.

- Do some "internal marketing" with your channel partner. Think of some creative ways to draw attention to your new partnership within your channel partner's business network.

Peer group

A peer group, within the context of this book, represents a selected group of partners who share roughly the same characteristics such as size, business type or capability to serve a particular market. Once you've formulated an action plan and you are confident to go ahead, then the potential channel partner becomes part of the peer group with whom you want to grow your business. Keep in mind however, that even after a lengthy selection process, often a lot of partnerships just don't work out.

The task of managing the peer group must now be passed on to one of your channel managers. They should ensure that there is the right number of active partners in each target market segment, and that relations with partners who are performing poorly are phased out.

I've explained how to select the right partners. My experience shows however, that only 20% of all partners will work out and contribute the agreed revenue. So it's necessary that we take a closer look at the "partner engagement lifecycle." The goal is to identify the most promising partners and make sure that your channel investments are not wasted on the wrong 80%. The partner engagement lifecycle describes the likelihood that a partner will contribute to the channel revenue (even after the screening process has taken place).

The following graph illustrates a typical example. Depending on the type of partner and expected average sales as well as the results of the screening process (which should be completed within the first month), the "partner development" stage can begin. During partner development your company, your products and your team must win trust. The "pitch rate" in the graph shows the likelihood of successful development with the partner within the first 3 months after screening. A successful development means that your partner's team is trained, your products are officially listed and that an action plan is in place.

Partner engagement lifecycle

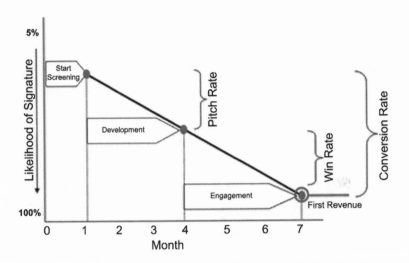

The next step is the "engagement phase" which starts after the development has reached a certain point and the active promotion of your product has begun. During the engagement phase, the focus should be concentrated on promoting your product with the partner. Make sure that the sales team understands your product; ask the right questions and work out solutions for any problems which appear during this period. The engagement phase is extremely critical for the success of the partnership, so it's important to try and ensure that your partner has early success with the product. Try to minimize problems - if they do arise then make sure they don't go unresolved.

The "win rate" describes the likelihood that a partner will contribute revenue in the next 3 months following the end of the development process. The timeline for this process really depends on the type of product you are selling. If you sell packaged consumer products your channel partners will be the type who only make low level revenue and the timeline will be much shorter. On the other hand, if you are working with a global alliance partner, the timeline will be much longer. The total "conversion rate" shows the likelihood of finding and developing a target account (channel partner), who successfully resells your product and reaches the expected revenue.

A simple example

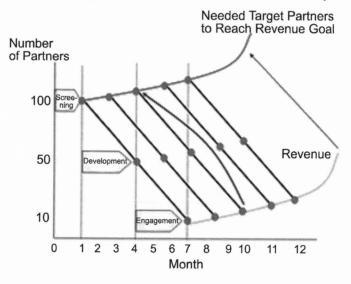

For revenue growth in October, the number of screened target accounts has to be increased in April

If your aim is to make US$1.2 million p.a. in revenue using the channel and you forecast that the average successful partner will buy US$10,000 worth of products every month, then you need 10 successful partners (10 partners buy US$10,000 per month = US$100,000 per month, which is US$1.2 million per year). If the conversion rate is 1:10, then you need 100 partners to pass the screening process.

If you plan on growing your channel revenue, then the number of target accounts needs to be constantly growing, as long as the revenue potential with the partners is stable.

Another way to boost channel revenue is to increase the revenue with the partners who are already successful. That's the next chapter's topic.

Overall, it's very important that you have realistic expectations and don't expect too much of partners that in the end won't deliver. With a clear channel partner program, you can create different partner levels and differentiate the channel partners based on their experience and their revenue potential. Once you've defined different partner groups, you need to make sure that your channel team spends their time with the partners who are committed, who serve an important market segment and, most importantly, generate the defined revenue. Channel partners who don't achieve agreed sales levels need to be either phased out or moved into another partner level where they don't get special treatment and receive lower discounts. Your partner account managers must always optimize the group of partners. They should actively create relationships with potential new partners so as to ensure that they build their own pipeline of partners.

Key Factors for Successful Partnerships

To make certain that your partners are successful and to keep those that are in your channel (which is often more important), it's vital that you try and identify what the drivers behind a successful partnership are. Before you begin to build a channel strategy, you should understand what motivates a long lasting relationship with a partner and what factors create real value from the partner's point of view.

Research conducted by Gartner in 2001 shows that there are many factors that are important and some are more important than others.[29] Interestingly, this study found that the most important factors are: quality of the relationship manager; revenue generation and executive level support/sponsorship.

---

[29] Gartner Dataquest, www.gartner.com (2001)

Value Drivers Rated Above the Mean (All Participants)

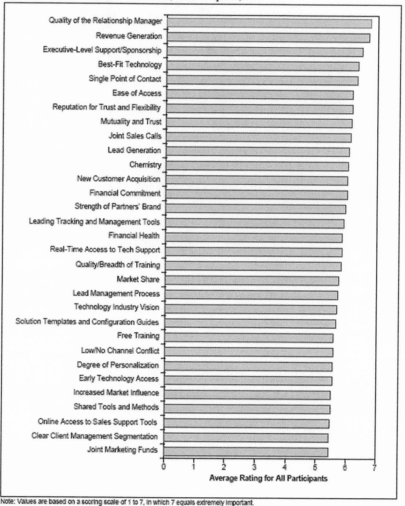

Note: Values are based on a scoring scale of 1 to 7, in which 7 equals extremely important.
Source: Gartner Dataquest (November 2001)

Why are these factors essential for a successful partnership? Why is it that only one of the 10 most important factors is technology/product related ("best fit technology")? The answer is easy: partners are aware that technology in the IT industry changes quickly - features will be added and new competitors or new technologies will come along very soon. Because of these reasons, the partners also know that they can't build a relationship based on technology alone, so they look for partners they can trust and rely on.

I want to take a look at some of these factors and explain why they are important for a successful partnership.

Quality of the relationship manager

The relationship manager or "channel manager" speaks for you (is your company's face) to the partner. This person is responsible for building and executing plans, working with the channel partner on specific deals and creating marketing activities to generate more leads. It's important that the channel manager understands the business of your channel partners and can provide them with the necessary support to reach their goals.

The channel manager should be the single point of contact for the partner and easy to get in touch with. Don't assign the channel manager with too many accounts though; otherwise they won't be able to support the channel partners more efficiently.

If the channel manager doesn't understand the business of the channel partner, is not reliable or revenue focused, the success of the whole partnership will be threatened.

Revenue generation/lead generation

Every partner begins their relationship with your company with the belief that they can generate additional revenue using your product. If your product doesn't contribute to their revenue goal, then you won't get the support you need from the sales team - they have to fulfill their quotas.

Successful lead generation is one step towards creating additional revenue for the company. Can your product drive leads to the part-ner's sales channel? Maybe your product can address a "hot" need and become the motivator for more business using complementary products. If this is the case, then you will get the attention of the sales and marketing team. They can use your product to generate new leads which creates mindshare.

Executive level support/sponsorship

An often overlooked but very important factor is executive level support and sponsorship from both sides. Most of the people I've worked with in the IT industry are always extremely busy and don't know how to get everything done. If business with your company is not high on their "to do" list, then it will be impossible to reach your goals as defined in the action or business plan. When this happens, the partnership can and will get off track.

Best fit technology

Your technology must fit into the partner's technology scope. Every company wants to leverage their existing resources in order to make more revenue. It will be very difficult however, to position a LINUX based solution in a Microsoft shop for example. It would be much easier to add a storage solution to the service portfolio of a channel partner who already serves this market.

It's also important that you give your channel partner early access to the latest technology. Most end users see their IT reseller, your channel partner, as their trusted advisor. It is therefore very important that the IT reseller always has the ability to impress the end user.

Low/no channel conflict

The protection of a market segment is always very high on the list. Channel partners often focus more on the discussion of channel conflicts and overlapping territories than on actual sales. The reality is however, that channel conflicts are very difficult to avoid - even the best compensation models can't avoid that different sales forces go after the same market or the same customer.

Joint marketing funds

When developing a market segment, it's crucial that both parties invest in marketing. Don't finance the marketing on your own. The channel partner must "show their skin" in the game and also make some investments. On the other hand, the channel partner often has the expectation that the vendor will help them with money for marketing material and additional discounts.

After the formation of a new partnership, the market penetration should start immediately. It's important that there are some early successes in order to encourage support from the partner's sales force. Joint marketing is a very important part of any new partnership.

This concludes part II of the book. Now that we understand how the channel works, we can look at what needs to be done to successfully build a channel, taking into account the newest trends and global competition.

Part III: A Revolutionary Approach

The difficulty lies, not in the new ideas but in escaping the old ones, which rami-fy, for those brought up as most of us have been, into every corner of our minds.

John Maynard Keynes

I hope I've made it clear in the previous chapters how important the channel is for the IT industry, which different types of channels exist and what you need to think about when selecting the number and type of partners you want to work with. So the foundation has been laid. Now I'd like to convince you to take a "revolutionary channel approach" and show you how it can be done. I'll talk about concepts and strategies. We'll then get down to the nitty-gritty in the execution part of the book. Proper execution can actually be seen as the first step in taking a revolutionary channel approach. It's not just about making promises to your channel partners and providing good marketing material. It's about keeping those prom-ises and doing what you said you'd do. You'd be amazed to know how many companies don't really follow through on their well thought out strategies.

Why is a revolutionary channel approach needed?

I've come to the conclusion, based on observations of current mar-ket developments and evolving technology trends, that the typical "follower" approach, when working with the channel, is no longer effective. If you simply "copy and paste" existing channel programs from your competitors or recycle old material from your previous business experience into your new project you will inevitably fail. Nobody will wait around for you to get it right either, since there are so many different independent software vendors (ISVs) in the market.

Now is the time to define new rules for working with the channel. Take an innovative approach and introduce a new business model. The internet is the key driver behind many of the changes in our daily business (and private) lives. It's also had a huge impact on channel programs. Social and business networks like LinkedIn, XING or Facebook have made it possible for the first time in history to directly and effectively get in touch with many channel partners. Tools such as Twitter can provide discussion forums for your product and blogs can disseminate information about your company to a previously inaccessible global audience. But beware, these tools can either work really well for you, or have a disastrous impact as they create more transparency about how you conduct your business.

You can, and should, harness the potential of these new times however. The internet and its information transparency allows you to design a channel model and program that is different from existing ones - bringing extraordinary value to your channel partners. Successful entrepreneurs have always revised and reworked the existing business models and rules; proposing something totally new and innovative which simultaneously increases end user benefit. The goal of the revolutionary channel approach is to increase the benefit for the entire value chain which includes you, your channel partners and their end users.

Please read this chapter with an open mind. Some of the ideas I lay out might seem crazy to you, but I firmly believe that without challenging the conventional wisdom it's not possible to create revolutionary products and services. This is especially true if you are entering the market as a new competitor because there will always be someone else who already owns the customers or can invest more money in conventional marketing than you can.

The following three short examples describe entrepreneurs who started small but by creating new rules became leaders in their market segment.

Henry Ford was not the actual inventor of the automobile. However, his innovations in automobile assembly line techniques and the introduction of standardized, interchangeable parts produced the first mass production vehicle manufacturing plant. This paved the way for the introduction of cheaper automobiles and turned the United States into a nation of motorists. [30]

Michael Dell revolutionized the personal computer industry by skipping the middleman and selling directly to the customer. He also innovated PC manufacturing by developing a process to mass produce individual, made-to-order computers. He then enabled customers to order these personalized computers directly online. His innovations in manufacturing and distribution have made him one of the most successful businessmen of our time. His direct sales model isn't working very well today however, and Dell is now facing a lot of challenges. In an interesting turn of events, they've now decided to invest heavily in building a channel. Only time will tell if Michael Dell can innovate the market again with a new idea.

Steve Jobs combined design and simplicity with innovation. After returning to Apple in 1997, Macs became more chic than ever, the iPod conquered the world and the iPhone became the market leader for smart phones. Apple claims that their newest product, the iPad, was the most successful technology product ever in its first month after market introduction. With its retail stores and cult-like following, Apple has become as much a lifestyle choice as a computer brand. Jobs recognized that style and ease of use are as important as substance for a certain type of customer. No one had built a computer for that type of user until he did.

The key lesson we can learn from each of these three entrepreneurs is that you have to analyze and then rethink what everybody else in your market is doing. If you simply follow the market leader and try to copy them you will fail. You can't beat the market leaders at their

---

[30] See "History of Automobiles" on Wikipedia for the full story of who invented the automobile.

own game. The Dell example also shows that what is right for the market at one point in time might not work out forever.

In the next chapters, I'll take a closer look at some well known business strategies, extracting the key lessons we can learn from them and applying this knowledge to the creation of a revolutionary channel approach. This book can't create a blueprint for every possible channel, but it will give you some valuable ideas for designing your revolutionary channel approach and providing unique value to your channel.

A "Me Too" Strategy Is Not Enough

In their book "Blue Ocean Strategy", authors W. Chan Kim and Renée Mauborgne describe why you'll only beat the competition once you've stopped trying to beat them.[31] Using tactics such as giving your partners a little more margin, raising marketing funds or adding another feature to differentiate your product simply isn't enough.

Once you've made your decision to use the channel for your business it's important to "burn your ships"[32] - making it very clear to your team that there is no other way for the company to become successful than building a channel. The vision and strategy for becoming a channel player must come from the top. If the company's status floats between being "direct" and a "small channel", the initiatives will fail. I will discuss this again in more detail in the execution part of the book. As shown in the chart below, it's important that you think about what can be reduced, raised, eliminated or created in order to generate a new value curve. These factors will vary

---

[31] Blue Ocean Strategy: How to Create Uncontested Market Space and Make the Competition Irrelevant (Boston Massachusetts, Harvard Business School Press, 2005)

[32] The phrase "burn your ships behind you" is derived from what Hernan Cortez did in 1519; he literally set fire to his ships when he arrived on the shore to let his crew know that there was no way back.

from product to product, as they depend on the type of business and the industry your products are aimed at.

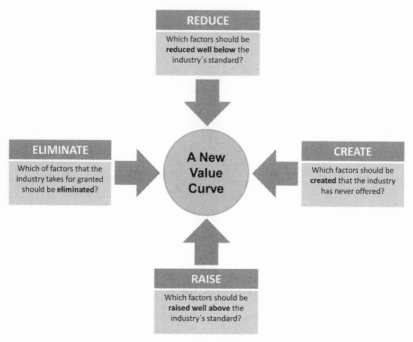

Source: W.C. Kim / R. Mauborgne, "Blue Ocean Strategy", 2005

Typical factors that can be *reduced* are the level of discounts to the channel or the marketing funding. Ask yourself: Is it really necessary to give almost 50% to distribution or 25% to every channel partner? Maybe you can *eliminate* certain product lines or limit the way you sell products to make the whole channel more efficient. Do all products fit the channel's need or is it better to start with a limited number of products? Do you need so many different product variations or is it better to reduce the items on your pricelist to make it easier to handle? Are there any possibilities to *raise* the bar and offer something totally new to your channel partners? Maybe you can offer "easy to read," competitive analyses that aren't focused on features, but put customer value at the centre. Even standard things such as free training, motivational videos, case studies and joint press releases can raise the bar significantly.

In order to *create* new value for your channel partners, you need to become more creative. This is because other ISVs have already tried just about everything to motivate their channel partners. Very often however, the channel partners themselves have so many restrictions in their business that they don't want to see new things.

This will require you to think "out of the box" and enter into new areas. Something I recommend is listing each potential area of value for the channel partner and then looking for ways that you can offer to create new value in these areas. For example, communication to the end user is an ongoing challenge and is very difficult for the whole channel value chain. This problem also costs the entire channel a lot of money. For example end users often don't buy maintenance and switch to other products. As a solution to this problem, why not offer "in-product communication" (messages that pop up when the software is being used) for your channel partners to help them reach the end user.

Another common scenario occurs when your channel partner's sales departments have difficulty with technical questions and their internal product managers don't have the knowledge or time to provide answers. I have seen cases where there only two technical staff members to support more than 50 products and more than 100 sales reps. Why not offer easy tech support via chat or phone that is dedicated to specific groups?

I'll go deeper into this area and show how you can avoid competing with just features alone in the next chapter. I'll also show you that it's possible for ISVs to develop a complete solution to bring more value to their channel partners. Your partners can also use other things such as services to win customers.

Always keep in mind that the most successful channel partners don't just sell technology, they sell solutions and this enables them to make more profit.

Moving from Product Features to Complete Solutions

In their book "The Delta Project", Arnoldo C. Hax and Dean L. Wilde II use a triangle to describe the different strategic positions.[33] The letter "delta" means transformation and, in this context, transformation means from the "best product positioning" to "total customer solution positioning" to "system lock-in positioning". The whole concept is about "customer bonding" and is based on the idea that it's only when a company reaches a high level of customer bonding that it can be extremely successful. Without customer bonding, most companies fail and they or their product will inevitably disappear from the market. I won't go as far as to explain the entire model and its underlying strategies in detail here, but I personally think that the core lessons we can take away from it are extremely relevant for building a successful channel business.

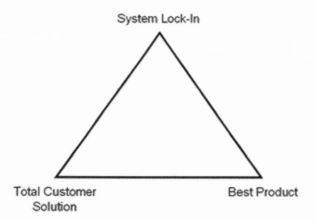

"Best product positioning" describes the classical form of competition; where the product itself and its functionality lie at the centre of the vendor's strategy. This means that low cost and unique features are the driving factors for development. The main benchmarks are the competitor products. Most of the product development, includ-

---

[33] Arnoldo C. Hax, Dean L. Wilde II, The Delta Project: Discovering New Sources of Profitability in a Networked Economy, Palgrave Macmillon (2001)

ing product features, is done internally without much interaction with partners or customers. The result is a commoditizing of the customers and the channel.

Make friends, not enemies

The "total customer solutions" strategy necessitates an entirely different mindset. This strategic approach does not solely place the product and its related features at its centre. Instead, the focus of this strategy is the customers and their requirements for an individual solution. The main benchmark is the ability to create solutions for specific customer groups. Companies who use this strategy are driven by customer needs. Their approach is no longer to be at war with competitors, but instead to focus on building relationships with customers.

The "system lock-in" strategy takes it one step further. This strategy makes use of "complementors", who deliver important products or solutions in order to create a complete solution for the customer. It's important to note that even in this strategic option, the customer continues to be the central focus. Together with the complementors, you can create a de-facto standard for a specific industry. A good example of a real world system lock-in strategy is the Apple iPhone with its Appstore. The Appstore hosts over 200,000 applications that increase the functionality of the phone itself.[34] For many people, the motivation for choosing an iPhone over a similar phone from another company (such as Blackberry or Samsung) is the availability of exciting applications. Most of the iPhone applications are developed by ISVs. This is a good example showing how a vendor can work together with complementors and different channels to create the perfect solution for the customers.

If you are following the "best product" strategy, there will always be a competitor who has more features or offers the same product at a lower price. The biggest pitfall of this strategy is that you are forced into a negative spiral of adding more and more features whilst low-

---

[34] Appstore: www.apple.com/iphone/apps-for-iphone (2010)

ering the price at the same time. This approach means that you can only target generic channels and mass distribution where there is no customer bonding and price dictates everything. This strategy can't be healthy in the long run because of the cost increase due to higher R&D and higher margins to the channel.

The "system lock-in strategy", on the other side of the spectrum, is very difficult to attain for most vendors. This is especially the case if you are a small software company because it's extremely difficult to convince complementors to build additional solutions based on your product. This will only happen once you've already started to dominate a market segment. There are many very successful "niche players" and it's a good strategy to try and become one of these vertical or geographical "heroes" in one market segment.

The most pragmatic approach is to focus on becoming a "total customer solution" and build your channel around this strategy. This means that your channel partners and their customers are at the center of your thinking.

Ask yourself all these questions: What will another price reduction or the bundling of goods really bring to my channel partners or their customers? How much success have I had from bundling a free copy of my software when the channel partner buys a package of 3 or 5? Will it confuse end user if I bundle a free photo book or a coupon for flowers to my product? Do I really believe I can gain any loyalty from my channel partner, knowing that they will leave me the minute another company offers something more attractive for free? I believe a feature or price driven strategy is bound to fail.

You'll be successful, on the other hand, if you implement the "total customer solution" strategy. In order to position yourself in this corner of the triangle, you must first change your mindset. Don't just think in terms of features and competitive comparisons, start thinking in solutions; solutions that can be sold with your channel partners to a specific group of customers. Your main goal is to provide your channel partners with a tool (your product and services) that enables them to add their products or services to create a total customer solution. Your channel partners should be in a position where they can create their own economic value and start earning money, not just from reselling your solution but from adding additional services.

If you want to reach this point, your focus must be on selecting the right channel partners and developing business solutions for their customers. You can enable them with marketing material, sales approaches and technical support to serve this market.

If you effectively shift the mindset from product features and actual competitors to complete solutions for specific market segments then, together with your channel partners, you can reach a dominant market position. From there it's only one more step to the system lock-in strategy. Empirical research has shown that companies who have reached the system lock-in position (even in small market segments) are significantly higher valued than comparable best product companies.[35] This is, however, another topic altogether.

Generating New Business for Your Partners

We have seen how creating new value and building a total customer solution will improve the relationship with your channel partners and how these two factors will create new business. But how can this actually be done? When I talk about creating new business, this also means that your partners will need to invest a significant effort to make this happen. There shouldn't be any "free lunches." In reality there is never a free lunch.

Companies who execute this aspect correctly can increase their market share without significantly raising their costs of sales, but they need to address how they can either help to increase revenue or decrease the cost of doing business. If you successfully decrease

---

[35] www.strategy-business.com (2009)

the costs then these free resources can be invested into the creation of new business.

I recommend that you analyze your partner's situation and identify each aspect where sales can be increased. Since it's often too difficult to make individual analyses of each partner, try putting your partners into different groups and then analyzing them group by group.

Here are my recommendations for points of analysis:

Communication

- Listen and learn from your partners. Communicate with all the different levels of your channel partners. It's crucial that you do a lot of listening and don't do all the talking.
- Make personal phone calls to the CEOs of your channel partners. As long as you talk to them about increasing sales they will be interested in what you have to say.[36]
- Summarize what you learn from this and create a real world plan. Never create a plan without first communicating with your partners.

Marketing

- Many channel partners are weak in the area of marketing. Help them to target their existing customer groups.
- Create a "partner demand service" to increase the speed and efficiency of their marketing activities. The service can provide specialist marketing skills, resources and co-marketing funds that will help create unique campaigns and stage successful events.
- Accelerate their growth by providing them with the tools and information they need to win and retain new business.
- Lend your brand name to the partners. Very often this gives them more reliability and visibility.

---

[36] An interesting blog: www.alextrain.com/inside-sales-telesales-tips-blog/bid/11869/3-Tips-to-increase-Channel-Sales-try-thinking-out-of-the-box (2009)

- Create mailers (templates and content) for your channel partners. These mailers should show how your product combined with your partner's services presents an ideal solution.
- Leverage your partners' domain knowledge in Google PPC campaigns or on social networking sites to promote a combined solution.

Sales
- Empower your partner's sales people. Think long and hard about what they are going to need to be effective at selling your products and services, and provide it to them in a concise, clear format - keep it short and to the point.
- Create an easy pricing structure so that your channel partners don't have to invest extra time just to learn your pricing. Don't forget that your channel partner's sales people are always very busy.
- Tell them how to compete. Be frank about your capabilities and how you fare against the competition. Tell the sales people where your strengths lie and forewarn them about areas of weakness.
- Help them empower their telesales and field sales or join forces with your partner.
- Build close relationships with the sales force. If they know you personally then they will be more likely sell your products. Let them know that they can always discuss their challenges with you and that you will help to solve them together.
- Help them to generate more revenue from the existing customer base - you will be astonished how you can exploit this for more sales and better revenue.

Education
- Educate your channel partner's team for free or for a low price. As said before, knowledgeable partners achieve higher sales.
- Offer professional services for the first couple of projects without extra margin. This means you as the vendor only charge what the actual costs are. The ISV shouldn't try and make money in every corner of the business.

- Allow your channel partner to sell your trainings and professional services as well.

New markets

- Expand your partner's existing solutions and create new solutions for similar markets. For example, if the target market is lawyers then you can expand it to include notaries.
- Build solutions together with your channel partner and other ISVs who work with the same group of channel partners.
- Expand the existing ideas from one channel partner to another - something that works in the east should also work in the west.
- Organize webinars or events where your channel partners can meet each other and exchange ideas.

General

- Less complexity when doing business is key. Many channel partners become frustrated if they deal with companies who have complex processes. If your processes are fast and easy, this forces the partner to move faster as well.
- Show commitment on all levels. Have your CEO deliver webinars for the channel partners to show that top management is committed to the channel strategy.
- Provide financing if this will ensure that your partner can close an attractive deal that will provide regular revenue streams.
- Share the risk. A form of risk sharing is when you allow the partner to return the product if the project fails. Or the customer doesn't have to pay if the project fails.

From "Techie" to "Skeptic": Understanding Your Partners

One of the major issues is how to invest your resources in the right activities to recruit the right channel partners, whilst avoiding the partners that won't contribute to your success. Or, perhaps even more importantly, how can you ensure that you don't recruit the right channel partners at the wrong time, which can eventually lead to loosing these partners to competition without ever seeing success from them. To help navigate this tricky stage, it's useful to take a look at the "chasm theory" developed by Geoffrey Moore.

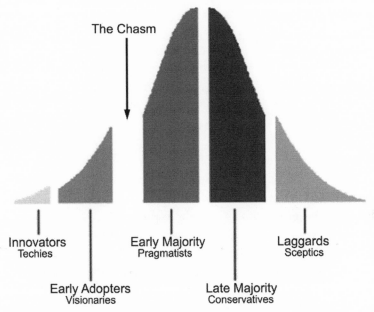

Source: Geoffrey A. Moore, "Crossing the Chasm", 1991

In his book "Crossing the Chasm", Geoffrey Moore describes that it's necessary to review each different customer group to implement successful, high-tech marketing for their technology products.[37] His book is widely accepted as the "bible" for introducing cutting-edge products to progressively larger markets. While Moore is talking about the end user, I have applied his findings to the channel partner, as they both show very similar behaviors. I've also adapted Moore's definition of the different groups to the IT area. I'll explain which channel partners fit into the different groups and how you can categorize your partners into the right group.

---

[37] Geoffrey A. Moore, "Crossing the Chasm, Marketing and Selling High-Tech Products to Mainstream Customer "(revised edition), HarperCollins Publishers, New York (1991)

Innovators or "techies"

The innovators represent approximately 2.5% of all end users. Typical innovators have a strong technology mindset and pursue new technology products aggressively. They sometimes seek them out even before a formal marketing program has been launched. This is because technology is a central interest in their life, regardless of what function it performs. There aren't very many innovators in any given market segment, but winning them is nonetheless key because their endorsement reassures the other players in the marketplace that the product does in fact work.

You find these kinds of people mostly in smaller, owner driven companies in the channel. They are mostly VARs that are in some kind of business relationship with you. Convince them that they should try the product and give them the best technical support you can offer for free. Don't expect much revenue from these innovators though. Use them as a tool for learning and apply the newly acquired knowledge to your product, pricing and marketing material before you target the next level of companies.

Early adopters or "visionaries"

Early adopters are very often also called "opinion leaders" and they represent approximately 13.5% of all end users. Early adopters, like innovators, buy into new product concepts very early in the product life cycle. Unlike the innovators however, they are not techies. Rather, they are people who find it easy to imagine, understand, and appreciate the benefits of a new technology and to relate these potential benefits to their own situation. Early adopters are the key to opening up any high-tech market segment because they don't rely on well established references when making their buying decisions. They prefer instead to rely on their own intuition and vision.

These early adopters are the most important group for the success or failure of your product. Winning the mindshare of the early adopters is the key to wider product sales and for spreading your product to the early and late majorities.

Early majority or "pragmatists"

The early majority represents 34%. Typically they are very pragmatic, benefit oriented buyers. Their concerns centre on their company, the vendor and the product quality. They value the service and support they receive from the vendor. Early majority buyers are not brand oriented and they are willing and able to become technologically competent where necessary.

The early majority share some of the early adopter's ability to relate to technology but ultimately they are driven by a strong sense of practicality. They are especially vertically oriented and communicate with others in their own industry. Normally they wait and see how other people are using a product before they buy in themselves. They will want to see well established references before investing substantially. Due to the fact that there are so many people in this segment (roughly one third of the whole adoption life cycle), winning their business is key to making any substantial profits and growth. Without a reliable channel however, you cannot win the early majority because you won't have the vertical knowledge or the insight into their markets.

These first three groups represent roughly 50% of the total market! If you are a startup company, using the channel for the first time or launching a new product, it's very important that you realize the need to focus on this group of channel partners first. They constitute a large group of potential partners and if you are able to convince a large portion of them, the "other 50%" will automatically take notice of you. The other 50% are typically followers who don't like taking any risk and are happy with only a small reward - in stark contrast to the first 50% who take more risks and look for more rewards.

Late majorities or "conservatives"

To reach the late majority, who represent 34%, the product must be widely available, easy to install and adapt, have many references and its vendor must have a recognized brand in the industry. The late majority are not willing and able to become technologically competent when necessary. If technical knowledge is necessary to run the product then a transition to the late majority will never really happen.

The late majority shares all the concerns of the early majority, plus one major additional concern: whereas people in the early majority are comfortable with their ability to handle a technology product, should they finally decide to purchase it, members of the late majority are not. As a result, they wait until something has become an established standard before they buy it. They also want to be provided with lots of support and therefore tend to buy from large, well established companies. Like the early majority, this group comprises about one third of the total buying population in any given segment.

To reach this group of buyers, you must have an established and very loyal channel. Some of your channel partners will need to carry big brand names and be considered as specialists in their vertical market segment.

Laggards or "skeptics"

Finally, the remaining 16% of the buying population is comprised of laggards or skeptics. These people simply don't want anything to do with new technology and only buy once it has been integrated into another product. This group carries a high risk of blocking purchases. Your main objective must be to neutralize their influence and find out what you are doing wrong. This is the reason why you as a vendor cannot build a channel network to reach this group of buyers. However, you should help your channel partners to neutralize them.

Getting the Majority to Buy

We have now examined the definitions of the different types of technology buyers. But, as Geoffrey Moore writes, there is a "chasm" between the early adaptors and the early majority buyers. It's only when a technology company can reach this early majority that their product will become widely accepted and they can generate profit with their products.

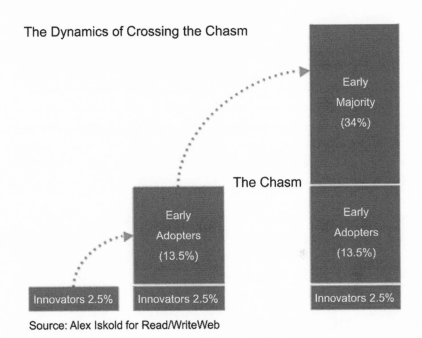

Source: Alex Iskold for Read/WriteWeb

I'll show you how the right channel partners can assist you with "crossing the chasm". It's important that you cultivate a diverse group of people that love your company and your product and start talking about it. You may have the best product and marketing machine, but if you are not able to create a group of evangelists, your product will never spread virally.[38] Viral marketing is essential for carrying your product into the mainstream market.

---

[38] Alex Iskold, "Rethinking Crossing The Chasm" (2007)

You can cross the chasm using these three steps:

Step 1: Focus on the innovators

Start offering your product to the innovators. Even if the product is not ready for the broad market and some documentation and functionality is missing, put it in the hands of some selected techies. Give them special treatment in the form of instant communication with your technical team (such as providing a forum or a blog where they can easily communicate). View this phase as the second beta phase of your product. The product might work but both you and the innovators know that there is still a lot to do.

Don't make the mistake of offering a brand new product directly to the end user market or providing it to your entire channel network. Many companies, especially smaller startups who might have just received some venture capital, make the mistake of starting to announce the first release of the product on their website or releasing PR material or promoting the product to their existing user base. If the product still has some bugs or the documentation is incomplete or the product lacks features or, or, or, then it's likely that the product will die during this phase or suffer a severe setback.

Step 2: Focus on the early adaptors

After you've invested some time in implementing the features and functions that are required according to feedback from the innovators, you should target the early adaptors. You'll find early adaptors either in smaller, technology oriented companies and channel partners or in the technical department of larger groups. If your product delivers significant economic advantages then you should also target the business owners of midsize companies.

Why target midsize companies? Midsize companies don't normally reach the level of revenue that gets the attention and preferential treatment from larger vendors. When approaching midsize companies, you'll find it's much easier to present your advantages to the business owner than in larger companies. Be careful though that you don't waste time and resources on complex decision making and RFP processes. Companies that require this type of information will typically not buy from smaller vendors, but prefer established, large companies. You should avoid them because they will not invest in improving your product and they will not provide you with the necessary reference cases to reach the early majority.

The course of action must be that you reach out to some early adaptors who show a need for the product and that you already have some relationship to. Provide them with the necessary technical support so as to ensure that your product works perfectly for them. Listen to their advice and make improvements to the product, its documentation and especially the technical support. In the event that you must choose between a horizontal feature and a vertical business improvement, always choose the vertical approach for the market segment where you want to reach the early majority first.

By the end of this phase you'll have learned where your product fits best and can offer real value to a specific customer group. Give yourself some time to finalize the necessary marketing and sales material, finish your website and review the product once more. Then you'll be ready to move to the next step and conquer the majority of your market.

Step 3: Crossing the chasm and winning the early majority

The early majority represents approximately 34% of all buyers. They are a very large group. If your target is the US channel then your target customer group is made up of 100,000 potential channel partners. If your target customer group is the SMB business in the US, then we're talking about millions of potential companies. This shows that market segmentation is the key to "crossing the chasm".

Moore advocates in his book that a company should focus on one single market. You should win domination over a smaller, specific market segment and use the success as a springboard to the larger market. Target the exact, specific market segment where your early adaptors have shown a need for your product. Reach out and win channel partners that are experts in this market segment. You can find these companies easily by using the internet (google the right keywords), searching industry conferences and events or studying the partners of complementary products who serve the target industry. There are many more ways to find these companies; some of these are described in later chapters of this book.

Once you've identified your target group of channel partners, select the most promising 10. Try to achieve success with around 10 partners first and if your concept works well with this sample of the partner network, you'll have a formula you can roll out to the market. If it doesn't really work with this smaller group of channel partners then you'll have problems to scale up to a larger group of channel partners. If you start with a large group right from the beginning, then you'll use up all your resources just to manage these partners rather than to make a smaller percentage of them exceptionally successful.

Together with this smaller group of channel partners you can streamline important elements such as your positioning, pricing, product features, marketing material and technical presentations. Analyze the customer's problem and work out a complete solution with your channel partners. If you find out that some of your selected channel partners don't know enough about the target customer group or don't invest enough time, replace them. You'll need 100% committed channel partners if you want to win the battle. Always keep in mind that the "early majority" are pragmatic - they have existing business, they have existing vendors and they won't wait for you!

If you've gone through the process as described, you'll have assembled a complete solution to solve the customer's problem. This solution should include your product, additional software or hardware, system integration, training, support and other elements that represent value in the eye of the customer. The next step is to define a value proposition versus the competitive solution in this market segment. Don't lose sight however, that you are targeting a pragmatic buyer. Therefore a competitive solution can also be an alternative way to solve the problem.

Now it's time to start communicating with this customer group on a broader level. Show presence at their events, focus on their magazines and publications and undertake other "lead generation" activities together with your channel partners. Don't communicate too widely though - focus on your fundamental competitive claim for this market segment. Don't forget, you are the challenger so you need to be clear in your communication and deliver an outstanding solution.

A lot of people believe that only their own direct sales force can create the demand in a specific customer group. But this direct sales force can also come from the channel partner's side - receiving support from a consultative channel manager who works with the partner's direct sales to identify projects and convince the end user.

The best approach for crossing the chasm is working closely with the direct sales force of targeted and committed channel partners. After achieving success in one market segment, you should start increasing the number of channel partners and add more market segments - always focusing on the "early majority" however. When you've won enough members from this group, the viral effect will begin and the later majority will start to follow.

Turning Resellers into Business Partners

Quite often channel partners, especially VARs, offer a very limited range of products to their existing customer base. The main reason for this is that they don't have the time or knowledge to research which solution fits their customer group best or solves a specific problem.

The "long tail" theory reveals a significant business opportunity for your channel partners.[39] Long tail business normally represents the 80% of products which are not as popular as the first 20%. But the total revenue of this 80% is very often higher than that of the best selling products. Even if this concept was created with the business models of e-tailers (Amazon or eBay) in mind, it also describes typical VAR business perfectly.

The Long Tail

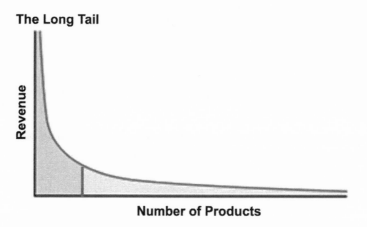

Number of Products

Source: Chris Andersen, "The Long Tail: Why the future of business is selling less of more", (2006)

Most typical VARs will have already made contact with their clients and now must offer them a complete solution in order to earn more of the clients' business. Large VARs often say "sell the whole truck" which means all products and solutions they carry. As the VAR wins more new projects the trust between the partner and the client will increase. In addition, the percentage of competing software products at the customer's end decreases since the partner is winning more projects with your technology - hence the VARs gross margin also increases.

The fixed costs of maintaining a relationship with a specific client (e.g. visits) already exist. In the online era, where a lot of products

---

[39] Chris Andersen, "The Long Tail: Why the future of business is selling less of more", Hyperion (2006)

are delivered digitally or on demand, the normal VAR has zero inventory costs. This means that with every sale they generate revenue and increase their gross margin.

One very important point to reiterate here is that you can enable your business partners to create more business within their customer group. You as the ISV are the expert in your specific market niche and you have knowledge about not only the competition, but also the complementary products, and you are well informed about what your partners and their customers really need. In most cases you also have a relationship with the complementary vendors already and know their product. Smaller VARs in particular, don't have the resources or the knowledge to carry out the necessary research and testing for new products.

So isn't it a good idea to tell your channel partners about this and become their business enabler? If you expand the total product range for your channel partners, most of them will honor the fact that you are taking care of their business. Once they know this, they won't try to push your product in a "fire and forget" mode only. They'll accept you as a "one stop shop". Even if you offer third party products, many partners will still buy from you - proving that you have turned the channel partners into business partners. In the next chapter, I'll describe how you can enable your channel partners to strengthen their brand within the customer base and how you can add emotion to your offering to strengthen the relationship between you and your channel.

The Power of White Labeling

One lesson that can be learned from working with different resellers is that every reseller, be they big or small, is proud to have their own brand and they want to deliver this brand to a growing audience of customers. Establishing a brand however, is very challenging for most companies, especially for the smaller channel partners. The ISV can help their channel partners reach this important milestone.

White label your product

Every size and type of reseller is proud to have their own brand. Your partner's brand can very often be an important asset in a geographic or vertical area. End users may know your partner as a specialist in a specific niche or geographic region.

The majority of smaller channel partners doesn't receive special treatment from the larger or more standardized vendors. These channel partners don´t want to sell commodity products that every end user can buy in a million other places, especially when the end user can easily research the cheapest price on the internet. When using standard products, the entire sales process can be reduced to a price war, forcing the margins lower and lower. It can also become a problem if there are many other resellers offering the same product for a lower price because the price for services will also be questioned.

You can stop this from happening though if the channel partner is given the ability to offer the product under their own brand. Even a "powered by vendor" approach can be very helpful. In this case, the end user is reassured that they are getting a standard product with maintenance in place and that the channel partner has a good relationship with the vendors and a lot of knowledge about the product. From the end user's point of view, they are getting a local service from their preferred reseller based on standard software. This creates a strong motivation to buy the solution from this reseller.

From your channel partner's point of view, they should offer their solution to their customers - proving that they are the specialists in this area and have a tight relationship with the vendor. Most resellers will also add further services or products, providing their customers with a more complete solution and therefore generating better margins. These higher margins also create a strong reason why you as the vendor can charge even more for your product, reduce the discount or ask for a higher commitment.

White label your marketing material

An interesting and effective way of promoting your partner is to offer "white label marketing". This strategy gives your channel partners the opportunity to use your material (mailers, promotion flyers, and data sheets) but deliver the message with their own individual design.

When you give a partner the opportunity to include their logo on an existing data sheet, it also represents a low form of commitment. Even though this service is offered by many companies today, it does not add the necessary emotions for ramping up your business with a partner.

A much better approach is to offer text and graphics to the partner along with examples of how they can use them. If you give them this material in Word or HTML format, then they can use it in their own marketing material.

For premium partners, you can also offer a service to help them prepare this marketing material and send it out to their customer base. This will clearly prove your commitment to the partnership and it will put the channel partner in a very good position from their customer's perspective. If you start having some influence on your partner's marketing department, ensuring that they use your material for promotions, you'll have taken a big step forward in the partnership.

White label collateral development

Consider working together with your channel partners to help them find out how they can position the product for specific buyer groups (who they already have relationships with). By working closely with your channel partners, you can combine their specific market knowledge of the product and the value they generate in real world use cases with your more generic knowledge. By aligning your technology with their domain knowledge you can develop client specific material and distribute it together with your channel partner's brand.

Normally, this requires a lot of work and it's not efficient to do this for only one partner. Group partners together to reduce the work and increase efficiency. One option is to cluster all the partners who serve a certain area and generate specific marketing material for them (e.g. white papers or case studies). If you do this well, it can create an unbelievable value for you and your partners.

The target customer group may also start to view your solution as the leader in the market segment - initiating your ownership of a niche market. Your partner also stands to make a lot of profit from this situation. If the end user believes in the partner's ability to deliver the right solution then their chances of closing a deal are much better. In addition, due to their existing knowledge, the partner can very often ask for higher prices and work more efficiently. This will result in a higher gross profit.

White label partner portal

Everybody is familiar with the typical vendor partner portal, which is very important for maintaining and strengthening the relationship between the vendor and their channel partners. I'll show how e-commerce can steer channel revenue a little later. Now I want to explain the concept of allowing your partner to use your infrastructure to promote their service (which is based on your solution). However, this concept will only work if you also allow them to use your infrastructure for other services that aren't related to your solution. Otherwise there can be a very high risk that the partners won't accept your offer in the first place.

For example, you can allow a separate landing page on your website for each partner to which all traffic regarding a specific topic is guided.[40] On this landing page, which can be part of a bigger web section, the partner can add their own content via content syndication (see the next section) which is "mixed" with your content. Since both of you want to make sure that the content is always up to date, this landing page will always have the latest content (e.g. product downloads, videos, marketing material), and will also be optimized by two specialists; you and your partner.

White label web syndication

Web syndication means that companies share their content with other websites. In our case, the ISV can produce content and then make it accessible to their partner to be displayed on their website. If the content is updated frequently and starts to develop value for both customer groups (ISV and channel partner), then many other people might link to your site. If the vendor's content appears on several partner's sites and content from these partners also appears on the vendor's site, then the website will be updated very frequently. This can generate significant SEO[41] value and help both partners' sites to show up on Google Search. Another important benefit this approach provides is that you can distribute your content (e.g. white papers, webinars, and news) to a larger audience.

Many other white label opportunities also exist. For instance, your sales and professional services team can use your partner's business cards on their projects, directing the end user to use a support team that is actually your support team acting in the name of the partner. Or your engineering team can build customized solutions for your channel partners. Always talk with your channel partners and think "end to end" (encompassing the entire sales process from beginning to end), this way more ideas can be generated. Before you start putting these ideas into practice, it's important to carry out a test of

---

[40] In online marketing a "landing page", sometimes known as a "lead capture page", is the page that appears when a potential customer clicks on an advertisement. The page will usually display sales copy that is a logical extension of the advertisement or link.

[41] SEO = search engine optimization.

the concept with a smaller group of partners. Don't just rely on the opinion of one single partner either, you need to put a lot of effort into this and acquire feedback from several of your partners. You will only see a return on your investment for this effort if you take on other channel partner's opinions.

I think it's clear that white label marketing can be used to motivate the channel partner's organization. The next chapter focuses on another set of motivational tools, namely rewards.

Revolutionary Incentive Programs

Usually, you and your close competitors will be in a very similar situation. You may have the same products, the same target customer groups, the same discount structure and even the same market approach. It's very common that the manufacturer responds to this dilemma by differentiating the product's features. The big problem here is that nobody really understands these differences. The typical reseller product manager and sales team are responsible for 10 to 20 different vendors - how can you educate them on the differences between the feature sets and the uniqueness of your product when they deal with so many?

The "old school" answer to this is an incentive program such as a weekend in Las Vegas for the sales managers and their families. Then a competitor counters with a cruise, so the Vegas weekend is replaced by a trip to Hawaii. Very soon you'll end up in an incentive war.

This example fails to take into account the real value of an incentive program. These programs should not just be a commodity or pricing strategy, but instead should be used to build better relationships with your partners. A good incentive program should enable your channel partners and their sales team to position your products correctly, move your products more effectively, build solid solutions for the customer and create more margin for your channel partner.

Please remember that a channel partner and their employees are driven by what's good for them. They will only move your product if it works well, or if they receive good support from you - resulting in them earning more money with your product than with others. This may be the bottom line, but you'll also need to wave a carrot to add some special motivation for your channel partner's team to focus on moving your product faster.

How can you create a really powerful incentive program that is different from the "old school" incentive programs? Here are some ideas.

Focus on the organization

Successful incentive programs don't target the individual sales people alone; they target the entire reseller's organization. There's nothing wrong with picking a "stand out" sales person or a small sales team, but if you chose a team you need to make sure they are successful and growing. In the end you'll only have greater success if the reseller can increase their business with your solution or if your solution generates a significant amount of revenue. When you start designing your incentive programs make sure that your business goals and your partner's are aligned.

Don't only motivate the winners

Just like everywhere, the 80/20 rule also applies to sales organizations. As a general rule of thumb, only 20% of the top performers make 80% of the sales and profits. There are two reasons why your program must be designed to inspire the masses: firstly, the top performers were already making good sales before you entered the picture so why should they start selling your product with a higher priority? The second reason is that if your product is easy to sell, then these top performers will start selling it anyway. The real challenge is motivating the next 20-30%, which can make a huge difference for you and your channel partner. If you are able to motivate the second layer of sales people, then the top management of your channel partners will thank you by investing more resources into selling your product.

Avoid complexity

I've seen many incentive programs that were unbelievably complex and required a lot of reporting. The ISVs marketing departments simply didn't understand the sales people they were working with. Most successful sales people just want to make things happen – they're always looking for the easiest way to make money. Don't get me wrong. This doesn't mean they're not hard working, just that they don't tend to think very long-term. "Keep it short and simple", otherwise known as "KISS", is a good motto to keep in mind. Install a program that has easy rules, clear benefits and is attainable.

Fast rewards

Designing a rewards program that promotes the best "partner of the year" is not the smartest solution for ramping up your sales. For example, if you want to promote the partner of the year for say 2011, the program roll out has to begin, at the latest, in Q4/2010. The rewards, however, will not be granted before Q1/2012 - at least 18 months after the start. The reward program therefore becomes uninspiring because the time span between the effort required and the reward are too long.

Try to design programs that grant rewards almost immediately or in an ongoing fashion over a certain period of time. This way you'll create clearly defined winners of the year, but also motivate everybody else to focus on your promotion.

Creative awards

What's a good prize for a winner? What motivates people the most? Money is the biggest motivator! The problem is, however, monetary rewards usually just get lost in people's household budgets. Money, as a reward by itself, has no "trophy value" which is important for

creating a long-lasting memory. Since money is still the biggest motivator why not combine a monetary reward with another reward?
Perhaps it could be something that is symbolic of their achievement
as an individual and implants a lasting memory.

Create certifications

As already stated, simply awarding money alone doesn't help to
motivate others very much. Something that does add an element of
personal achievement value for the sales person is a certification.
Certifications such as "Best Sales 2011", "Presidential Cup Winner"
or "First Sales with Product XY" can be of great value. But always
be careful with certifications – don't inflate the value. If everybody
wins without achieving real success, it can have a reverse effect.

Put the winners on stage

Making people feel special is very motivating. Give them something
they can't buy for money like a meeting with a celebrity, a private
tour in a winery, a seat in a historical car race or something else.
Even "free" prizes like getting to shake hands with the CEO at a
company party, listing their name on your website or giving them a
trophy will make the winner feel special. Encourage the winner to
talk about the prize and make sure that you include information on
your website, in press releases and other media. If you're seen to be
offering interesting prizes that people can't just buy for money and
communicating about the winners, then the partner's organization
will talk about your incentive program.

Focus on execution

Very often, the only thing that's discussed on the manufacturer's
side is the budget for the incentive program. As an ISV, you need to
spend time on designing and executing motivational programs. This
not only means that someone must be put in charge, but also that
you must track whether the channel partners are aware of the program, that milestones are being reached and the prizes are being

delivered quickly. The program should also be flexibly designed so that if the goals are not reached it can be changed without being compromised.

Partner council

Another powerful motivation tool for the entire partner organization is to build a partner council. This council invites your best channel partners to discuss the future direction of your products and your channel initiatives. Larger ISVs have their own independent organizations, such as user groups, but what can smaller ISVs do? Whatever you do, it's important that you don't just invite everybody. Make it exclusive enough that the channel partners see a real value in getting an invitation.

Steering committee

Every ISV, small or large, can create a steering committee. These help to decide on a strategic product roadmap, as well as pointing out the most necessary improvements in the channel program or working out how to enter a new market segment. You can create different steering committees with different topics - some of them being more technical and others being sales or marketing orientated.

Technical advisory board

It can be of great value for the more technical people within your partner's organization if they are invited to technical workshops or webinars with your product management and R&D team. Having access to the people who design and develop the product is something really special for most people and is also something they can't get with bigger vendors.

Alpha testing group

Since the "beta" group is very often open to almost everybody, including end users who've bought the product and are waiting for the newest release, the "alpha" testing group can be designed to become an exclusive circle of people who get very early product versions. The vendor can still change the product's design and also add or remove features based on the alpha group's feedback. This group can be given access to the R&D department of the ISVs organization and get answers from the top technical experts, while the beta group is normally handled by the support team.

Effective Lead Generation

Whether it's considered a revolutionary approach or not, effective lead generation with and for your channel partners is one of the most important aspects of building a successful channel network. I'll discuss lead management in more detail in the execution part of the book. This chapter will take a look at what smart methods exist to create leads together with your partners.

In-product marketing initiatives

In-product marketing initiatives can strengthen the relationship between the end user and the channel partner. This strong relationship can help the ISV to generate more business. However, hardly any ISVs make use of these initiatives.

As a manufacturer, your main purpose is to create and deliver innovative products to the market. Very often this is done in a "one-way street" fashion. Build the product, fire it out to the market and forget about it. You won't know if the end users are satisfied with the products, nor will you generate maintenance revenues. There is no link between the ISV and the end users. But this link can be an asset that should be nurtured.

One way to do this is to use your product as a communication centre. Build a product messaging system into your product that communicates with the end user and can also actively sell products and services to them.

Some vendors of packaged software today have a high number of product downloads (for example, certain anti-virus programs count more than one million downloads per week from www.download.com alone), but they often can't sell or communicate directly to the end user due to high volume, low average selling price (<$100) and the fact that many sales are made indirectly through online stores or other channel partners. Contacting end users with sales reps is not economically feasible. Research shows that the conversion[42] rate of downloads to customers is not very high, it is seldom more than 1%.

But people who have downloaded your product have already proven their solid interest. They have your product on their machine and this alone represents a huge business opportunity that you can share with your partners. Instead of just depending on sales models which are lacking the human element or an acceptable alternative (online store), are imperfect (VARs) or not focused (distribution & DMRs), start implementing in-product marketing elements and let the software work for you and your partners. Examples of this could be improving the product registration and aiming for double opt-in registration, or up-selling products for complementary functions etc. If you build the proper messaging and sales mechanisms into your product, you can accomplish the following:

- Direct communication with end users.
- 24/7, 365 day sales presence (the hardest working sales people).
- Introduction to new revenue streams.
- "Sweet spot" communication with end users.
- Dynamic content.
- Integration across multiple communication platforms.
- Perceived value - departure from commodity.
- Cross promotional success.

If you are a hardware manufacturer you can bundle software with your hardware to achieve these goals.

---

[42] Conversion rate: Percentage of customers who actually buy software after downloading a free trial.

Helping your partners generate leads

Today, in the online era, the internet is the ultimate information source for many buyers. To "google" something is now a common phrase for finding the answer to almost any question. Social media is becoming increasingly important – social sites such as Facebook have more than 500 million members who spend a substantial portion of their time talking to their friends or sharing pictures and information. Connections over business networks like LinkedIn or XING are also becoming more and more important for business success.

People are searching the internet for high quality content, which makes content creation and promotion the most valuable customer engagement tools for anyone marketing online.[43] High quality content is also an important driver for effective search engine marketing and optimization. If people start viewing you as the expert in one field, they'll start buying your product or working with your channel partners.

Many channel partners don't have the content, resources or experience necessary to generate qualified content. However, they very often have a customer relationship that you can use to generate qualified content. There are many different types of content driven marketing material. Avoid using the "old way"; don't just fire out your content to your channel partners. Generate the content in conjunction with the channel partners to motivate their customers to buy the combined offering.

- **Press releases:** It's not only about writing a press release, it's also about distributing a press release and measuring the results. You should also use your relationships with journalists to place press releases.

---

[43] Keith Holloway, "How to Dominate Your Space Online with Content Marketing," www.onedegree.ca (2009)

- **White papers:** Generate qualified content based on your technology and your partner's vertical or technical experience. White papers are not just about technology but also about business solutions (e.g. how to make your business more effective). Sometimes you can reuse content (generic technology content) and combine it with the specific use case of the channel partner.

- **Webinars:** These can be used to educate your channel partners, promote new products or present interesting solutions. Webinars or videos are great tools - you can offer them "live" with Q&A or record them in order to make them available 24 hours a day. Together with your channel partner or a group of channel partners, you can invite a specific audience and create well targeted webinars.

- **Case studies:** There is nothing more valuable for customers than to read a case study about a solution in a comparable environment. Buyers normally trust their peers. You can help your channel partners to use their relationship with the end user and motivate them to do a case study. You can produce the content and distribute it together with your channel partner.

- **Competitive analysis:** Most ISVs have some kind of competitive analysis which compares their product to other leading products. It can be even more valuable if you compare a solution based on your product (implementation done by your channel partners) with other existing solutions or even with the "status quo". Your channel partners have the vertical knowledge to make the advantages of your specific solution clear.

- **ROI/TCO calculators:** This is a very interesting tool for most end users and they often base their decisions upon it. If you combine knowledge with your partners, you can provide ROI/TCO calculators for specific solutions.

- **Blogs/social media content:** Many channel partners don't know how to use blogs and other social media websites to promote their content. The content itself must be specific though. Educate your partners about this and you will profit from their networking.

- **Newsletters/mailers:** If you've already produced all this valuable content, why not create newsletters and other mailers to promote combined solutions. Very often, ISVs have a superior mailing system in place and more experience with sending mailers than the average channel partner. Help your partners by "piggy-backing" them on your mailing system.

A content driven lead generation program can be a substantial help for driving more business to your channel partners and improving your partnership with them. If you work together on this program, analyze the information needs of the target customer group, generate and promote content, it can be a very powerful tool. Make sure that you have someone in your team to manage the project, create a game plan and keep everyone on the same page. A content driven lead generation program can produce outstanding results and lay the foundation for a robust, ROI driven conversion program.

Activate channel partner communication lines

Trust is a significant factor for success. End customers tend to trust the people they already know and perhaps have already done business with. There are many ways that you as a vendor and the channel partner can work together to generate leads, as long as you begin with using the channel partner's communication lines.

- **Share email lists:** Each one of your channel partners has an email list that can be targeted. Why not use these lists to invite their contacts to webinars? Or create special offers together with your channel partner to deliver valuable content such as white papers or case studies.

- **Speaking at events:** Contact the regional chamber of commerce or any other organization your channel partner works with for opportunities to speak at their events or functions.

- **Work with business partners:** Your channel partner might have some interesting business partners from other industries. These contacts can be used as a great inroad to some other interesting customer groups.

There plenty of things you can do. By combining your contacts with the contacts of other partners you can end up establishing a huge contact base. Always remember the "six degrees of separation" theory (also referred to as the "human web") which states that everyone is, at most, six steps away from any other person on earth. A chain of "they're a friend of a friend" statements can be used to connect any two people in six steps or less.[44] Working with your channel partners in this way can establish a huge network of potential buyers.

Build lead generation groups

You can create a lead generation group together with your channel partner. The group can help to generate leads using outbound cold calling, inbound lead follow up or account profiling. However, the term "cold calling" doesn't simply mean to pick up the phone and call somebody from a long list of names. There are many different ways of cold calling today. Smart organizations also use their company website, Google Search, LinkedIn or other resources to prequalify accounts and then make introductory calls to relevant or very specific customers.

It makes sense to share resources with your channel partners because you are the expert in your field. You know how many leads you can generate in a specific period of time, which methods are effective, which questions should be asked and so on. You also should put an automation and CRM system in place to make sure that all leads are managed correctly.

Another method is offering lead generation to the channel partner and then sharing the costs. It's only normal that the channel partner

---

[44] http://en.wikipedia.org/wiki/Six_degrees_of_separation (2010)

should pay for leads – remember there's no free lunch. Every partner needs to show their "skin in the game".

Lead generation is an important activity, but you might find yourself in a market, where lead generation as described above is not an option. Maybe you don't have any strong partners in a region or they're simply not interested in generating leads with you. In order to deal with these types of situations I want to introduce the concept of "flag partners".

Using Flag Partners to Expand Market Reach

Your market analysis may show that there are areas, regional or vertical, which you cannot reach or serve efficiently with your own channel team. One innovative solution to this problem is the implementation of flag partners to serve these markets.

Definition of "flag partner"

A flag partner is a company that represents you as the vendor in a geographic or vertical area. A typical example of this is when you work with a channel partner who represents you in a country like China, India or Brazil. These countries might have huge potential for new and interesting business but are not geographically close enough to your business. So rather than invest more resources to physically reach these regions, you invest in the education and support of a flag partner instead.

A flag partner represents your products in clearly defined markets or customer segments. A geographic market does not have to be limited to just a country; it can also be a region for example, Southern California or a metropolitan area for example, Moscow. It's important, however, that these market segments have enough potential to justify an investment from your side. Flag partners are not just another type of channel partner, they represent your company and become an integrated part of your sales and channel strategies.

The perfect flag partner must have the ability to reach a minimum 50% of the revenue the vendor makes in a comparable area or market segment. This means if you earn US$2 million in California, your flag partner should be able to generate a minimum of US$1 million in the Northeast US territory.

How to know when a flag partner makes sense

Many of us have, at some point in our business lives, targeted a far-away market where we knew there was demand for our product.

Typical examples of these markets are:
- A geographic region that has similar characteristics to other regions where you have been successful.
- A vertical market segment where you've already been successful, but are not able to grow further.
- A target market that can't be served directly using your normal channel via a branch office.
- A region where you already have reference clients or customers.
- Vertical markets that can be clearly defined. This can be very complex though, if a channel partner wants to serve a vertical market in a region where you have a strong presence.

The following requirements will have to be met for a flag partner strategy to make sense:
- Your product is saleable in this region (e.g. support for the language, legal restrictions etc.)
- The target market has a decent size.
- You need to be willing to invest the necessary amount of time and money in this market.

Be careful not to install flag partners in market segments where you have no experience or that you are not willing to put any effort into. For example, you could assume that most of the products which are sold through the channel in Germany could also be saleable in France or Greece. You could also assume that if you sell your product to vertical market segments such as lawyers or doctors in one area, that this target customer group will also buy your product in another area, providing that you can offer the same quality of service.

It's a totally different story, however, if you are looking at markets whose local language your products don't support or at vertical markets that are completely new to you. In these cases, I would recommend that you start by signing up a "normal" channel partner and move into the market slowly. Don't get me wrong though – it's important to invest some resources into new ventures to expand your market reach and growth. But if you want to serve a market seriously with a flag partner, that flag partner will require a substantial amount of help and support. So don't take on too much at once. Only take on the number of partners that you can serve properly.

Responsibilities of a flag partner

As defined previously, a flag partner represents your company in a region or vertical market. This means that the flag partner can also start behaving like a "master distributor" or "exclusive distributor" in this region and begin building their own channel.

There are some important differences between a flag partner and a normal channel partner:
- The flag partner represents you in a defined market.
- They are treated like a subsidiary - meaning they are given access to a lot of internal resources.
- All business in this market area will be done by the flag partner.
- Flag partners build and maintain their own channel network.
- They often operate under your brand.
- They organize events and represent you at major fairs.
- The flag partner has direct access to your organization.
- The partnership is visible to everyone.

Selection criteria for flag partners

Selecting the right flag partner can be quite difficult and time consuming. But you need to invest effort into this. Don't just select the partners who are right in front of you or where "somebody knows someone in the company". It's important that your potential flag partner is willing to invest in the partnership and has the ability to deliver the necessary results.

A flag partner must meet the following criteria:
- Ability to invest time and resources in your target market.
- Be a financially stable company.
- Doesn't work with your direct competitors.
- Already has customers/partners in the target markets.
- Has experience in the market and sells similar products and solutions.
- Gives you easy access to management level.

When you begin the selection process, it's important that you set clear goals about what you want to achieve with this flag partner and what the milestones will be. It will be a challenge to reach a revenue goal with your products that is higher than the total revenue of the flag partner in the current year.

Characteristics for a suitable flag partner:
- Technical knowledge.
- Regional experience.
- Appropriate company size.
- Language (can they communicate with you?).
- Actual business focus.
- Marketing know-how and budget.
- Existing partnerships - talk with them about their success with these partners.
- Membership in organizations.
- Required resources.

Flag partner business plan

Once you've found a potential flag partner and the first contact has been made, the next phase involving a closer working relationship begins. The starting point for this should be the creation of a partner business plan (by the way, you can download business plan templates at www.channel-revolution.com). The plan must include a method for reaching the defined goal. Appoint someone from your side to be accountable for the success of the partner. For this situation I highly recommend creating a detailed business plan rather than just a simple action plan. This is because you will be working much more closely with the flag partner than other types of partners. The resources you will be required to invest to reach the goals are much higher. It is essential to establish right from the beginning that you and the potential flag partner have the same expectations.

It is also imperative that the partner business plan is finished before you start promoting this new partner internally and externally as your flag partner. Again, this is to ensure that both parties are clear about what the goals are and the expected revenues. You don't want to find yourself in the situation where you start a new partnership only to end it after a short period of time. If you have some doubts or uncertainty about the outcome of the partnership, you can always start the business and just promote them as a main partner who hasn't been given exclusivity yet.

Make sure that the partner business plan outlines the necessary commitments and deliverables from the potential partner and from you.

A flag partner must be committed to:
- Promote you prominently on their website and other marketing material.
- Provide a marketing budget for promoting the solution.
- Provide the sales people with quotas on your products.
- Have a dedicated accounts manager and technical support staff.
- Be willing to create a partner network.

- Report on leads and revenue.

Necessary commitments from you:
- Have a dedicated account manager with defined goals.
- Have dedicated technical and marketing staff.
- Provide access to top management.
- Provide free training for the sales and technical team.
- Assist at a reduced price for the first projects.
- Provide marketing material (reference cases, sales tools, data sheets, pricelists etc.)
- Forward any leads from this region/market segment.
- Provide discounts and NFR licenses.

Another important part of the business plan should forecast the costs and revenues involved in the partnership. Don't underestimate the investments and be sure to plan your revenue stream conservatively. Be aware that the costs will begin now and the revenue will come later. A good rule of thumb is that you will need three months to form the partnership, prepare the marketing material and train your partner's staff. It then takes another three months to establish the new partnership in your partner's community. Based on the product's sales cycle you should see the first real revenue stream after six months. If you are selling enterprise products, then don't expect too much until 12 months after starting the partnership.

The costs are always very high in the beginning of the new partnership. You have to build the partnership (plan, contract, management involvement), train the sales and technical people, prepare the required marketing material and begin sales and marketing initiatives.

Typical costs involved in the support of a flag partner:
- Labor costs for sales, administration and technical support.
- Travel costs (flights, hotels etc.).
- Costs for customized marketing material.
- Marketing funds.

- Additional discounts if the flag partner takes over existing customers.

Typical revenues that can be expected when working with a flag partner:
- Licenses
- Training
- Support
- Professional services

A necessary step in the process is to draft and sign a contract or LoI (Letter of Intent) which includes the goals, commitments and the partner business plan. The main purpose of this document is not to be legally binding but to be emotionally binding - ensuring that both parties are on the same page.

Typical points to address in the contract:
- Goals of the partnership.
- Type of partnership (cooperation/independent from each other).
- Rights and obligations of both parties.
- Termination clauses.
- Confidentiality agreements.
- Transparency of information.
- Quarterly planning.
- Discounts, payment terms etc.
- Milestones for the partnership (perhaps there is interest for capital investment by you or your partner).

Working with flag partners

After you've selected a potential flag partner and formulated the business plan, the real work can begin. In the beginning, the required support for a flag partner is much higher than for a normal channel partner. This is the main reason why the flag partner needs to contribute significantly to your revenue.

When you start working with your partner, try to identify the "low hanging fruits" that can increase the motivation of their team to work with you. Once the sales team generates their first revenue or gets their first commission on a project with you, you'll start owning a piece of their mindshare - this always makes things a lot easier.

Typical activities in this phase are:
- Announcement of the partnership.
- Identification of potential projects.
- Positioning the product in the partner's solution portfolio.
- Joining your partner on sales calls.
- Internal marketing in your partner's organization.
- Co-marketing activities (e.g. workshops, webinars, and events).
- Premium support on the first projects.
- Forecasting, lead tracking and milestone tracking.

A real world example of flag partner cooperation

When Allaire, now part of Macromedia, entered the European market in 1999, they didn't have the scope or the budget required for the roll-out of their channel concept - they needed a flag partner. They started with a small, but smart team in Brussels and a clear channel strategy. My company (at the time) had worked on some projects with Allaire's Cold Fusion product; the leading web development tool at the time. We had also just begun to work on some cross border projects with companies all over Europe. Allaire saw this as a reason to select my company as one of their flag partners. They also appreciated that we were very committed and had no conflicts with other strategic partnerships or competitors of Allaire. Together, we created a strategy for the German market, held local workshops for corporate end users and also provided professional services and technical training for smaller resellers of Allaire. To gain an even better insight into Allaire and gain access to their knowledge, we acquired a company in Boston that hosted the local Allaire user group. We also formed a strategic partnership with a Canadian company that developed some of the code for Allaire's core products.

A typical example of work was the European launch of Allaire's new product line. We organized the launch at the Frankfurt Messeturm, a very recognizable landmark, and invited partners and important end users from all over Europe. Allaire sponsored the event and sent their product managers and speakers, but we took responsibility for the event's organization and made sure that the visitors came away with a great experience.

This cooperation was successful for all parties involved. Allaire now had a partner in Germany that they could rely on and who could act as an extension of their technical and sales forces. We were able to showcase their technical experience to a totally new customer group and could therefore begin hiring more people.

Part of the evaluation process for potential flag partners also needs to entail taking a very close look at your product's channel in terms of general trends. In the next chapter, I'll examine some trends we are seeing now and which in my opinion will shape the future. I'll also show you how to benefit from these trends.

Embracing Software as a Service (SaaS)

As described earlier in the book, more and more channel partners are beginning to offer Software as a Service (SaaS) and many ISVs are providing their services online via the internet (cloud computing). The channel in SaaS times works fundamentally differently than the channel in brick and mortar times. These good old times (only 2 years ago!) are gone and won't come back. Even though the SaaS channel only represents a small portion of the entire reseller channel today, this portion will grow very fast and the rules for doing business will change even faster. I think that we'll see many resellers working in the hybrid model (selling products and offering managed services) in the near future, and that they will continue using this model for a couple of years.

Please note that when I write about SaaS, I'm actually referring to two distinct models. One is the more obvious SaaS software distribution and licensing model, where the ISV hosts the application and the channel partner resells the solution. In the other model, the ISV functions as a business enabler, selling the software to managed service providers (MSPs) who host it in their own data centre and deliver it to the customer. In both cases, the SaaS solution is a single instance, multi-tenant application, which means that every customer logs into the same application.[45]

The major difference between a reseller of SaaS applications and their counterpart in the brick and mortar software world is the mindset. Resellers of SaaS applications can't just sell products to the end users to get their margins; they have to provide the solution to the end user on a long-term basis. As already shown in the chapter "Channel Trends", the revenue streams when providing SaaS solutions are totally different because this model normally requires an initial investment to set up the solution and become an expert in the area.

How can the ISV and their channel exploit this great market opportunity? What adaptations do they need to make to their existing business model and how can they work together in the future? I'll point out some ideas how to create a win-win situation for ISVs and their channel partners.

Stop thinking like a software company / reseller

The first point I want to make is that ISVs and their resellers have to stop thinking in old fashioned reseller terms. The SaaS model represents a real revolution in the distribution of software. The channel partner may be the one selling the solution but the ISV controls the system.

But the collaboration between the ISV and their channel partners also needs to be totally different. In the first model, where the ISV hosts the application, the channel partner is the trusted advisor to

---

[45] "Rethink Your SaaS Channel Strategies", www.sandhill.com (2010)

the customer and the specialist for the different business models. In the second model, where the former reseller morphs into an MSP and starts delivering the software on their own, the channel partner becomes an integrated part of the value chain.

ISVs and channel partners (VAR or SI) need to make a major decision. Do you as an ISV want to adopt the reseller model and sell your license to the channel partners so they can start offering the solution to their customer group? Or will you insist on hosting the solution in your own data centre? While this may seem to be the easier business model, there are some hurdles. If you host the solution, you'll need or have access to all the end user data. And that's something most channel partner will struggle with. This challenge becomes even bigger when dealing with complex solutions where the target market involves larger companies/enterprises.

You can find a middle ground to motivate the resellers by giving them a rebranded solution, but the challenge of acquiring the customer data is still unsolved. Don't underestimate this aspect - every reseller will try to protect access to their enterprise customers.

Integrate new groups into your channel model

Some customers don't search the internet for the best solution, they use their regional VAR or SI as trusted advisors instead. You should expand your channel model and not only focus on the technology savvy IT resellers who can integrate software systems. Integrate the vertically specific players such as business consultants, business process outsourcers (BPO) and people with specific business knowledge into your channel model. Anyone who is viewed as a trusted advisor by a specific group of customers can become your reseller. In this case, the ISV can host the solution or even better, the ISV can point to a trusted channel partner who runs a local data center.

Slice the subscription pie

Help your resellers move into the SaaS world. Every reseller has to make a substantial investment in education to learn about the product and attain the required business knowledge. And don't forget the other necessary investments in sales and marketing. If the reseller wants to become a SaaS provider and wants to host the application on their own, which means becoming an MSP, then this also requires an investment in technology.

In the SaaS world on the other hand, the revenue stream is substantially different from traditional licensed software business. SaaS providers need to make larger upfront investments and the revenue from the service will be lower in the beginning, but will grow over time. In the SaaS model, the customer pays a monthly fee for the period of software use instead of paying for the software outright.

For example, let's say the price of the software is US$12,000. In the "old" model, the customer has to pay this upfront and the reseller's share is perhaps US$3,000 (25% commission) and you (ISV) get the rest (US$9,000). This money is in the bank on day one. Now, in the SaaS model, let's say the customer only pays US$750 per month, meaning the reseller gets US$250 per month and you get US$500 per month. The monetary gap between the upfront price and the monthly fee is missing from both the reseller's and your bank account. How can you and the reseller build a business model around these smaller fees minus the large upfront investment? You as the ISV can't finance the normal payment to the reseller out of their monthly revenue because until you have reached a significant number of customers, your revenue stream will not be substantial enough (e.g. the reseller gets only US$250 instead of US$3,000, so the ISV needs to finance the US$2,750 which is basically impossible with only US$500 per month in revenue).

There are different solutions to this problem and you should evaluate each one. Here are some ideas (perhaps a combination of these will also work):

- Acquire substantial funding from an investor.
- Make special offers to your end users (e.g. pay now for 1 year and get 1 month free).
- The reseller should ask for an upfront implementation fee.
- Offer business and technical consultant packages.
- Combine your offer with other solutions.

The revenue push can come from two sides: firstly the sales cycles for SaaS solutions are often much shorter because the upfront investment is much smaller and the decision can be made on department level. Secondly, a SaaS solution is attractive to a much larger group of customers as the upfront investment is smaller and therefore complies with smaller IT budgets. This second point is the reason why you can reach more customers, especially smaller ones.

Find the right compensation for the sales team

The problem of the revenue stream goes along with the challenge of finding the right compensation model for the sales team. Most sales people's compensation is based 50% on revenue. In the traditional license model, however, the sales teams are compensated only when the deal is done. In many SaaS models, the "break-even" point is reached after 36 months of recurring revenue, meaning that after this time the revenue is the same as in the traditional model.

Here are some ideas for finding the appropriate compensation for the sales team and, at the same time, generate sufficient profit:

- Calculate the "break-even" point and then calculate the quota for the sales person based on this.
- As the sales cycle becomes shorter, you can increase the quota and give lower commissions.
- Build a sales team that targets new customer groups. For every experienced account manager, you can hire inside sales who will help to standardize the sales process.

- Increase the portfolio of the account manager. Let them sell the complete solutions, which include not only training and implementation but also third party products.

Free education as part of the business model

Many traditional channel partners, especially broadliners and e-tailers, don't have deep product knowledge. In the SaaS channel, it's not possible to become a trusted advisor to the end user without having this knowledge; so it's critical that you train your partners. It's equally important to educate the end user. This should actually be easier than training the partners, because every end user uses the same application - therefore the process can be more automated.

Make sure you offer free education in the form of webinars, training videos or web based certifications and make these available free of charge.

Focus on the customer relationship and trust

As I've already pointed out, all resellers want to protect their relationships with their customers. In the traditional model, there was no doubt that they were the ones responsible for customer satisfaction. But if the reseller decides not to become an MSP, this situation changes. The end user becomes the customer of the SaaS vendor (ISV) who is providing the service; and the channel partner is "only" the intermediary. It's important for both the ISV and the channel partner to keep the end user happy for a long time, since profitability is only achieved after a longer period of time. Every ISV should keep a close eye on the end users' relationship with their channel partners and on end user satisfaction in general.

The best way for an ISV to create trust and establish a long-term relationship with their channel partners is acknowledging the value each channel partner brings to the end customers.[46]

---

[46] "Success and the SaaS Channel": www.ebizq.net (2010)

Typical benefits a channel partner can provide:

- **Domain knowledge:** Similar to the traditional software model, the channel partner will have either vertical, regional or technological domain knowledge. All end customers want to work with a partner who understands their business and can communicate in their language.

- **Business consultancy:** Before deciding on a new system, most customers want to see a breakdown of the value the new system can provide, the associated costs and how long the implementation will take. This can be a challenging task, especially in the case of larger systems such as ERP or CRM. When the customer makes their decision based upon the channel partner's recommendation, they expect the partner to support them through the next steps.

- **Data migration:** A tricky aspect for every new system implementation is the migration of data. Here, the new SaaS world hasn't changed anything. Data migration from the existing to the new customer solution requires the same amount of work or sometimes even more. Very often the rules that apply to the SaaS vendor are even more restrictive, because data from different customers has to be migrated to the same database structure.

- **Implementation:** If the SaaS system requires implementation, then this needs to be carried out by a local channel partner. The integration of other solutions or the education of end users may also be part of this implementation.

- **Maintenance:** As most customers don't like talking to someone in another language or in another time zone, local maintenance from a channel partner provides substantial value to the whole solution.

Invite new participants to your SaaS partner network

As previously stated, there are many different channel partners involved in the delivery of the SaaS solution. Not all of them just do sales, business process consulting and implementation. Some of them also develop value adding tools such as applications. Others are specialists in third party applications that normally work in conjunction with the SaaS application.

Every SaaS vendor can expand their channel model by integrating new partners who for example, maintain the target customer group's "legacy solutions". You can also invite vertical business consultants into your channel. They can be very helpful to the more technically driven channel partners for winning new customer groups.

By creating this type of SaaS partner "ecosystem," in which new roles are created that allow new partners such as the vertical business consultant to earn money, the ISV can not only increase the share in the customer's IT budget but also generate upfront charging opportunities and market their solution to new customer groups. This approach can be used to expand your target market and, with a growing market penetration, the brand will become more familiar. This will, in turn, give you access to new groups of channel partners and other vendors who will want to add your solution to their portfolio.

Boosting Your Channel Business with E-Commerce

Many people describe the internet as the second coming of the industrial revolution. I agree that the internet represents a new era of globalization. Just as the end of the Cold War revolutionized relationships between the East and the West, e-commerce is revolutionizing the business world. It will also revolutionize relationships between ISVs and their channel partners. It won't stop there

though, it will also change the relationship between channel partners and their end users since almost all information (very often
including the products and prices) will be or already is available
online.

How will ISVs and their channel partners respond to these changes? Some ISVs might consider selling only directly to their end customer base. Personally, I would advise any ISV not to choose this
strategy, especially if they sell more complex solutions. The tempta-
tion is strong because you can get closer to the customer and don't
have to pay large discounts to the channel, but there is a downside
involved. By cutting the channel out of the supply chain, ISVs will
not only lose volume, they will also lose the vertical knowledge and
valuable feedback from the channel partners about how to improve
their offering. They will also create a large sales force for their competitors since channel partners they used to work with will begin
selling competitor solutions to their existing customer base.

My advice is to implement a specialized platform, consisting of an
e-commerce system and a partner relationship management (PRM)
system.[47] This way you can start developing e-commerce offerings
that include the channel partners.

Advantages of e-commerce

- An online platform will allow you to promote your entry level
  products to end users. This should make your products better-
  known and will result in greater demand for your entire product
  range. Just make sure that you don't undercut the channel in
  terms of pricing.

- It will enable you to manage a much larger network of channel
  partners, giving you better control. This is also better for the
  channel partners since many challenges such as license management, maintenance selling and lead distribution can be
  solved more easily.

---

[47] There are many solutions available from different vendors such as Avangate,
Cleverbridge, Netsuite, Relyware and others.

- E-commerce can lower your operating costs significantly. Working efficiently with hundreds of smaller partners is nearly impossible without an online platform.

- It creates a unique, 24/7 global shopping experience. Channel partners can pay using their currency, language, time zone and preferred payment method. They also don't have to invest before their customers want the software.

- Integration into your (the ISV's) website makes partners visible to their customers as specialists for your products, and it helps you to attract further channel partners.

- Powerful reporting tools allow you to optimize your whole channel management and your offering to the channel.

- It allows you to work with affiliate networks and other ISVs to promote your product to each other's channel partners.

As you can see, there are plenty of reasons to implement an e-commerce system to help boost your channel sales. Depending on your individual business (what kind of products you sell, their average price point, the target user group etc.), the system needs to have different functionalities. I'll look at some of the options that are commonly provided by most professional systems on the next few pages. Nowadays channel partners and end users expect a professional shopping experience, so I highly recommend using a standard system that is specifically designed for software sales. Try to avoid developing your own platform. It'll only cost you a lot of money and it's unlikely you'll be able to develop something that's actually superior to "off-the-shelf" solutions.

Necessary functions for an e-commerce platform

As I just said, the system you select should be designed for software sales. That means it needs to be optimized for an ISV to run their business online. Since almost every ISV works with a channel that wants to be served online, this also means that the system should involve some type of reseller management functionality. Below is a list of requirements an e-commerce system must meet.

E-commerce system requirements:

- Order management: The web-based software should allow the resellers to view their order history, give instant access to all sales information and analyze the history and product details within seconds.

- Partner management: The partner or reseller management functionality of the software should help the ISV to build and easily maintain a database of resellers and the reseller's network of contacts. Furthermore, it should help to optimize the relationship with the resellers by providing transparent data and order history information for each reseller. It should have the capability to define credit limits, partner types, and different margins to manage the various types of resellers. It should make trends easier to identify so you can optimize your offering or even your channel partners' programs.

- Product catalogue management: The product catalogue management area should make it easy to edit all product details - from prices to delivery text and product attributes (product code, name, description, category, price lists, currency etc.). Using this, you can also create "special" products that are only available online, in specific countries or only for specific resellers.

- End customer registration: The system should give the vendor the ability to easily collect information about the end user. In fact, both the vendor and the reseller should have access to this end user information. This not only gives full control over the sold licenses, it also allows cross selling for the vendor and the reseller.

- Customer support: It should be possible for every ISV (and their resellers) to instantly see the language chosen, currency paid, browser used, emails sent, subscription payments paid/scheduled and communication history for all orders. This way it's much easier to manage large order amounts. If you delegate more tasks to your resellers, you empower them to serve their customers more efficiently and create new revenue streams.

- Marketing campaigns: Increasing revenue from the existing customer group is normally much easier than winning completely new customers. An e-commerce solution should enable you to cross-sell, up-sell and sub-sell to your existing resellers, bundle products with other companies (e.g. hard drive and backup software), make special offers and generate unique URLs for your channel partners so they can use your platform to sell the products. This way the partners are handled more like affiliates and get their share of the revenue after the end customer buys over a specific link.[48]

- Powerful reporting: It's a simple fact that if you can't measure something, you can't manage it. Any professional e-commerce system can give you instant statistics and reports on resellers. It can also help you analyze the results using various criteria or visualize them by using pie charts, bar graphs etc.

Why ISVs should outsource their online shops to e-commerce providers

Using a professional e-commerce platform and outsourcing the management of their online shop sales has many benefits for ISVs. I've listed the most obvious ones below. But I also encourage you to do your research and talk to different providers such as cleverbridge, Digital River or others to identify the benefits for your specific situation.

Benefits for the ISV:

- Focus on your business: A home grown, self developed e-commerce solution can waste your team's valuable time because

---

[48] http://en.wikipedia.org/wiki/Affiliate_marketing (2010)

of all the adaptations they will have to make to deal with the challenges you will face when selling your products globally and managing your reseller base. I'm not only talking about supporting different payment methods, addressing different tax systems, managing different merchant accounts and the chargeback management. I'm also talking about the human resources required to manage the system. Using these resources to develop and market your products instead is a much better investment.

- Increase international sales: If you can display your product in each channel partner's native language, as well as listing the prices in the local currency and accept their preferred payment method, this will definitely help motivate international channel partners to join your sales force.

- Increase spending: Channel partners will buy more frequently from you if they can use a professional system with a superior shopping experience, hassle-free processing and no hidden fees.

- Running promotions: The e-commerce platform offers a lot of features for new marketing campaigns and opportunities. It'll allow you to run campaigns using coupons, product discounts, bundles etc. without any new development. This makes it easy to set up campaigns and measure the results - both for you and your channel partners.

There are many more benefits but going into more detail here would only distract from the focus of this book. Instead, I'd like to give a brief example of how NovaStor, the company I'm running today, implemented an e-commerce system and what steps we are taking to improve customer satisfaction for our resellers and their customers every day.

An example of an e-commerce system (NovaStor)

NovaStor started using a standard e-commerce system at the beginning of 2009. After a long evaluation phase we chose cleverbridge[49]

---

[49] cleverbridge: www.cleverbridge.com

to provide the system. Since then, we've consistently been improving the buying experience for our channel partners.

After implementing cleverbridge, NovaStor managed to bring its channel partner program ValueCREATE! in line with the company philosophy: "Easy to do business with" - not only in theoretical terms but in practice. When a channel partner works with us, we want them to be able to concentrate on their business. We'll help them grow by providing not only the products but also marketing, sales and technical support. We wanted this philosophy to also be reflected in our e-commerce platform for channel partners. This meant that certain factors were absolutely mandatory, such as:

- Simple and fast order placement with individual partner conditions.
- Immediate order processing.
- Instant delivery of license key.
- Direct access to orders completed and information about the licenses (including entered customer data).
- Self service: Partners should be able to update and change their account data themselves.
- 24/7, 365 day availability: The channel partner's login gives them access to their account at any time or place.

The following screen shots will show you what a system could look like. A good recommendation, based on my experience, is that you work on improving the system over time. Don't expect everything to be perfect from day one. And even if you launch a great platform, expect to make changes going forward. Working with an e-commerce provider who listens to your requests and adapts the solution accordingly creates additional value for you and your channel partners.

Easy registration

New channel partners either find us as a result of their own research or because they've received one of our promotions. Normally, we'll guide them to the partner registration through our website, but we've also used special landing pages or links in mailings.

NovaStor ValueCREATE! e-commerce platform

NOVASTOR

Microsoft
GOLD CERTIFIED
Partner

Online Store

McAfee SECURE
TESTED 11-SEPT

This site is SSL SECURED

Verisign Trusted
VERIFY »

Language: English

Partner Signup

In order to become a registered partner, please fill in your details in the form below.

♥ Already a Partner with another cleverbridge Client?

Are you already a registered Partner with another cleverbridge Client? If so, please use the following link to login: Click here to login.
If you are not a registered partner in the cleverbridge platform yet, please fill out the form below.

🔧 Address

Please enter your address information below.

*First Name:	Stefan
*Last Name:	Utzinger
Company:	NovaStor Corp
*Country:	United States
*State / Province:	California
*Address:	29209 Canwood St.
Additional Address Information:	
*City:	Agoura Hills
*Zip / Postal Code:	91301
*E-mail:	stefan.utzinger@novastor.com

🔒 Choose Login Data

Please choose a username and password for your new partner account.

*Username:	stefanutzinger
*Password:	•••••••
*Re-Type Password:	•••••••

The goal during the registration process is to make a highly professional impression and make registration as easy as possible. Supporting several languages is very important for conveying this professionalism. In fact, we found that once we had implemented a process that allowed the potential partner to navigate the pages in their native language, the drop-off rate went down significantly.

After new partners have entered the necessary information on the registration form, they are asked to go through a quick verification process. This important step helps to reduce spam.

Verification

Verification

Enter the characters shown in the picture below:

After you have finished reviewing your data, please use the "Save" button below to complete your signup.

Confirmation process

NovaStor receives an automatic notification when a new registration comes in and we are then asked to review and confirm the registration. This gives us the opportunity to provide important information about the reseller relationship.

As you can see in the screen shot, we can input the partner status and add the reseller to a group of resellers who receive a standard discount or give them an individual discount. This is an especially helpful system if you have to manage many partners from all over the world.

Once we've accepted the registration, the reseller receives an automatic notification. They also receive a first partner package including price lists and NFR codes to use our software in their environment and marketing material.

Partner Update

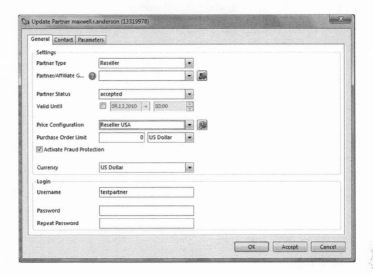

Partner login

Hopefully the new channel partner already has a good client base and wants to start reselling our products immediately. All they need to do is login. Once they've done that, they can buy every product offered in the online shop taking into account their specific discount rates.

Login screen

Companies who use an e-commerce platform such as cleverbridge, can maintain an overview of all registered partners; their current status, what they buy, when they buy and so on. You aren't only able to generate reports regarding the last few days, weeks or years, it's also possible to generate reports on previous and current campaigns. This will allow you to optimize the campaigns and run them again. Thousands of partners can be monitored and supported individually, making it possible to customize the process for every single partner or partner group.

This can really boost revenue as it allows you to reach specific customer groups and drive business to your channel partners. Without access to this type of analysis you won't be able to optimize your effort or the results for you and your channel partners.

Purchase workflow

The e-commerce platform lets you adapt the system for selling products to partners instead of end users, for example, to change how products are presented and the purchase workflow. However, this may not be necessary because channel partners very often behave like end users and it's important that they have the same professional shopping experience as end user customers.

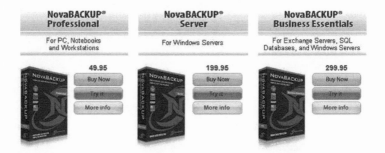

In our example, the partner chooses a product from the online shop and clicks on the "Buy Now" button. As shown in the screen shot, the channel partner in this case has started the buying process directly from our website and the end user pricing is still displayed.

After making their selection, they can click on "registered partners click here to login" and enter their access data as a reselling partner. The shopping cart now shows partner prices. (They can also login right from the start and immediately see their individual prices.)

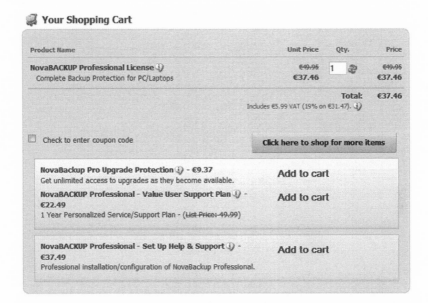

The next step is very important in the channel business — I've seen many home-grown solutions break down at this point. Resellers normally buy the products and resell them to their end customers. It's absolutely essential that you as the software vendor give your channel partners the opportunity to manage their end users using your system.

The channel partner can enter a licensee and billing address for every end user. This address is important for assigning the license to a customer. The licensee address is not used by the company running the e-commerce platform, but it's important for the vendor and channel partner when it comes to maintenance and support. For example, using this information you can ensure that the software is always up to date and the end user receives support when they contact the vendor's team.

Licensee Address

Please enter the information of the person to whom this product shall be licensed below.

*First Name:	
*Last Name:	
Company:	
*Address:	
Additional Address Information:	
*Zip / Postal Code:	
*City:	
*Country:	Germany
Phone:	
*E-mail:	

Billing address

Please enter your billing address information below. If necessary, you will also be able to specify a different delivery address later.

*First Name:	Test
*Last Name:	User

After selecting the payment options, the channel partner just needs to review their data and submit the order. The order will be processed immediately and a confirmation page with all important information including the reference number will be displayed.

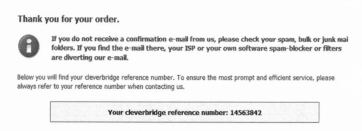

Thank you for your order.

If you do not receive a confirmation e-mail from us, please check your spam, bulk or junk mail folders. If you find the e-mail there, your ISP or your own software spam-blocker or filters are diverting our e-mail.

Below you will find your cleverbridge reference number. To ensure the most prompt and efficient service, please always refer to your reference number when contacting us.

Your cleverbridge reference number: 14563842

Channel partners are given a reference number for each order and also receive a confirmation email with order details.

The entire process is optimized and it will continue to be improved further by the e-commerce platform provider. The fact that the cleverbridge system is so standardized is a real advantage. Many other ISVs use the same platform or a very similar system; therefore most end users and channel partners are already familiar with it. This significantly increases the acceptance of your buying process, which is very important when using an e-commerce platform to work with the channel.

Building a Multi-Channel Strategy

In the next chapter, I'd like to focus on the different channel types and describe how most ISVs can build and maintain a multi-channel strategy. A multi-channel strategy is in place when the ISV works with a variety of different channel partners who sell different kinds of products.

Why multi-channel strategies exists

Whenever I hear the word "multi", I know that something complicated will follow. Why do most vendors, not only in the IT Industry, work with a multi-channel strategy? There are many different reasons, but the availability of global information, thanks to the internet, is a key driver here.

We've seen that the typical ISV today sells their solutions in different ways:

- Direct to the end customer via their own sales force.
- Traditional software sales via a channel partner.
- Sales of packaged software via the internet, using their own store or via different distribution chains.
- SaaS solutions direct or via channel partners.

To be successful, most ISVs will have to run these different sales methods in parallel. This is because they very often have different products that require different sales models or the market requires different models. There are still many resellers who only buy boxed products from distributors, but more and more resellers now use online stores and buy directly from the ISV.

In most cases, this will sooner or later create channel conflicts. These have to be managed very creatively because there are so many different parameters to take into account. In a "multi-channel" conflict, two or more sales channels will focus on the same market segment, which means they target the same customers. In the case of a horizontal channel conflict, more than one partner competes for the same project or customer. This very often results in a price battle and inevitable price dumping.

A typical example of this is when the distributor, who gets the best margins, not only sells to resellers but also sells to end users ("multi-channel" conflict). Or when two VARs compete for the same customer and give huge discounts ("horizontal channel" conflict). Don't try to find the perfect solution to these conflicts! You'll only fail. It's much more effective to take a different approach and encourage cooperation across the channels instead.

Cooperation across channels

The key to success when running a multi-channel strategy is to break down the barriers between the various channels and to encourage cooperation between the different partners.[50] Every company striving for multi-channel success will soon notice a trend towards becoming "customer centric" and not "company/channel centric". Customer centric partners are good for your business because they focus on the right solution for the customers instead of their own business model. Studies from retail organizations have shown that customers spend over 30% more per year with customer centric companies. Also, customers of a customer centric business will return to the same vendor with a probability of 75% when they need an additional product.

Here's a list of things you can do to motivate your different partner types to cooperate:

---

[50] Jack Schmid, "Seven Strategies for Breaking Down Silos" (2006)

- **Top management support**: Top management must support and drive the multi-channel strategy. They must also motivate the channel partners to join forces to win new customers. If top management doesn't demonstrate the benefits and the various ways to team up, this strategy will fail.

- **Break down the barriers:** Make sure that your "org chart", which maps the responsibilities and the power within your organization, reflects your strategy. Motivate each one of your resellers to join the channel network. You will soon see that once more resellers join, it becomes easier to motivate people to co-operate.

- **Set goals and give incentives:** "What's in it for me?" This is a question both your team and the channel partners will ask. Give additional discounts for channel partners who choose to work together to win a customer, or allocate extra marketing funding if two partners start promoting their solutions together. If you can create win-win incentives then the partners will follow.

- **Carry out customer research:** Help your channel partners to provide the service their customers are asking for. Communicate with the customers - most customers like being asked what the vendors could do better. This feedback can be of real value to your channel partners.

- **Push cross-channel promotions:** Whenever success happens as a result of channel partners working together make sure you spread the word. Utilize your PR, case studies and special promotions. It must be clear to everyone in your channel network that cooperation within the channel will lead to success.

- **Be aware of brand identity:** It's especially important in a multi-channel strategy that your brand is always consistent and doesn't confuse the customer. Make sure that all the design elements (layout, color, typeface etc.) look the same. Your message must be clear and consistent, otherwise you risk losing channel partners and customers due to your lack of appropriate attention to the brand details.

By the way, one more reason to pursue a multi-channel strategy and push cooperation between the channel partners is that most channel partners are actually aware of the fact that a multi-channel strategy reflects the current market trend.

Success factors for a multi-channel strategy

So we've seen why multi-channel strategies are important and how to motivate partners to go along. But what do you actually have to do? Here's a list of necessary steps:

- Clear definition of the channel strategy; including responsibilities, pricing strategies and also client/market segmentation.

- Well balanced ratio between the number of channel partners and the market potential.

- Invest in high quality channel management that acknowledges the requirements of each kind of channel partner and actively communicates with them.

- Ensure clear communication lines with the channel. The channel must understand your strategy and learn how you can help with selling the solutions.

- The goals of your internal channel managers and the channel partners must be in alignment. Focus on the commission model because money drives the relationship.

- Provide the same level of support to the different partner categories (e.g. marketing material, pricing and pre-sales resources). Don't treat one channel better than the other.

- Create focused action plans and strategies, controlling the results together with your channel partners.

- Integrate your channel partners in joint marketing activities (e.g. to promote specific customer solutions).

- Build a channel community. Boost the communication between channel partners and point out the value of a working channel community for everybody.

Even if the multi-channel approach makes the channel harder to manage (in terms of handling various different channels to sell the products) there is a huge market opportunity associated with this strategy. Vendors, who get it right and establish a working partner network that serves their customers through different sales channels, will win in the end. This alone should be a huge motivation.

The Revolutionary Rules

Everything I've laid out so far in this book points towards taking a new approach to your channel strategy. You can choose the "old" way or the new "revolutionary" way - it's as simple as that. The table below highlights the differences between the traditional old way and the revolutionary new way. When you look at it this way, it's pretty clear which way to go.

The Old Way	The Revolutionary Way
Fire and forget sales approach	Recurring revenue
Compete directly online	Develop channel e-commerce offerings
Home-grown e-commerce systems	Standardized, professional e-commerce platforms
Stock channel partners	On demand sales
Business plans and contracts	Action plans and actions
Charges for training	Free education
Product thinking	Solution thinking
Focus on all channel partners	Focus on specific verticals
ISVs focus only on own products	ISVs implement cross-selling promotions
Channel partners only resell	Channel partners are part of the value chain
Generic marketing material	Reseller specific marketing material
Certifications from big names	Industry leading certification

The Old Way	The Revolutionary Way
(e.g. Microsoft or SAP)	(SaaS)
Beta groups for testing	Partner councils to develop strategies

Okay, that's it for theory. The next part of the book will focus on the nitty-gritty, namely execution. We all know that the best laid out plans aren't worth the paper they were written on if they aren't executed properly.

Part IV: Execution

When everything seems to be going against you, remember that the airplane takes off against the wind, not with it.

Henry Ford

Command Like a King

Execution is the discipline of getting things done![51] John S. Reed, the previous chairman of CitiGroup, once said "A CEO has just two jobs; deciding what to do and making it happen. And ninety percent of the job is making it happen. When you are running a company, execution becomes everything."[52]

Hopefully, parts one and two of this book have helped you rethink your existing channel strategy and have given you ideas about strategies to implement or adapt. But maybe you've already drawn up a strategy and made some key decisions. So now comes the execution. As Guy Kawasaki wrote in his book "Rules for Revolutionaries": "Command like a king: for a revolution to succeed, someone has to take charge and make the tough, insightful, and strategic decisions."[53]

Commanding like a king is even more important if you want to create a powerful channel. Someone must set the strategic guidelines, create the sales messages and define the rules. If the channel doesn't understand the strategy, the message needs to be adapted or the rules need to be more clearly defined. Otherwise it'll be impossible

---

[51] Larry Bossidy & Ram Charan, "Execution - the discipline of getting things done," Crown Business (2002). This is a great book that provides a very clear and pragmatic approach to building a strategy and executing it correctly.

[52] "MIT Tech Talk," April 29, 1998

[53] In his book "Rules for Revolutionaries" Guy Kawasaki says "create like a god - command like a king - work like a slave". These are the key factors for creating and marketing new products and services.

to build a reliable and productive channel. Not everyone will follow however, not every channel partner will understand and accept your channel strategy. Someone must break down the barriers and explain why the channel strategy is healthy for your company and your channel partners. The only person in a company who can really do this is the CEO and it's very important that this key decision maker is in support of the channel strategy. Only if the channel is embedded in the corporate strategy, will there be any chance for a good channel implementation.

I'll point out how to execute a powerful channel strategy in this chapter. In particular, I'll address the following issues:

- How to create the right channel strategy for your company.
- Why the right team setup and the right people make a difference.
- Which tools are absolutely necessary for success.
- The type of education your first channel partners should receive.
- How you can profit from these first experiences and grow your channel.
- Which key drivers will increase sales with your partners.
- How the channel account managers should report and how they can drive revenue.

Setting the Right Goals

The first step is to define a clear channel strategy. The project manager or the person most strongly supporting the idea of building a channel should work out this strategy plan. It's important that the strategy is constructed and owned by the people who will execute it. I recommend viewing the channel business as a business unit within the company. The strategic plan should lay out the direction for this business unit: where it is now, where it will be going and how it will get there.

Make sure that the strategy is straightforward and not too difficult to understand. If it takes a long time just to explain the strategy then there is a high likelihood that it will fail. Always remember, the human brain has tremendous limitations when it comes to processing capacity! Most people cannot process more than five elements at one time. If something becomes too complex then the average person won't be able to execute it correctly. If your business requires "regular Einsteins" to run it then it will never fly!

A good strategic plan should cover the following points:

- Today's situation (channel revenues, number of partners etc.).
- Corporate vision for working with the channel.
- Goals and action plan.
- Team setup.
- Who are the competitors and how you can win against them.
- Necessary investments.
- Major milestones.
- Reporting - how you control the milestones.

Always keep in mind that creating a powerful channel is not a part-time job. You can't expect big success in a very short time frame. Creating a powerful channel is based on taking little steps and getting little wins. There must be a clear trend though; if the trend isn't positive then you'll have to change your plan quickly. You can download an example of a channel strategy plan for a smaller to mid-size company at www.channel-revolution.com.

Building a Partner Centric Organization

One of your most important goals should be creating a partner centric organization. If you want to be successful in the channel, the channel must be at the centre of your business and must be supported by your top management. However, this doesn't mean that a partner centric organization can't also sell directly, but it needs to know exactly when to choose which sales channel and give partners a high priority.

The most important aspects for building a partner centric organization are as follows:

- Hire the right people. They need to want to work with the partner to achieve joint success. That means, they should be service-oriented, hard working, good communicators and results driven. If you find that their skill set or work ethics don't match your requirements, then don't wait too long to replace them.
- Draw clear lines between the direct and indirect organization. It's very important that there is a clear differentiation between these sales methods in your business.
- For larger organizations, all functions from account management, marketing, education and professional services should report to a head of partner management either directly or in a matrix organization.[54]
- The head of partner management should have a compensation plan that is connected to the revenue of the channel. This will keep their interest focused on promoting the value of the channel inside the company and helping the channel partners to become successful in selling your products.
- In smaller organizations there should be designated employees working "for" the channel in every department.

If you are a very small company, you won't have enough employees to build up whole departments and teams, but you'll have to focus on making sure that the following jobs/functions are taken care of:

- Partner Account Management
- Partner Program Management
- Partner Business Development
- Partner Services
- Partner Project Consulting

---

[54] Matrix organization: Multiple command-and-control structure in which some employees have dual responsibilities and dual bosses. www.BusinessDictionary.com

- Partner Sales Consulting
- Partner Education
- Partner Product Marketing

You may assign a team of people or a single employee to each of these jobs. Or, in smaller organizations, you might have one person covering all of these tasks. The next pages will describe these roles in more detail.[55]

Partner account management (PAM)

Partner account managers control all aspects of managing new and existing partners. They manage a defined group of partners and are the first point of contact for the channel partners in the company. PAMs create value for the partners by cultivating and fostering the relationship as well as developing and implementing strategies to grow the business with these partners. A PAM has a sales quota and their main goal is to boost revenues with the partners. The main difference between a PAM and a direct sales manager is that they have to build and maintain relationships to generate ongoing revenue streams. They look for long-term revenues in contrast to short-term revenues which are the main interest for direct sales managers.

It's important that the PAM department has support from the other channel departments so that they can focus on working with their most valuable partners. The PAM should control all aspects of integrating and managing the partners.

Partner program management

The partner program management is made up of a group of employees with different skill sets. It includes the partner marketing group and is responsible for the organization of "partner days" and

---

[55] I list key requirements for each position/job. You can find more detailed job descriptions for these positions on recruiting websites such as www.monster.com or on LinkedIn.

other events. They host the partner website, the internal partner web and communicate with the partners about webinars or newsletters.

They will also compile the necessary statistics to control and optimize the channel program. Every month, they should provide lists of the top partners, the low producers, the best and worst selling channel products etc.

The partner program management creates website promotions, works on joint direct marketing initiatives and joint event participation. On the whole, they provide the marketing tools for working with the partners.

Partner business development

The partner business development creates business cases that show how the partners can combine your solution with services they offer and then sell them into different markets. They create business cases to convince the customer, marketing material and also set pricing guidelines. Another role of the partner business development is to identify and create material for the acquisition of new groups of partners and also for the cooperation with strategic partners.

A special team within the partner business development should be responsible for the selection and acquisition of new channel partners. They are responsible for locating new potential partners, collecting information about these partners, making the first contact and presenting your company and solution to them. They take responsibility for the potential partner until the level of "expertise fit" is reached and then hand the most promising ones over to the PAM. The remaining potential channel partners are handled by the partner program management who will make sure that these partners all receive standardized information such as product documentation or promotions.

Partner services

Partner services takes care of all aspects in the partner's lifecycle. They manage the partner's special requirements, ensure that the discounts, finder's fee or any other fees are paid and that all questions regarding order processing are sorted out.

Very often, partner services also manage all the other smaller partners who don't generate enough revenue to justify working with a dedicated PAM. This aspect of their job becomes especially important if you run your own online store, since many smaller resellers with little or no knowledge about your product will start buying directly and they will need a kind of first level support.

Partner project consulting

The technical side of the partner centric organization is represented by the partner project consulting and the partner sales consulting groups. Their typical tasks are the facilitation of project planning workshops with the end user, the creation of technical specifications, reviewing existing specifications and giving assistance to the partners when deploying the application (e.g. code review, help coding different parts).

It's important that the partners view this group as an extension of their capabilities and not as competition. It's really critical that you make sure your organization never goes around the partner and deals directly with the end customers. The partner project consulting group needs to understand the project from the channel partner's perspective - their job is to deal only with the channel partners and this is an important difference from dealing directly with the end user.

Partner sales consulting

The partner sales consulting group also belongs to the technical group. They provide important tools to the partners for winning new customers such as ROI (Return on Investment) or TCO (Total Cost of Ownership) tools. By using these tools, you can educate your partner about what kind of projects deliver the best ROI for the end user and enable your partner to identify possible projects at their customer base. It's only once the channel partners understand the concept and the value of the offering that they will sell it.

The partner sales consulting group can also build prototypes or market/technical requirement documents to make sure the project can be estimated and executed properly.

Partner education

I've already argued that only educated partners will contribute the necessary revenue to grow your business. Therefore a separate education or training unit is necessary. If you are a smaller vendor without a specific training department, appoint your technical presales as responsible for training the partners.

Typical responsibilities of a training department are developing the training material, organizing technical courses and performing certifications. Training should usually be done via webinars, but for more complex products face-to-face trainings might still be necessary.

Partner product marketing

The partner product marketing is a very important group who works with the partners and provides them with information about the entire product range as well as tools to generate new business.

A typical tool is market research about technical and industry trends, which provides information about the market and the competitive landscape. Partner product management not only conducts competitive analyses but also identifies the different solutions that exist to solve a particular problem (not necessarily just technical solutions) and provides the reasons for why your solution is the best. It's important that this group also consults the channel partners because if your solution doesn't fit, then the probability of losing the project is very high.

Further responsibilities of the partner product marketing group are the creation of price lists and case studies and helping to put together presentations for specific projects.

The Channel Partner Program

Apart from having the right team on board, it's also important that the basic tools are in place before you start building a larger scale channel network. I believe there are two tools that stand out from the rest and are worthy of closer examination, these are the channel partner program and the channel website.

The channel partner program describes the framework of the relationship between the ISV and their channel partners. In most cases, it's a marketing document; nevertheless, it should provide a clear definition of the benefits a channel partner receives in return for selling the manufacturer's product. A channel partner program should outline and demonstrate the value for the end users that you and your channel partners can create together - showing how to make your solution (the product and the reseller's services) more attractive. However it's important to be aware that no channel program can fit the needs of all the different types of channel partners. Distribution partners think completely differently to VARs or OEM partners. Therefore you need tailored programs and dedicated teams for the different groups of partners.

I highly recommend creating a channel partner program from the perspective of creating additional value to the end user and not, as many vendors still do, from the perspective of defining partner levels (benefits and discounts within the various levels). Even if these aspects need to be included in the channel program, the focus must be how to create additional value for the channel partners and their end users.

How can you do this? Start by getting to know the business world of your target channel partners - understand their business, their lingo and their typical way of doing business. By gaining a better understanding of your channel partner's business, you'll be able to think of ways to add value by adapting your product or service. Usually, the relationship with a VAR is characterized by the ISVs product being sold as part of a larger solution that is offered to the customers by the VAR. The VARs and similar partners will add value for the end user by implementing the solution, integrating it with other products or building a specific solution in conjunction with or complementing the ISV's product.

Always keep in mind that a channel partner will only do business with a manufacturer if the ISV's specific type of technology or product will help increase their revenue. None of the benefits you offer for joining the channel program (including product and marketing training, discounts, technical support, lead generation tools and other important perks) will be of any help building a good channel network as long as the partners can't increase their revenue with your solution.

Your channel program should not only help the channel partner increase their revenue, but also drive down the costs of doing business by providing easy access to the benefits. The channel partner program should outline your core vision for the channel partners such as building long-term relationships or how your team will work with the channel partners.

If you are a smaller player, you can work out a clear vision for becoming stronger by cooperating with the right group of channel partners. If you have limited resources, you can combine your products with the knowledge, services and customer access of the channel partners. Identify the main factors that you can provide to your channel partners to make them more successful or to make them feel more confident about starting to sell your products. It can be especially hard for smaller ISVs to convince channel partners to come on board for the first project with them.

One strategy you can implement is the delivery of high class technical support to your channel partners. This type of support is especially important at the beginning of a relationship, when the channel partner doesn't know your products well enough. Don't even think of outsourcing your technical support to countries that offer cheaper labor. Add value instead by delivering local technical support in your main territories. Try to offer something unique to the industry in terms of this support. Take a different approach than your competitors. For example, you could offer pre-arranged appointment times with technical support executives. This could be particularly helpful when your channel partner is installing your software at their client's site because you will be ready and waiting in the background to answer their technical questions. This will also create a risk free implementation experience for the channel partner, saving them time and money.

Another innovative example is providing easy access to resources for product training. You can provide all partners with free access to web-based technical training, NFR copies that they can familiarize themselves with and any additional training such as workshops free of charge. It's important however, that you assure the channel partner that this training is not a profit centre for you. Let them know you don't aim to earn any money with training before the channel partners have first made money with the product. I know that many vendors handle this differently, but my personal view is that the vendor should enable the channel partner to make money - therefore technical support and product training are absolutely necessary.

Another step you can take is appointing a personal sales associate, even for your smaller partners. This means you have a dedicated employee who is a reliable point of contact for the channel partner. The associate is someone who they can discuss business plans with, special marketing initiatives, product plans, promotions, discounts, accounting issues and especially potential customer situations where your product could fit. Even if this costs you some resources, it can be very valuable for learning more about the channel partners and helping them to sell your products or include them as part of a solution. You can also leverage this knowledge across your partner network and ultimately lower the cost of doing business with you for the channel partner.

Your channel program should outline how you as the vendor will help your channel partners to sell the products and the total solution of the channel partners. Therefore the marketing and sales support should be clearly defined. This is important since many smaller resellers only have limited resources available for marketing - very often these companies are not as marketing driven as most ISVs. Typical things you can provide is free web-based sales training, templates for marketing collateral that your partner can easily convert to their own brand and use in promotions.

It's also important that you as the vendor become the specialist in a specific market segment. This means you should publish white papers and research that supports your partners with sales arguments for your product in specific sales situations. Sometimes it's necessary to allocate marketing funds for special initiatives, but this should be done on a case-by-case basis. It's more important, from my point of view, to make sure the channel partner knows who they can contact in the marketing department and that they can get help easily.

In my opinion, helping your partners so that they can help themselves is the first step in lead generation. It's also what partners expect most. Just about all research shows that "lead generation" is the top answer from channel partners when asked what they expect from their ISV. Technical support, free education and marketing/sales support are all major steps for generating leads together because they enable the channel partner to appear more knowledgeable in front of their customers and to articulate the value of your product. When they can do this, it creates a much higher probability of generating a lead, exploring an opportunity and closing a deal. To reward the effort of your channel partners you should direct leads generated through marketing initiatives such as your website, attendance at fairs and other activities to your most qualified partners.

Discounts come at the end of the list of benefits that should be covered in the channel program. The main reason for this is that the channel partner should not only focus on getting more discounts off the product, they should try to make money selling the complete solution. They should be encouraged to include their services and to put all their energy into learning what kinds of solutions they can build with your products.

The channel partner program also needs to be specific about the ISV's expectations. If the ISV expends a lot of effort on delivering an outstanding product and providing a lot of support to their channel partners there must be some return coming in - winning is always a team effort. If the ISV pushes but the channel partners don't react, then there will be no success. The channel partners must feel obligated to become knowledgeable about the product - not just their technical team, but also their sales and marketing departments. That means partners must take part in a certain amount of technical training and allocate dedicated resources for marketing and sales.

Last, but not least, the top management from both sides should be involved in the partnership and support it. I recommend you include this aspect in your channel program and make it a requirement for anyone starting a partnership.

The Web-Based Partner Portal

Earlier in the book, I already discussed how important a web-based e-commerce portal is for channel success. The focus of this chapter is to show how you can use such a portal to generate a web presence and enable channel partners to sell your products. If an ISV really wants to demonstrate their commitment to a channel strategy, then the channel partners should have their own section on the ISV's website. You should be able to find it promoted in a prominent position on the ISV's homepage. This shows that the channel plays an important role in the ISV's business concept and demonstrates management's strong support of the channel partners, its employees, the customers and the channel itself.

I would recommend listing the benefits for channel partners directly on the front page. From there, it should be easy to sign in to the partner program or locate the web pages with marketing material.

A channel partner should not only be able to find the necessary information about the partner program, but should also be able to locate all the material required for their marketing and customer communication at first glance (updated datasheets, pictures, events, trainings etc.). The goal must be to establish a professional, self service channel portal and to automate as many processes as possible. This is an absolutely necessary step if you want to build a channel network with thousands of resellers.

A partner portal provides the following benefits:

- Dashboard with current partner status, contact information, current promotions and important news.

- Easy access to current marketing and sales tools such as datasheets, graphics and others.

- Up to date information for channel partners. For instance, you could have a section called "Partner News" containing information about new releases, white papers and case studies.

- Invitations to events, webinars and training. Registered partners should also be given access to recorded webinars and training events.

- Preferred access to support information (FAQs, contacts, RMA etc.) with a direct link to the technical support team.

- Channel partners should have access to their profile and be able to update information or logos themselves.

- Information about the contacts within the vendor's organization. It's important to make it easy for channel partners to communicate with the vendor.

- Sometimes an online chat section can be a very good addition. This enables real time chat sessions with channel marketing, partner account managers or even technical support.

- For many channel partners the most important function will be the partner locator. This allows end users to easily find and contact channel partners.

The partner locator

Since the partner locator is such an important tool, let me go into a bit more detail here. Obviously, the partner portal needs to work properly on your own website, but it should also come up on Google searches. Some partner locators require the end user to select the product or the competency area they are looking for.

I recommend that only certified partners with specific product knowledge, reference customers and a minimum revenue level are listed and that these partner contact profiles are closely reviewed. Always ensure that partner information and profiles are up to date. End users will tend to trust these vendor website listings; it can therefore really hurt the vendor's reputation if the end user contacts a listed partner who doesn't know much about the product or even the partnership.

The vendor, not only the partner, also benefits from a partner portal and can use it to gather information. This information can be used to further optimize the channel page as well as the entire channel program. It's very useful to know which partners have used the portal (last login), how often a particular partner uses the portal or what kind of information the partners are actually downloading. You can also view reports on how much traffic the partner portal is getting and how often end users are contacting the channel partners. This can provide you with a good overview of the actual lead generation and how to improve it.

Education and Training

I've already pointed out that education should be part of the channel program. However, educating channel partners is a big challenge for almost every ISV. This is a typical "chicken and egg" problem; most channel partners are very busy with their core business and don't have any time to spend on "non revenue generating" activities. Larger ISVs, who have a big brand name and "popular" products can fairly easily convince channel partners to invest time in trainings, but smaller ISVs will have a much harder time to do this.

Training & Webinars

NovaStor offers a variety of Workshops, Trainings and Webinars to NovaStor partners and customers. Register today and learn more about our products and solutions.

Schedule Table & Registration

Date / Time	Training / Workshop	Topics	
2 Dec. 2010 9.00 AM (PST)	Webinar: NEW VERSION: NovaBACKUP xSP v12 – Introduction	NovaBACKUP xSP v12 – 1 new product, 1 complete managed backup solution. Learn how the new version can provide Solution Providers and MSP's a complete centralized managed backup architecture and a fully hosted online backup service combined!	REGISTER NOW
9 Dec. 2010 9.00 AM (PST)	Webinar: NovaBACKUP 12 xSP: Upgrade Process	NovaStor would like to give you an overview of the upgrade options. Please attend this webinar before upgrading to the new version to avoid any trouble.	REGISTER NOW

In reality, there are quite a few reasons why a channel partner should consider solutions from smaller ISVs. For example, they often provide a more unique solution, better service, better pricing and also a better relationship. In fact, the relationship factor is a key explanation why many channel partners give smaller ISVs a chance. These days, the channel partner usually has to offer a fixed price project to the end user. This means that the financial risk for the implementation is carried 100% by the channel partner. While larger vendors often charge big bucks for training and assistance during the implementation stage, they often don't care if a project fails. Smaller ISVs can take on some of the risk and actively help their channel partners with projects. This not only builds trust, but also ensures that the end user doesn't return your product. By helping your channel partner win and master a project, you're created another source of revenue potential.

I don't want to go into all the details of successful project management, but instead want to show you how to structure your organization in such a way that you can support your channel partners throughout the entire sales and implementation process.

Create partner consulting packages

The first course of action is to define the roles of the channel partners more clearly and begin to offer standardized consulting packages. It's essential that you always maintain a professional approach and that you guide your channel partners through the process.

Here are the most important things to keep in mind:

- **Best practice:** You are the expert in selling and implementing your products. Only you have a complete overview of all projects that have been implemented by you or one of your partners. Don't create any material or strategy for your partners without including the best practices.

- **Quality assurance through standardization:** When you start developing the packages you need to make sure they are as standardized as possible. Always keep in mind that you have different parties involved in each process.

- **The internal team:** They need to deliver the product and service. I've experienced situations where the price list and packages weren't understood by the internal team. This can create a lot of confusion for everyone; your team, the partner and also the end user.

- **The channel partners:** They need to understand the packages. Often, the channel partner has to include these services into their offering, so it's very important that they understand the package. They must also know what they can expect from the sales process right from the beginning. It will lead to big frustration if your channel partner has worked on an opportunity for months only to find out that they will not be able to deliver the solution on time or on budget.

- **The end users:** They often expect some kind of teamwork between the vendor and system integrator - especially if you are talking about enterprise projects. In situations where the system integrator doesn't have many references with the product or the end user must be involved (providing project critical parts such as specifications or interfaces to other systems), then making the project successful can become a real issue.

- **Covering all project critical issues:** You as the vendor should be able to identify the typical pitfalls and challenges in your projects and have solutions ready for most of them. If the type of project is new for you (e.g. your first vertical implementation for a special industry or a complex integration with another product) then you need to be honest about this information and discuss the possible solutions with your partner.

- **Synchronization with education program:** If you've identified the specific basic knowledge a partner requires, then you must ensure that your education program provides it. You'll also have to offer specific training frequently enough (or with enough flexibility) so that your partner can access the knowledge when they need to. Your education program should also offer on-site trainings.

Coach your partner through the first few projects

A very successful way to work with partners is accompanying them during their first projects. Often the partner can't invest their time and resources in all the education without seeing some revenue coming in. The problem is, however, by the time the partner has won their first project, there won't be enough time for the necessary education as set out in the project plan.

The software vendor and the channel partner should undertake the first project together in order to kick off their partnership and make the first project a mutual success. Even if you or your channel partner make less money on the project, you can ensure that the end user will be satisfied and that the project becomes a success.

Either the vendor or the partner can take the leadership role on the first project. But if the vendor does 50% or more of the work on this first project, it must be understood that this kind of leadership will be an exception.

The main focus of the vendor's involvement in the project is to provide coaching to the partner. Make sure the partner also understands that you are not going into competition with them, but instead that you have a plan to educate them. Your plan involves handing over future project leadership and the majority of the professional services to the partner as soon as possible.

On the second project, the partner should take project leadership and the vendor should be responsible for a maximum 30% of the project. The main focus for the vendor's involvement is assuring quality and training the partner on some "specifics." This kind of involvement can continue until the partner has reached a sufficient level of knowledge and they can master projects on their own. As a good rule of thumb, you should assume that the partner should be ready to take complete control after the fifth project.

From now on, the partner must take on project leadership and the vendor should only be involved in special tasks. This makes the partner feel secure that there is always somebody to help them when needed. It also allows the main focus of the vendor's business to remain on software and not service revenue.

**First
Project**

**Project
No. 2-5**

**Project
No. 6-15**

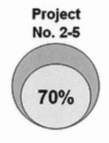
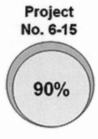

50%   70%   90%

The above graph illustrates the progression of this strategy. My experience with channel partners is that they are very protective of their client base and will quickly become critical if there is direct interaction between the end user and the vendor. If you present them with a visible and reasonable strategy, however, the partner will understand your intentions. This kind of understanding and openness on a project is the first step towards success.

Secure a revenue stream with "partner project insurance"

Partner project insurance is especially appealing for new vendors, new technologies or very complex projects with a high risk of failure. The main idea of this concept isn't to offer your channel partners insurance in the style of a traditional insurance company, but instead to give the partner a guarantee that you will support them and see that the projects with the first few customers will be a success.

Partner project insurance doesn't require an upfront financial commitment from your partner. It only requires that they possess the necessary resources to win first projects. During these first projects you will educate your partner and provide the resources to guarantee that the project will be delivered on time and budget. Costs to the partner will be in the form of lower margins on the licenses in the first phase, and that the vendor will deliver a substantial part of the professional services. This insurance concept is built upon the fact that the vendor possesses the resources for each phase of the project, that they will take the risk and that the partner will participate in the revenue stream. If you want to make this work, you need to listen to your partners' opinions about the concept and see if they provide good ideas.

The next chart illustrates the concept of partner project insurance. In the first phase, the end user can conclude the contract directly with the vendor. This makes sense, if the partner hasn't received enough education/training yet and doesn't want to take the contractual risk of a project failure. The vendor takes the project leadership and the partner receives a small commission on licenses sold and for providing service in the project.

Partner Project Insurance

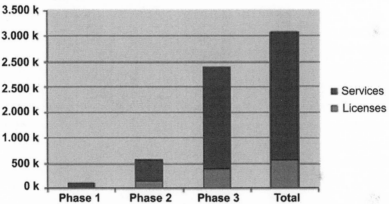

In the second phase, so projects number two to (max.) five, the partner will sell the license to the end user and will provide a substantial amount of services defined in the project. In this phase, the partner will not receive the entire commission on the licenses, since you as vendor have to provide much more support to ensure that the project is successful.

From phase three onwards, the partner will provide almost all of the services and will also receive the highest commission on licenses sold. It's important to show the partner that your goal is to put them in the leadership position, and that they will get most of the revenue in every project.

Using this concept of partner project insurance might work for you "as is" or you might have to adapt it to your situation, but don't underestimate the importance of showing your partners the safe route to success. This is also one of the reasons why you should have a clear plan for the first year or for the first 10 projects. The partner will only invest the necessary amount of time and money if they can see the return on investment in a relatively short time frame.

Create a "partner competence center"

Over the last couple of years, more and more vendors have started to build professional service units and some of them have even purchased large system integrators. This strategy was based on the fact that an increasing amount of professional services is required for each software implementation.

Personally, I think this strategy is in total conflict with fair channel play and will cause tons of channel conflicts. I would recommend creating a "partner competence center" instead of a large professional services unit.

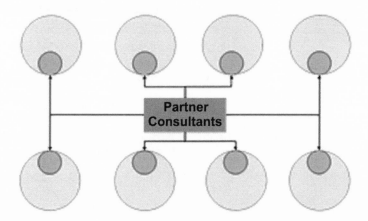

The partner competence center is organized in such a way that a specific group of partner consultants work on several projects at once. These partner consultants have specific knowledge to support and educate the partner on a running project.

There's a big differences between a professional services group and a partner competence center. The partner consultant's goal is to educate and support the partner so they can begin to master large, complex projects on their own. The key measurement of success for the partner competence center is not revenue! It's the number of successful projects completed by the partners. A professional services group always uses the amount of man days sold as a measurement of success, but this will only be understood as a competitive move by you against your channel partners.

The knowledge required to educate and support the partners is totally different to actually running a project. While the partner competence center is focused on assisting the partners in specific situations, a professional services unit must master complex projects end to end. The partner consultants don't require vertical knowledge but they need to be able to teach the partners.

I don't believe that a channel driven organization should have a professional services unit. If a channel partner asks for help, the professional services unit will always try to maximize their profit and sell as many man days as possible. In most cases, the professional services unit will also try to take the leadership of the project. Partner consultants, on the other hand, will always try to work as efficiently as possible to support the partner in generating a profit with the project. They will never try to take the project leadership.

The advantages a partner competence center has over a professional service group are:

- **Higher average rate per man day:** The average rate you can charge for a partner consultant who provides education or solves specific problems can be much higher than that of a normal project consultant who works on every phase of a project.

- **Lower project risk:** More than 50% of all software projects fail. There are many reasons for this; such as having inadequate specifications, changing requirements, bad project management or missing features. In order to win new customers today, you have to offer fixed price projects with very aggressive pricings. This significantly increases the risk of losing money on projects. When utilizing the concept of a partner competence center, the channel partner leads the project and assumes the project failure risk. Most channel partners also know their end user much better because of previous business with them or because of their vertical expertise. This knowledge, in conjunction with the vendor's technical ability to support the partner in critical situations, reduces the risk significantly.

- **Bigger commitment from partners:** If it's 100% clear that the vendor won't compete with the channel partner, the vendor will receive a higher commitment from these partners to sell the solution. Channel partners can "smell" their competition. If the vendor starts looking like a competitor, the channel team will spend their time holding discussions about potential channel conflicts rather than about new projects. Your competitors will also relish the opportunity to point out that you are stealing projects from your channel partners.

- **No vertical knowledge required:** On almost every project, substantial vertical knowledge is necessary to achieve good results. The channel partners, together with the partner consultants, can achieve great results. Their communication is always much better than the communication between the channel partners and the vendor's professional services group.

- **Partner consultants can act as presales for the channel partner:** This is something that technical consultants from a professional services unit can never do. The channel partner will never use them as a "door opener" to their clients since they see them as a competitor.

In general, educating channel partners is challenging and never easy. Obviously, vendors can't offer everything for free forever. So the

ISV's channel team has to figure out a specific strategy to educate the channel. Keep the 80/20 rule in mind. There is no solution that will please every channel partner. See that you find the right solution for the channel partners who can contribute the most value to the end users and the most revenue for you.

The last few chapters have focused on building or rather starting a channel program. Now it's time to win market share! You need to roll out the channel program on a larger scale and win more partners. Read on to find out how.

Growing the Channel

One of the biggest shortcomings when building and maintaining the channel is controlling the effort you expend on increasing the channel network, selecting the right partners, building a lead pipeline and closing business with them. Effectively controlling the expenditure of this effort and its progress on almost a daily basis is just as important as it is when you are selling direct.

Building a reliable channel is no different to building and managing a solid account pipeline. I've seen lots of channel concepts fail because the channel management either thought potential partners would find them or because they only wanted to talk to people they knew from the past and therefore didn't evaluate their ability to resell the products.

Partner recruitment

The first step is the recruitment of the right channel partners. Earlier in the book, I wrote about the importance of the partner selection process. Since this is meant to be a pragmatic guide, let me use an example here. Let's say you want to generate US$2 million in channel revenues and half of that should come from your top twenty partners. If each of your top channel partners can contribute a minimum of US$50,000, you'll need 20 top channel partners. In reality, the remaining selected partners (the ones that worked on an action plan with you) will also produce some revenue, and some of the 20 top partners will hopefully contribute more than US$50,000. In the end, total revenues could exceed US$2 million - but that isn't the main point of this example. The important point I want to make here is that you need a solid process and good management tools to select these top channel partners.

Using the selection funnel describe earlier in the book, you should build your own easy-to-manage funnel. The first phase should be "prospecting/potential leads," which represents all the potential channel partners your team has identified and selected for qualification. These are the partners you know a little bit more about than just their name, and they have some connection with your business. You can ask an assistant or educated temp to locate these partners. It's an important research job because the main prerogative is to build a list of promising potentials.

The next, and very important, phase is "qualification/expertise fit." During this stage, your channel team needs to put a lot of effort into finding out as much as possible about the potential channel partner, their business model and what the main focus of a partnership would be. This job should be carried out by your partner business development department.

The companies that have passed the expertise fit stage will be handed over to partner account management. The account managers will then define an action plan with these companies and select their "peer group". You'll be surprised how many companies will pass the expertise fit and work with you on an action plan, but never really take any action. A good partner account manager (PAM) should be able to see this coming, and only invest in the partners where they see real potential to deliver the revenue.

The partners who will deliver the revenue are the "producers." These companies are classified in the "win" segment. The benefit of working with these companies is that there is a high probability they will produce even higher revenues in years to come.

Prospecting / Potential Lead	Number of Potential Channel Partners	1,600
Qualification / Expertise Fit	Prospects / Qualification	1:5
	No. of Pot. Partners	320
Action Plan / Peer Group	Qualification / Action Plan	1:4
	Partners in Peer Group	80
Win	Peer Group / Producers	1:4
	Number of Partners	20

Let's return to the example I used earlier. We said that the ISV will need 20 partners in the win category. Here comes the reality check. In general, between 70% and 80% of your partners will never generate the promised revenues. This means that your peer group needs to be 4 times the size of the win group. So in this example, you need to have 80 companies in your peer group.

Based on my experience and discussions with other people who've worked with the channel, I can say that the same 1:4 ratio applies at the next level which is expertise fit. There are some fairly common reasons why some companies who have the qualification and expertise fit don't want to work with a new vendor. Either it's because they're already in a relationship with another vendor, or they want to remain independent or they simply don't have the resources to evaluate another product.

It can take some time before the ISV and the channel partner make the decision that it's worth progressing to the next level and creating an action plan. If you consider the 1:4 ratio, then you'll have to evaluate over 300 companies in order to select the 80 that are necessary for the next level.

Prospecting for potential partners forms the basis of the selection process. You can either "steal" names from your competitor's partner list or research resellers on the internet. Whatever you do, you'll need to build and manage an extensive list of partners. This is very similar to managing a lead list; if you don't build your leads today you won't have any business tomorrow. Assuming a realistic 1:5 ratio, you need to initially identify approximately 1,600 potential channel partners. It's hard work to build the list and it has be to maintained constantly.

I've observed many companies who decided to start selling over the channel. They begin building a list of potential channel partners, then select a few and start working with them. Besides a lot of effort and wasted time, nothing comes out of it. To avoid this situation, make certain you have the right selection criteria and processes in place. Take care that your channel team knows how to select the right partners and that you make this a consistent and unchanging process.

Investment in the early stages pays off

Let's take a look at two different scenarios: one where there is a moderate investment into the first two stages of partner selection and another with a bigger investment in the process. It's just like building a house; if you spend more time on the planning, you'll have less headaches during the construction phase.

As shown in the chart below, if you put more effort into the prospecting/potential lead phase, you should be able to generate a much higher quality list of potential partners. Instead of just copying their address from somewhere or doing basic web research, you should invest time to read their latest press releases and find out where their business focus is. Contact someone who knows this partner and look closely at what kinds of customers they have. A very helpful source for finding channel partners in your area are business networks like LinkedIn or XING.

Stage	Scenario A: Normal Investment in Prospecting & Qualification				Scenario B: High Investment in Prospecting & Qualification			
	Time / Partner	Ratio	Part-ners	Total Time	Time / Partner	Ratio	Part-ners	Total Time
Prospecting / Potential Lead	0.25 h		2,000	500 h	0.5 h		320	160 h
Qualifica-tion / Expertise Fit	0.50 h	20%	400	200 h	2 h	35%	112	224 h
Action Plan / Peer Group	8 h	20%	80	640 h	12 h	35%	39	470 h
Win	32 h	25%	20	640 h	32 h	50%	20	627 h
TOTAL				1,980 h				1,482 h

Even more important than doubling your effort in the prospecting phase is quadrupling your effort in the qualification/expertise fit phase. Instead of just "ticking the boxes," get in touch with people who work for the company. Present your solutions and the possible business model and allow the potential partner to do the same. Encourage them to invest some time and you'll find out how serious a potential partnership can be.

When you work on an action plan, make sure that you organize personal meetings with the most influential people. If this isn't possible due to the time or effort involved then conduct phone or video conferences to ensure that you find out more about the company. An action plan needs to include your "gut feeling" about the company and its most important people, otherwise it will not work. Ideally you should visit the company personally, but quite often this just isn't possible at this stage because of time and expense constraints. But take care that you are both on the same page and have the same understanding of the partnership. Be very clear about what you expect and what you are willing to invest. Always remember that if you select this partner to join your peer group, you'll need to invest a lot of time to help the partner generate the required revenue.

Even if my calculations may only be approximations, they demonstrate that if you invest more time in the beginning, you'll save more time in the end and achieve better results. But you'll also build a much more reliable partner base which will make your forecasting more reliable. There will also be a high probability that even the second tier of partners will produce a significant amount of revenue because you've already begun to build a relationship with them. Investing 12 hours, for example, with everyone in the peer group is a significant amount of time, and you can only afford to give this time if your pre-selection is high-quality.

PRM (Partner Relationship Management) system

It's crucial for the proper execution of a larger channel network to have a system and process in place for managing the indirect channels. In this context, I already described the advantages of a professional e-commerce platform. There are many different definitions of a PRM system. Some describe a PRM "simply" as an adaptation of a customer relationship management (CRM) system with identical processes and mechanisms. Personally, I don't agree with this definition because managing a multi-tier channel strategy is totally different from dealing directly with the end customer. Most CRM systems are focused on managing the relationship between the vendor and the end customer. The focus of a system to manage the partners should be on the business processes between the vendor, the different partners and their customers. A PRM system must allow the partners to feed information back into the system.

A typical definition of PRM

"Partner Relationship Management is a business term used to describe the methodology and strategies for improving communications and relationships between companies and their channel partners. Partner Relationship Management solutions include key features for selling, commission, opportunity, marketing campaigns, inventory access, and other features designed to facilitate the relationship between manufacturers and their channel partners."[56]

---

[56] www.webopedia.com (2010)

Since it can be assumed that most companies currently don't have a PRM system (homegrown or purchased) in place, I want to describe the necessary processes for building and managing a growing channel network in a bit more detail. Obviously, you can also initiate and grow a channel network based on Excel spreadsheets and use Outlook for the communication. But if you want to manage a larger channel network with multiple channel managers, I highly recommend that you consider implementing a PRM system along with a professional e-commerce/mailing system.

Lead management with the partners

As already said, generating leads with a partner or forwarding leads to a partner is one of the most important areas in the relationship of an ISV and their partners. During every discussion about a new or existing channel relationship, the topic of lead management will come up and very often results in heavy debate. This is normal, however, because generating new customers or selling new solutions to existing customers constitutes the essence of every business partner relationship. This should also be reflected in the action plan where most of the activities are geared towards lead generation. For example, the channel partners will try to involve the ISV in generating leads by supporting or running marketing programs.

This is all good in theory, but in practice, things can often turn out differently than expected. Sometimes, when the marketing program results in producing many leads for the partners (which are provided by the channel manager to their respective contact person) there is hardly any feedback from the partners. We all know that only hot leads count. If you don't go after leads as soon as they are generated and close deals by supporting the customers in their buying decision, these leads quickly become cold. Once they're cold, business with this customer is no longer likely. So what's the problem here?

I am a fan of Axel Schultze's description of a typical process within a channel organization: "The lead is given from person 1 in marketing to person 2 in channel sales. Person 2 then divides the leads into groups and gives them to the regional channel representatives. Person 3 (the channel rep) gives a few leads to person 4, who is the key contact from their partner organization. Person 4 takes the leads and gives them to their sales manager, person 5. After person 5 reviews the leads and throws 50% away, they give the rest to their team, which lands on the desk of person 6, the sales assistant. Person 6 takes the leads to their local office in Omaha, Nebraska where the office manager, person 7, receives them and gives them to the local salesperson, person 8. Person 8, however, is too busy to follow up, and asks the sales assistant, person 9, to call the prospect and find out how they could help them."[57]

Perhaps this description will make you smile, but it also points out the real problem here; nobody is taking responsibility. Without building a solid pipeline, every sale occurs by accident only. This shouldn't be the foundation on which to build a solid partnership. Always keep in mind that relationships between channel partners are about increasing sales! If you can't prove that a relationship with you will result in sales, you'll never build a solid channel business.

The main challenges involved are:

- Recruitment and focus on the "right" resellers.
- Knowledge of the reseller's business model.
- Building personal relationships with product management and sales people from the channel partner.

The following tools and processes will help to build your channel business using the "right" resellers.

Prospecting/building a list of resellers

As I think I may have stated more than once already in this book, it all begins with finding the right resellers. As described in previous chapters, there are many different ways to research and get in touch with potential channel partners in order to start a business relation-

---

[57] Axel Schultze, "Channel Excellence" (2007)

ship. I've also shown how many resellers you'll need to find and how to design a funnel for selecting the peer group that should generate the planned revenue.

This is only planning and theory though. Execution is about actually building a pipeline, managing the process, ensuring that what you learn along the way is fed back into your system and, most importantly, it's about controlling the results. Without putting a proper assessment and analysis system in place, you can't be successful in the channel business.

Even though I recommend using a web-based system for this, I'll also describe how you can implement the whole process with Microsoft Office tools. If you're just beginning to work with the channel or you only have a small team to manage, then using Office tools might be the most efficient method to start out with.

Set realistic and measurable goals

This first step is perhaps the most important one. It's easy to talk about setting goals but in reality it's a step that requires good judgment and knowledge. First of all, goals need to be "realistic" and "measurable". In order to set realistic goals for the channel team and each of its members, you must define your company goals first.

Let's say an analysis has revealed that you need 20 new, active and producing channel partners next year. As described a few pages ago, to win 20 new, active producers you'll need 500 - 1,000 potential partners in your database.

In order to identify the "right" partners, you need to make members of your channel team accountable for certain defined tasks and certain sub-goals for each of the necessary steps. These people must be focused and have the time to work on their task. If the job becomes just another task on top of their normal work, then that is a warning for you to stop right now! It simply won't work. It is only when your team is 100% focused and capable that you'll see success.

Typical goals for a channel sales team can be:

- Research 50 potential resellers every week.
- Get in contact by phone or email with 10 resellers every day.
- Add 5 new channel partners to the peer group each week.

To be successful, the objectives must be tied to a manageable time frame and this must be assessed on a regular basis. I would suggest setting bi-weekly or monthly goals and assessing their progress on a weekly basis. If there's no time for face-to-face meetings with your team members then using web-based conferences such as GoToMeeting or WebEx can be very efficient.[58] These solutions make it possible for all participants to view the same computer screen and discuss progress over the phone.

It's necessary to avoid easy mistakes such as having no single person being responsible for a certain task or failing to assess the work progress. If you set up an assessment meeting each week then it must happen each week. Otherwise these important tasks will not be taken seriously.

Make sure that you listen to your team and feed the information they give you back into the whole process. To get a better feeling for the channel, get in touch with the actual potential and existing channel partners who are in every stage of the funnel - from prospecting to building the business plan. Your team will only follow when management shows a 100% involvement and commitment.

Maintain one, central set of files/databases

It's very important that the channel team works with one, central system. It doesn't really matter if this is a database driven, web system or a set of Office files such as Excel. You can also share Office

---

[58] WebEX: www.webex.com; GoToMeeting: www.gotomeeting.com

files via programs like SharePoint or via web-based services like Google Docs, ZoHo or Peepel (there are many similar services and they are improving at light speed).[59] Be sure to define rules and processes regarding how to work with these shared documents, otherwise you'll have chaos.

One of the biggest problems can arise when different people start working with their own files. They might change the structure or add information into their personal files which makes it impossible to combine all files or integrate local information into the master file. The result will be an unmanageable situation and frustration within the team caused by an accumulation of varying lists with outdated information. To avoid this outcome, you need to set clear guidelines for using the files. This rule applies whether you are using a web-based system or simply a set of spreadsheets. People might want to use their own method of collecting and summarizing information, especially sales people, but this is not in your best interest. You must ensure that all information about the channel is available and easy to access. It's vital that you stay on top of this and put clear processes in place.

Managing the Partner Database

The next pages will look at ways of working with your resellers and creating a typical reseller database. You can download an example at www.channel-revolution.com. In fact, in order to follow this example, you'll really need to download the spreadsheets. For simplicity, I've created them using Excel. All in all, there are three spreadsheets:

- List of existing resellers
- Reseller contacts
- Target resellers

---

[59] Google Docs: http://docs.google.com; ZoHo: www.zoho.com; Peepel: www.peepel.com

List of existing resellers

The list of existing resellers should include all partners that are enrolled in your partner program. This means there will also be resellers on the list who have met the basic criteria of your selection funnel but don't currently belong to the peer group. If there are too many of these partners or if there is a group of partners that don't require a lot of attention, then they can be separated into an extra file.

The list of resellers contains detailed information per partner, such as company name, website, address, partner status, partner revenue, etc. Every reseller, regardless of status, should have a clearly defined key or partner account manager (KAM or PAM) who is responsible for progress with this partner. Progress, in this context, can also mean realizing that continuing to work with this company doesn't make sense.

The status of partners in your channel program is also very important - this should give you an overview of the structure of your channel partners. For example, you might have three levels of partnerships (gold, silver and bronze). The gold partners should contribute US$50,000 p.a., silver US$20,000 p.a. and bronze US$5,000 p.a. If the quota for the channel is US$1 million, then you'll need to create the right mix of channel partners based on your experience with the product.

Here is an example of how to build the right mix of channel partners: If you know that the typical sales cycle of the enterprise version of your product is 6 months and the average sales volume per deal is US$5,000 (what you get from the reseller), then you have different options for structuring the "partner mix". Let's make it easy and say that a possible mix could be US$300,000 from the gold partners, US$300,000 from the silver and US$400,000 from the bronze. Based on the assumption that only 20-30% of the partners actually deliver results, you can make the following calculation: US$300,000 needs to come from gold partners, and the average active gold partner makes US$50,000. This means you will need 6 active gold partners. But since only 20-30% actually deliver results, you'll need around 25 gold partners in reality. Continue to apply this calculation for every partner level and you will see that you'll need an additional 60 silver partners and over 300 bronze partners in the peer group of your channel program.

A combination of the partner status and information provided by the KAM will allow you to see where you stand with the channel program. The status gives you the number of partners in each category and the total revenue potential. Every KAM should deliver additional detailed information about the progress with these partners (e.g. revenue, leads, certifications, and marketing activities). Spend some time analyzing this information and use it to make improvements. Don't assume that you'll have the best recipe right from the beginning.

If the database also includes partners who don't belong to your peer group, then it's advisable to add the funnel stage to the database. When applied to the database, the funnel stage indicates the status of where you are with the partners and how many of them are in the peer group or can reach that status shortly. Only partners in the peer group should be counted as revenue generators. They should also start generating revenue quickly, otherwise something is wrong and you'll need to go back and find out what.

Having the channel partner's address and region is important for different reasons. You can visit these channel partners when you are in the area. For example, if you have business meetings in Chicago, but have half the day off, then visit a few channel partners in the area. Even if they are smaller companies, a face-to-face meeting will give you a lot of information about the market and special insights regarding what your company can improve to work better with the channel. Another reason this information is important is that you can map out where your partners are located. If you're selling enterprise software that requires implementations and you have successful partners in Chicago, Miami and Austin, then there is no reason why you shouldn't have these kinds of partners in Boston, New York, Los Angeles and every other metropolitan area in your sales territory. Beginning the search for these partners is an extremely valid action point.

The next part of the database provides details of your main point of contact within the partner organization such as name, position, direct email address, direct phone line, mobile phone etc. This main contact should be the counterpart of your KAM/PAM and is responsible for the business relationship with your company. Make sure that this person is motivated to work with you and make the relationship successful. This motivation could be that they receive an extra bonus, or have a quota on the revenue with you or that the relationship will help them in their career. Very often, the main contact will either be a marketing person, business developer or a product manager. There's nothing wrong with any of these positions, but it's good to keep in mind that often a marketing person will try to sell you expensive marketing programs, a business developer isn't necessarily very sales driven and a product manager is often a technical person who has many vendors to look after. If your contacts within the partner's organization are not focused on developing successful relationships with new vendors or generating additional revenues and are not supported by management, the relationship will never work out. At the risk of sounding repetitive: remember that every channel partnership is about increasing sales and without the right relationships it will not work out!

The next part of the reseller database is mostly concerned with numbers and results. This will help you estimate whether or not the partner has the potential to reach the target revenue with your products. Even if you have to make some "guesstimates", that's okay in this stage. If the partner becomes more important for your business, then you'll create a partner action plan or, for even more important partners, a business plan.

A simple example: If your PAM plans to generate US$50,000 in revenue with a partner and you have a 1:5 ratio between software and professional services, you can make the following calculation: US$50,000 + 20% reseller discount = US$62,500 + 5x (times) this amount for professional services = US$375,000. In general, any new partner will not contribute more than 10% of their total business to a new partnership. This means that a perfect partner earns total revenues between US$3.5 million and perhaps US$10 million. If that's the case, your part of the total business is large enough to get management's attention and the partner should have the ability to sell projects of this size. You should place big question marks behind companies who are much smaller (how can they reach the required revenue?) and companies who are much bigger (why do they want to do business with you?).

Next are the actual and target results with this company. This should give you an overview of what the partner has done last year, what their target is this year and where their actual revenue is. These numbers should be provided by your accounting system. Don't make your PAMs search and enter all the information for every partner into the file. If you can't automate this process, then just focus on the most important partners. Normally a monthly review of the numbers is necessary. If your channel team has to enter the numbers manually, then a quarterly review can be sufficient.

The section that covers certified employees should give you an overview of how many people within the channel partner's organization have good knowledge about your products. Make sure that you differentiate between the different product categories and between a technical and sales oriented certification. For this overview, providing just the numbers of trained people is enough - their details should be in the contact database.

The "last contact" section provides information about interaction with the reseller (when and how). If important partners aren't contacted often enough or only via email then you should question this relationship. A gold partner should be contacted at a minimum every two weeks, silver partners at a minimum once a month and bronze partners once a quarter. I know that some will say this is too often, but always keep in mind that our goal is revenue. We all know that good relationships drive revenue.

Something else you should know and include in the database is if the reseller lists you on their website? This reflects commitment, encourages the reseller's customers to ask about your product and is important for web marketing like SEO. If the reseller doesn't show this commitment, I would not list them on your website or forward them leads, because you never know whose product they are recommending. Partnership should always be a two way street.

I also recommend that you include in your list (on the same sheet) the next planned activity with the partner. This makes every channel manager aware of what is planned for the reseller and the information can be assessed in the weekly update meetings. You should also list the date of the activity and who is responsible for it. The activities listed here should only be special activities for this reseller or for a very small group of resellers. Broader activities such as emails to all partners shouldn't be listed here.

Reseller contacts

Having only one contact person at a partner / reseller company is not enough. Here are the reasons why:

- A partnership must be organizationally driven - with only one contact at a channel partner, the partnership becomes purely relationship driven. This makes it difficult to maintain the partnership if the contact either leaves the company or changes their focus.

- You product and your company must be visible throughout your channel partner's organization. This is only possible if you have many access points into the different departments. You must have the ability to invite sales and technical people directly to trainings and other events.

- Success means direct relationships. It's only when people know each other that they will do business with each other. It's very important that your channel partner's sales team has direct access to your team. They must feel certain that they can get an offer within a few hours or that someone from your team can join them on a sales call. The same goes for the technical team; a presales engineer or a professional service consultant will only recommend what they know and where risk is limited. This type of confidence can only be provided by your technical support to the partner's technical team.

- Be in front of your contacts. Today's world is very fast paced and your competition is only "one mouse click" away. If you don't inform your contacts about new solutions, others will. The consequence will be that the channel partner spends less time with your products and you lose their mindshare, resulting in slower and lower sales.

You should have at least 5 - 7 contact names for every gold partner, 3 - 5 contacts for silver partners and 2 contacts for bronze. The information about each contact shouldn't be limited to necessary personal information. Apart from name, address and email, there should be information about their position, their certifications and some more comments about their view of the partnership (how they can help) or what other relationships to other companies exist.

Target resellers

It's advisable to have separate lists/databases for the "target resellers". These are the resellers that are still in the selection process and don't belong to the peer group yet. These companies might be registered in the channel program but have not gone through the complete selection funnel to be part of the peer group of partners you want to generate the revenue with.

Depending on the number of partners, the target resellers should either include all potential partners or just the potential partners that are in the prospecting/potential lead stage. Personally, I prefer the second alternative; the target reseller list should only include the potential partners who are either in the screening, prospecting or qualification phase. As soon as they have reached the qualification stage, they should be transferred into the main list.

The target reseller file should look just like the "normal" reseller list. If you have a web-based partner portal, you should take the information provided there and enter (or transfer) it into the target reseller file.

Please do go to www.channel-revolution.com and take at look at the sample file. It will give you an idea of how a list can be structured. Obviously, every business has its special requirements and there may be other details that you will have to include. Feel free to modify the spreadsheet and add the necessary columns. But make sure that the database doesn't become too complex and that it can still serve as the working file for your team.

Partner Recruitment and Retirement

Many companies that want to begin selling their product via the channel underestimate the time it takes to become "channel ready". They're also not fully aware of how long it will take from making the decision to sell through the channel until the first partners sign up and start contributing real revenue. That's what this chapter is about.

"Channel ready" implies that, based on a decision made by top management, an ISV is prepared to sell their products through the channel. The company must have everything in place to be channel ready; including a channel strategy, price lists, website, marketing material, selection criteria for channel partners, training material and a dedicated channel team. As already stated, if you don't take the channel seriously, revenues generated from the channel will be accidental and it'll be impossible to build a reliable channel. Always remember that there is a big difference between just working with a handful of resellers and building a proper channel program. There is nothing wrong with working only with a handful of partners, but if you want to scale things up, you have to do it right and assign the necessary resources to this important task.

If you want to become channel ready, and you are "starting from scratch", it will take between 3 - 6 months to make all the necessary decisions, put all the necessary materials together and get your team trained. This may not be enough time to make everything perfect, but if you have people with channel experience on board, it is possible. If you don't have these people already, I highly recommend enlisting external help. The minimum resources you'll require in this phase is a channel lead, people to create the marketing material and a small budget for this material (covering things such as a website, graphic design or translations).

After this 3 - 6 month period, the real acquisition of the channel partners begins. As already shown, there are basically four different phases in the process from tagging the partner as a potential to seeing them produce revenue. Depending on the kind of products you sell, your company brand, the stage of the technology and many other factors, the time it takes will vary. To avoid putting together an overoptimistic business plan, it's important to understand the different phases of a partner's lifecycle. The lifecycle of every channel business can be broken down into four key phases:

1. Recruitment
2. Growth
3. Maintenance
4. Retirement

1. Recruitment phase

The recruitment phase is defined as an ongoing process of identifying and recruiting the best breed of partners in the given territory. These partners should have the highest available market potential for your solutions. The recruitment phase ranges from "screening" to "expertise fit."

2. Growth phase

The growth phase is defined as the time when the partner has proven they meet the criteria of the selection funnel and have agreed, in theory, or have demonstrated through limited revenue streams to support your solutions. This phase is focused on enabling and maximizing the potential of the partner to sell your solution. In this phase, you should see an accelerated pipeline growth, first revenues and an increase in the technical competency of your solution. The growth phase spans from "action plan" to "win."

3. Maintenance phase

The maintenance phase is described as the ongoing period of supplying maintenance and support to the partners which enables them to contribute regularly to your revenue. Good relationships should be established across various personal and organizational levels. The partner now has the ability to sell and support your solutions. Key goals within this phase are ongoing education, increasing the pipeline and expansion into new areas of vertical or geographical customer groups. The maintenance phase extends from "win" to "retirement."

4. Retirement phase

The retirement phase is a necessary process of retiring partners from your program because of poor performance, market changes or if the partner no longer represents a good investment of your resources. This very often happens to the ones who signed up early to your channel program and received your full attention and special treatment during the build up phase. Often these companies are typical innovators or early adaptors (technically orientated and visionary) but not able to provide the necessary growth. The retirement phase focuses on smooth account transition for shared customers and a mutually agreed exit from the partnership.

Let me give you a calculation example for building and maintaining a channel over time. It's based on a typical channel business where an enterprise product is to be sold over the channel.

A typical channel partner is a value added reseller (VAR) who adds professional services to your solution. This will make the average deal size between US$40,000 - US$60,000 of which your solution is US$10,000 - US$15,000. For this example, I'll set the ISV's annual target revenues from each of the partners at US$50,000 which means that they have to close one project every quarter.

The average sales cycle for these kinds of solutions is between 3 - 6 months (in an optimistic case). To reduce the complexity of this model, I've used a 3 month sales cycle once the action plan is in place and the channel partner belongs to the peer group of partners. There are some valid reasons for this assumption; the VAR may have started to position the product during the partnership evaluation process and very often the first customer is relatively easy to find. In fact, the new channel partner may have already had this first project in mind and it was the motivation for the partnership.

The model also quantifies the necessary resources for the channel program. Overall, you'll get a realistic overview of the main factors for a channel program; the number of VARs in the funnel, the necessary investments and the forecast revenue.[60] The percentages used in the partner selection funnel are the same as in earlier examples. The success ratio from the screening phase to the prospecting/potential lead phase is 50%, which means that one partner out of every two will become a potential partner. From this stage to the qualification/expertise fit phase, the ratio is only 20% and out of these potential channel partners you will create an action plan with

---

[60] You can download the calculation at www.channel-revolution.com. It's easy to change any parameters and adapt the model to your needs.

25%. From this peer group of channel partners 25% (every fourth partner) will contribute to your revenues.

In real numbers, these selection funnel percentages mean that out of 1,000 companies in the screening phase, 500 will be considered as potential partners. Then only 100 potential partners from this group will meet the qualification criteria, and a realistic action plan will be created with just 25 of these partners. Based on this calculation, approximately 6 out of this peer group will deliver the defined revenue. The reduction from 1,000 to 6 is the "distillation factor," and this determines how many partners you require in the screening process in order to gain just ONE revenue producer.

If you are a well organized company and you can complete the entire funnel selection for the most important partners in one quarter (from screening to building an action plan or, as we will see later, a real "partner business plan"), then the first revenues can be expected in the next quarter. If your average deal size is US$12,500 and you have around 6 producing partners, then the revenue will be approximately US$80,000 in the second quarter after you have begun screening.

In the following quarters, the new producing partners will be added to the already existing base, which hopefully will result in a fast growing revenue stream from the channel. To illustrate this, I've added the second year to the calculation. The revenue jumps from around US$80,000 in Q2/Y1 to over half a million in Q4/Y2. But this will only be the case if you're able to maintain the same speed in developing new producing partners over almost two years. In reality you will always lose some of your producing partners and it will become more and more difficult to find new partners to screen. We will revisit this topic later.

We have seen the possible outcomes of good channel management and how much revenue you can expect in a more or less short time. On the other hand, there are costs associated with building this channel. As already described, you're going to need a team of a minimum of 3 people for 3 - 6 months who will generate the basic material and this team has to be strengthened by channel managers over time. To maintain the status quo, in the first year after the basic material has been generated, there should be two people responsible for channel marketing, one person dedicated to the screening process and two channel managers who are responsible for the stages from qualification to helping the partners make sales.

Parameters	
Partner Revenue p.a.	$50,000
Working Time per Day	8 h/MD

Sales Funnel	Screening	Prospecting/ Potential Lead	Qualification/ Expertice Fit	Action Plan/ Peer Group	Win	Distillation Factor
% in Next Stage		50%	20%	25%	25%	160
Effort	0.15 h	0.5 h	2 h	12 h	32 h	176 h
			Sales Cycle 3 Months from Action Plan / Peer Group			

Year One (Y1)	Q1 / Y1	Q2 / Y1	Q3 / Y1	Q4 / Y1	Total Y1
Screening	1,000	1,000	1,000	1,000	4,000
Prospecting / Pot. Lead	500	500	500	500	2,000
Qualification / Exp. Fit	100	100	100	100	400
Action Plan / Peer Group	25	25	25	25	100
Win (New Partners)	6.3	6.3	6.3	6.3	25
Producing Partners		6.3	12.5	18.8	18.8
Total Revenue	$0	$78,125	$156,250	$234,375	$468,750

Year Two (Y2)	Q1 / Y2	Q2 / Y2	Q3 / Y2	Q4 / Y2	Total Y2
Producing Partners Y2	25	31.3	37.5	43.8	137.5
Total Revenue Y2	$312,500	$390,625	$468,750	$546,875	$1,718,750

Effort Y1	Q1 / Y1	Q2 / Y1	Q3 / Y1	Q4 / Y1	Total Y1	Total MD Y1
Screening	150 h	150 h	150 h	150 h	600 h	75 MD
Prospecting / Pot. Lead	250 h	250 h	250 h	250 h	1000 h	125 MD
Qualification / Exp. Fit	200 h	200 h	200 h	200 h	800 h	100 MD
Action Plan / Peer Group	300 h	300 h	300 h	300 h	900 h	113 MD
Win (New Partners)	50 h	50 h	50 h	50 h	150 h	19 MD
Producing Partners	0 h	50 h	100 h	150 h	150 h	19 MD
Total Hours	950 h	1000 h	1050 h	1100 h	4100 h	
Total MD needed	119 MD	125 MD	131 MD	138 MD	513 MD	513 MD

The chart above outlines this process and calculates the necessary effort that is involved. You should apply this calculation to your strategy and, even more importantly, adjust the numbers based on your own experience. A system like this will help you structure your approach and can give a firm idea of the goals for the channel team.

The Channel Partner Business Plan

As you may remember, I mentioned that the first thing you need to do with a "real" channel partner is to create an action plan. This message still holds, but sometimes when you are dealing with larger projects or with very important partners who will generate a decent amount of revenue, the action plan just isn't enough.

You as the vendor have set up your partner program so that it supports partners along the entire engagement life cycle (selling, marketing, integrating, maintaining and improving), making projects based on your solution easy to sell and deliver. The most profitable projects for channel partners are the ones with the least risk involved. By reducing the risk of implementation, you as a vendor can offer huge value to the channel partners. The first step in reducing this risk is to create a business plan together. A "channel partner business plan" is not only a planning and reviewing tool to define and follow up on common goals, measures and strategies for the negotiated time period, it also provides a clear understanding of the vendor and its partner's positioning in relation to the desired business targets. Even if the channel business plan creates no legal duties, responsibilities or rights, it will provide a clear understanding of the necessary skill sets, and definitions of the goals and guidelines for doing business together.

There are many reasons why you should implement a partner business plan with your most important partners. It will help you to engage your key partners and assist them in becoming top revenue generators by engaging strategic planning and creating clear expectations right from the onset. The channel partner business plan provides a clear outline for your joint business and sales strategies, and creates a living and breathing sales execution plan based on the partner's specific strengths.

Here are some other good reasons why a channel partner business plan with your key partners is important:

- **Same vision/same goals:** When developing the plan, it will become clear if you and the channel partner share the same vision and goals for the partnership.

- **Top level involvement:** With the channel partner business plan you create an official document that requires signatures. This ensures that top level staff from the channel partner will be involved.

- **Knowledge about the channel partner:** While you're working on the plan, you can ask questions about your channel partner's organization; how they make money and who the key people are. Very often, account managers don't actually have enough knowledge about the channel partner. The plan provides a framework for them to ask the necessary questions - especially regarding technical skills and if they normally deliver successful projects. Based on this information, your education programs can be better defined.

- **Business model information:** In order to be successful with your key partners, it's important that you understand their business model and the verticals they are selling into. On the other hand, the partner must also understand your business model and what kind of value your solution can offer to the market.

- **Chemistry between the key players:** It's essential that the key players on both sides work closely together. The channel partner business plan is the first project where they can learn how to operate as a team. The act of formulating a detailed outline for working together over the next 12 - 24 months will strengthen the personal relationships between the teams. Their signatures will also ensure that you have a personal commitment from the people who created the plan.

You can download an example of a channel partner business plan at www.channel-revolution.com. Remember that every vendor requires slightly different information and will set other priorities. The example should give you a good framework that you can easily modify. I'd now like to take you through the most important parts of this document. It might make sense if you download it now, it'll be much easier to follow my explanations. If you're not interested in the details right now, then feel free to skip to the next chapter.

The first part of the channel partner business plan should give you a very fast overview of the actual business relationship. I would recommend including information that is important for the partnership such as revenue (target, last year, actual), certified people or next activities on the front page. It should be possible to get an overview of a partner within one or two minutes. If you have 100 partners in your peer group, it can be a big job to review them all in the quarterly analysis of your channel business. This overview serves as a useful management tool for these reviews. The main purpose of the document is to be a working tool for the PAMs.

Do spend some time putting the channel partner business plan in a professional format, laid out in the vendor's design and formatted with headers, footers, confidentiality notes etc. It's the official document of the partnership between two companies. If you host all the information on a web-based partner portal or on any other database, make sure that it has an export function. You need to be able to produce the document as a PDF that can be delivered to your channel partners. If your channel partner business plan doesn't have a professional look, then nobody will take it or the partnership seriously - especially if you represent a smaller vendor.

On the first page of the example plan, the *Partner Status (Level)* shows their current status such as Gold, Silver or Bronze, and the field *Since* shows recent changes. The *Main Contacts* should give details of the PAM from the vendor side and a business focused person from the partner side.

Region is an important field because it shows the geographic areas where the partnership is relevant. This is important if the partner receives a special discount because of their region. For example, sometimes a channel partner gets a special price in South Africa or India because the total price level in this market is lower than in other countries. The region field helps you avoid the situation where a reseller buys the product for a lower price and resells into countries with a higher price level.

The *Introduction of the Channel Partner Business Plan* should give clear instructions about how to use the plan, who owns the plan and where to find the plan and other relevant documents. *Company Facts* gives a company overview of the channel partner. Sometimes you'll have to provide rough estimates here, for example regarding financial figures. Many privately held companies will not give out this information in the beginning of a partnership, but over time they will give you the information or you can narrow down your first guess.

Spend some time on filling out this information because it gives you a very good overview of the structure of your channel partner network. Perhaps you'll discover that most of your successful partners are making between US$10 - $20 million and are focused on government or telecommunications. It might then be worth focusing your partner recruiting activities on this group of partners.

In section 1.2, the *Executive Summary*, the *Partner Focus* describes which solutions make up the business focus of the partnership agreement. Be aware that there is no channel partner who can resell every kind of solution. If you have a range of different kinds of solutions, such as a boxed product for the SMB market, enterprise-like products and SaaS solutions, then you'll need different channel partners. For every product (or product line) the channel partner wants to sell, make sure that they have the capability to reach and serve the defined target. Don't let them sell into every market just because they want to.

In almost every company I've worked with, there was always big confusion surrounding the different contracts that exist with the partners. Try not to let this happen in your organization by including a section such as 1.2.2, *Overview of the Signed Contracts*. This is also a good opportunity to take care of any side letters that are you not aware of.[61]

Another important field is the list of *Contacts in the Partner Organization*. You should list detailed contact information for each of these contacts. Even if you have an enemy within your partner's organization, list them and rate the relationship with a minus sign (-) as negative. Very often, there are logical reasons why people won't support your solution. Sometimes technical people have received all their certifications from a bigger vendor and now have to support your "unknown" solution, or the sales team simply doesn't see new business with your solution. If you know who your opponents are, you can work on neutralizing them. This is a typical internal piece of information that should not be made available to the partner. Although I believe that you should build and share the plan with your partner, it's clear that some parts should not be shared.

If you think about the huge amount of information that needs to be entered per contact, it becomes clear why a web-based system is a necessary and sensible tool. Even if you only have 1,000 channel partners with 5 contacts each, this means you have to actively manage 5,000 contacts. Without a web-based system this is impossible.

The *Partner's Core Competencies* shows how the partner makes money and where they place their focus. This also relates to the next two fields; *Competitive Market Positioning* and the *Key Facts & Objectives of the Partnership*. It's important to be realistic when you fill this out and ask the tough questions about where you and your partner can provide value to the market. If your partner's business model is that of a typical VAR, and they consider their core competency as reselling software and hardware together with professional services, then you should look at where they place their real focus – selling products or projects.

---

[61] Very often when working with channel partners or customers you need to make agreements regarding special terms (e.g. delivery). These are often defined in so-called "side letters". A side letter can be in the form of an email or any other "informal" correspondence from the ISV.

How does your solution fit into the partner's business model and where is the "competitive market positioning"? Using an example, I'd like to describe a typical valuable partnership that can offer a competitive market positioning. Let's say you are offering a range of data protection software that includes enterprise backup solutions and hosted "storage as a service" solutions for a managed service provider. Your strategic goal is to become the market leader in some verticals where your solution fits perfectly. Based on your experience, you will need channel partners with domain knowledge in these verticals. One of the channel partners you've selected for your peer group has government vertical experience and services the public sector with total solutions. They already offer a suite of government solutions, have customers in this area and their domain knowledge not only includes the professional services for these vertical solutions, they also offer vertically oriented training. The goal of this partner is to add data protection to their offering so they can provide external governmental offices with a way of protecting their distributed data more efficiently. This seems to be a perfect partnership because it combines your and their core competencies to create a valuable offer for data protection for the customer.

After you've established that the partnership can provide real value to the market, you need to work on the *Partnership Action Points*. The *Key Milestones* cover important achievements. Typical examples are proving that the solutions will work together or, especially in some verticals, that a joint pricing strategy is necessary. Very often the partner is already communicating with customers who have a need for the combined solution. In this case it's important that you win this reference customer to prove your concept.

The *SWOT Analysis* is a strategic planning method used to evaluate the Strengths, Weaknesses, Opportunities and Threats involved in a project or in a business venture.[62] It involves specifying the objec-

---

[62] The technique of SWOT analysis is credited to Albert Humphrey, who led a convention at Stanford University in the 1960's and 70's using data from Fortune 500 companies. A lot of literature on this subject exists; see for example Menon,

tive of the business venture or project and identifying the internal and external factors that are favorable and unfavorable to achieving that objective.[63] The channel partner business plan should be a tool for helping you and your partners increase sales. The SWOT analysis can help to find out where the real opportunities and challenges are (what the action plan is for reaching the "low hanging fruits" first). I've entered some typical strengths, weaknesses, opportunities and threats in my example.

The next three fields provide a much better understanding of the real intentions for the partnership.

The *Opportunity Creation* outlines why both companies are entering into the partnership and how you both think you can generate more revenue by working together. For the channel partner, a very obvious reason for this is to increase the revenue per customer because they are already selling to this customer and are acquainted with the decision makers. If they can offer a broader range of products, they can increase revenue with a limited sales investment. Another common reason is that the customers are already looking for a more complete solution and the partner fears losing this customer group. This is important information for the vendor - if the vendor knows the real motivation of the partner they can use this knowledge for pricing and discount discussions. On the other hand, the vendor is often very interested in finding experienced partners to enter a new vertical market segment to avoid the price competition of the horizontal market. Another motivation for many vendors is that they see a demand or an increasing customer group from a specific customer segment, but due to their limited vertical knowledge and market access, the vendor can't figure out why the product is attractive to this customer group. The most efficient way to enter this market segment is with an experienced partner.

A. et al. "Antecedents and Consequences of Marketing Strategy Making". *Journal of Marketing* (1999)
[63] See also SWOT analysis method and examples with a free SWOT template http://www.businessballs.com/swotanalysisfreetemplate.htm (2010)

In the *Sales Engagement* field, both companies show their commitment to building a successful partnership. These commitments need to be as specific as possible and should produce measurable results. When entering new market segments, activities such as the set up of a demo case, winning first customers, creating presentations or educating the partner's sales force, are all very important points that should be included here.

The last field in this section is *Joint Unique Selling Propositions Due to Partnership*, which includes reasons why the customer should buy your combined solution. Typical reasons are cost reduction, new laws or that it's easier to operate.

The *Partnership Strategy* should define the strategic initiatives. What are the long-term strategies for becoming a leader in the target market segment? The main difference between this section and the partnership action points is that the partnership strategy includes more long-term initiatives. This section shouldn't always be used right from the beginning if there is no market experience available. It's better to "test the waters" first and then put more effort into the strategy after some initial experiences. Typical initiatives concern the joint development of vertical solutions, long-term marketing initiatives or vertical product offerings.

Addressable Markets provides a more concrete definition of the sub-segments of the market the partners should focus on. Even just focusing on the e-government market still presents a very broad range of potential customers. By giving the target group and the business model deeper definition, the vendor can support their partners much better with targeted marketing material and announcements. The target market segments also reflect the business model and the potential revenue streams.

This is also taken into account in the *Reseller Discount / Kickback Model* where, based on the business model, a discount, kickback or revenue share is described. It makes a significant difference if the channel partner resells a boxed product or if the vendor's product is a part of the total solution. In the first case, the reseller gets a discount and negotiates the price directly with the customer. In the second case, the vendor's involvement is much larger, since they either receive a fixed price per license or a share of the sales price of the total solution. An excerpt from this section should also be listed on the front page along with the partnership overview. An important recommendation is not to make the model too complex and not to work with many different models for the same reseller. This confuses the reseller's organization and will become a nightmare for your administration.

The *Staff Training Plan* lists the channel partner employees who should be trained regularly. You must make it easy for people to see the value in your certification. Most people view certification as necessary for the progression of their career, therefore they prefer to get it from bigger vendors such as Oracle or Microsoft. If you're not one of the large vendors, then make sure that the title of your certification describes what the course provided. Informative certification titles such as "Selling SaaS Solutions in the Government Market" or "Developing Web-Based SaaS Solutions" really add value to a CV.

The *Joint Marketing Plan* lists every activity planned within the period of the contract. This should be updated in each review. The columns for Direct Responsible Individual (DRI) and the Costs are both very important; they ensure that there are clear responsibilities and that a budget and resources for an activity are available. I recommend that you update the marketing plan at least once per quarter to be sure that the activities are done in time.

All the activities defined in the channel partner plan should also be included in the *Partner Action Plan*. Someone from channel marketing should be put in charge of the various partner action plans and oversee the progress on each task. Don't give this task to your PAM though, because they are responsible for the revenue. Their focus should be on generating leads, supporting the partner during the sales process and closing deals.

Another thing to define before the plan can be signed off is the *Reviewing Process*. Based on the importance of this partnership or the revenue generated, a review should take place every three or six months. If you decide that an annual review is sufficient, then you don't need this plan at all - it will only be outdated by the time of the review and the partner is obviously not important enough to justify investing the time.

Partnership Achievements is a compressed overview of the results from the current and previous period of the partnership. Necessary information regarding the number of projects, the revenue generated for both partners, the number of leads, the average sales cycle and the status of product knowledge inside the partner organization becomes transparent.

Projects Based on Vendor's Solution gives a more detailed overview of all the projects that have been implemented during a certain period of time. This type of detailed overview should only be made if the number of projects is not too large and the average deal size is big enough to justify the effort.

The *Information Checklist* should record all of the marketing material that all contacts, or at least the key contacts at every channel partner, should know or be made aware of. My experience from working with hundreds of channel partners and thousands of contacts inside these organizations is that most of the information/material a vendor produces will never come to life in the partner's sales process or be used in the marketing material. This isn't because your contacts don't like the material, it's simply because they are not aware this material exists. (There are many reasons why this can happen; a change of staff or an incorrect email address are just two of them). It's important that your information reaches your contacts. Again, at the risk of sounding repetitive: people will only sell and support what they know.

Information gathered from the reviewing process can really help to improve not just the relationship with a partner, but also to streamline and improve your whole channel program. Take your time when working with the committed partners to find out how you can perform better. You can also apply this information to other committed, but perhaps not yet successful partners. This is also a time to begin phasing out all partners who haven't reached their goals due to a lack of effort.

Finally there is the *Sign off Sheet* which documents that the review process was carried out. With their signatures, the responsible people from the channel partner's and the vendor's side show their commitment to the review. Someone from management level should be asking questions during the whole review process and also sign the document. This makes the whole team aware of the importance of the plan and that it's not just another piece of paper.

As already stated at the beginning of this chapter, the channel partner business plan I've described here is used to define the relationship between a software vendor (enterprise or higher value software) and a value added reseller (VAR). But it can also provide a framework for all other relationships and can be modified easily. If you work with channel resellers who resell products in volume or only products of lower value, then you'll need to remove some parts of the plan and add others - but make sure that you state clearly why this relationship makes sense for the channel partner. Always remember that channel partners will only do what is good for them. If a relationship with you doesn't provide value, which means money, they will not invest in selling your product; and then your investments in this partnership are lost.

Increasing Sales

Okay, you've recruited the right channel partners and written business or action plans. Now you really want to push your sales. Thousands of books have been written about sales techniques, how to manage direct accounts and how to make direct sales. This book is not about sales techniques and not about direct sales. Instead, it focuses on indirect sales and pipeline management, which is very different from working with the end users directly.

The main goal of this chapter is to help you:

- Set up and manage an indirect sales pipeline.
- Improve "bid to win" ratios with partners.
- Create more effective resource allocation.
- Increase sales per partner account manager (PAM).
- Shorten the sales cycle and keep account control.
- Optimize forecast accuracy.

Channel partners have their own agenda

Creating and maintaining partnerships is about making more money together than you could alone. Most of the channel partners you work with will have had partnerships with other companies before and either had positive or negative experiences. Most likely they also have many other partnerships with companies similar to yours and perhaps also similar products. These other vendors compete with you for the partner's mindshare and they have their own marketing and sales strategies to optimize their revenue stream from this partner.

Sometimes the partners have relationships with vendors that offer complementary solutions or they want to replace an existing vendor with a competitive solution. In both cases, the fact that accounts already exist or that other vendors are generating leads for your channel partner is very positive.

As a vendor, you have to realize that every channel has their own agenda and is driven by their own personal and organizational goals. They will only do what you ask them to do if they see profit for themselves or their organization. The goals will vary from reseller to reseller; some may just be looking for leads from new partners to help them resell more products, others may want to complete their offering or some might aim to create their own brand in vertical niches. This all depends on the type of reseller you are working with. Each person within their organization will even have different goals; a product manager is probably seeking innovative products and business models, technical people want to improve their technical knowledge and sales people want to make more money.

You will find thousands of individual reasons why some resellers want to work with you or why some people within their organization don't like you. The easiest and only way to win the reseller's mindshare and loyalty is to increase sales.

To be successful with a channel partner, a vendor has to create a "win-win-win" situation. This is only achievable by winning new accounts and increasing the revenue. Every real partnership begins and ends with sales numbers! Your key contacts on the reseller's side have to win (make more money or get recognition), the reseller has to win (increase their revenue by selling your solution or help selling higher value solutions) and the customers have to win (getting better value for money). These win-win-win situations will also increase the bonding between you and the reseller's organization.

Setting up and managing an indirect sales pipeline

The setup and management of an indirect sales pipeline is very different from selling direct in many ways. The first and most important difference is that you are not dealing directly with the end customer, where your main focus is to close the deal within the shortest possible time. You are dealing instead with channel partners and hopefully many deals can be made with the same partner.

In the case of a direct sales approach, the end customer and their specific project is the focus of your account manager. In the case of most direct sales, there will only be one deal possible with the same end customer. You might be able to follow up with some more licenses, maintenance and professional services to this customer, but this is minor stuff. This situation results in a focus on making as much revenue with the end customer in the beginning and in the shortest possible time. It's a typical "fire and forget" sales method. It may always be the case, but in general, a direct account manager will move on to a new potential end customer once he or she has closed a deal.

The indirect sales approach differs from this way of doing business completely. Growing an indirect sales channel is about the farming and developing of your channel partners. The focus of your PAM should not only be on the first deal, but on the total revenue potential of the partner within a defined period of time. The account manager has to find out who the most active partners are with the best revenue potential and undertake every possible activity to leverage the potential of this partner. I call this process "farming and scaling".

Consider this comparison: a direct account manager can work on perhaps 20 - 30 deals at the same time whereas a PAM can work on 20 - 30 channel partners with 10 deals each. The difference is clear. If a PAM works with the right channel partners then they can work on 10 times more projects than a direct account manager. The ultimate goal of the PAM must be to locate and build a relationship with the active group of resellers. We will see that the partner sales channel is a great help for achieving this.

Filter and focus the active partners

The first challenge for every PAM is to build a group of active channel partners that can be scaled and leveraged. How can they find this group of partners?

One way of doing it, is to push your marketing to undertake the maximum number of activities (e.g. banners on popular channel sites) to get as many resellers as possible to show interest in your solution and sign up for your channel program. This is what most companies actually seem to be doing. They treat each new partner equally and wait until the most active ones stand out. This is certainly one way to do it, but look at the challenge: If the PAM's quota is US$1 million p.a. and the average license revenue per project is around US$10,000, they will need to close around 100 projects with their channel partners. Even if every active channel partner has the opportunity to close 10 projects (a very high number, especially in the buildup phase of a channel), the 80/20 rule still applies - meaning that only 20% of all selected partners will deliver the required result. The PAM has to recruit, qualify and build action plans with a minimum of 50 partners in order to filter out the 10 active partners that will deliver the revenue.

Here's a better way to go about finding and working with the really active partners. We live in a world of limited resources and therefore need to focus in order to become successful. Your focus should be on the partners that serve your target market segment. If your solution fits the public sector and you see a target customer group of around 100,000 organizations, your PAM should only select partners who already serve this market from the pool of newly signed-up partners. An additional advantage of this is that your PAM will gain a better understanding of the market segment as well as the necessary approach the channel partners have to take. In the end, this knowledge will lead to a much better result. The remaining partners should be managed by channel marketing who can provide them with all the necessary material. This process can also be more automated and frees up time for the PAM.

Another way to save resources is by grouping the channel partners into three different categories. The first category with the biggest potential should be managed by the PAMs. Partners with business potential fall into the second category that should be managed by partner services. The rest of the channel partners should become channel marketing's responsibility. While the group of partners being looked after by the PAM should never exceed 20 or 30, a person from partner services can manage around 50 to 100. Using automated processes, channel marketing can then take care of the rest.

If you are a small organization and don't have the resources to create a complete channel team, you can just "cherry pick" and focus on the partners with real projects first. Any partner who doesn't have a project in a later sales stage should be the responsibility of channel marketing or technical support. The PAM needs to be freed up so he or she can focus on supporting the most important channel partners.

Managing the Sales Process

Having a well structured sales process with clearly defined sales stages is necessary for identifying the channel partners with the most solid pipeline and best revenue potential. Asking the right questions will help you to classify the projects. For example: What stage are they in? What help is required? Are they genuine or fake? When is a closing possible? (I feel I should point out that this chapter should not and cannot substitute sales training or other books on the topic of sales techniques.) The main goal you can achieve with a well structured sales process is transforming your forecasting from "anecdotal forecasting" to methodological forecasting. You've probably heard statements such as "This partner is going to close the deal in two weeks because the customer needs the solution urgently", only to end up one month later without any progress. Then you find out that there was no product demonstration given by the channel partner, no other compelling events and not even a formal offer. Hence, the importance of using a clearly defined sales funnel with the following 10 sales stages:

1. Prospecting
2. Potential Lead
3. Qualification
4. Discovery & Development
5. Proposal
6. Short-Listed
7. Selected
8. Negotiation
9. Won
10. Lost

A "chance of success" factor (percentage) is assigned at each stage reflecting the likelihood that you can win the project within the defined period. Even if it requires some work to keep all the projects updated in this detailed breakdown, it's definitely worth the investment of your time.

I'll now look at each sales stage more closely and will use some examples to demonstrate why this approach makes sense. The examples use the model of an enterprise deal with a channel partner implementing the solution. It's worth noting, however, that pipeline management with distributors, e-tailers or SaaS partners is significantly different.

1. Prospecting

The prospecting phase follows directly after a lead is generated either by you or the partner. During this phase, the key parameters for the opportunity become clear: What is the involvement of the channel partner? Is there a key account manager from the channel partner involved? What is the project type? What are the requirements? Can the end customer's requirements be met? Is the project interesting for the channel partner and for the vendor?

The chance of success factor is 0% at this stage because there isn't enough information about the project yet. The project volume multiplied by the chance of success describes the weighted project volume. The total of all weighted projects is the weighted pipeline.

As I've pointed out before, the channel partner may be very secretive about the end customer. The customer's name is not that important at this stage, but can become an issue from the qualification stage onwards. Try to convince the channel partner that trust is an important component of a real partnership and to prove their trust they should list the details in your deal registration program which is explained in more detail later in the book. The partnership will only lead to success if your PAM can create open and trusting communication. In order to win a deal, neither party can hide information or keep a hidden agenda. If you feel that this is happening, then it's better to end the partnership.

2. Potential Lead

The objective during this phase is to find out if there is an opportunity - not only for the partner but also for you. There is a big difference between the two! As described earlier, on many projects the investment in professional services can be several times higher than the investment in software. If we are talking about enterprise class solutions with bigger project volumes (>US$250,000) and long sales cycles (>six months), then several tasks need to be completed (concept, ROI calculations, specifications etc.) before the actual software or hardware purchase happens. Each PAM can only take on a certain amount of projects. If the project seems to be far away on the horizon, you must decide how to deal with it in the later sales stages.

The main difference here from a direct sale is that in a direct sales scenario, you're already in contact with the end customer and you are able to qualify the opportunity. In an indirect sale, you have to trust the information you receive from the partner. Every partner and their account managers have their own style of doing business and forecasting an opportunity; some forecast too positively and others too negatively. As already stated, they each have their own "game plan". Your channel partner's account managers are not your employees, they don't receive their paycheck from you and they won't just do what you ask them to do. They'll only prioritize projects using your solution or sell your solution if it's beneficial for them. This demonstrates the importance of maintaining a good relationship with your partner's account managers.

One of the biggest problems with a forecast from a channel partner is the lack of knowledge about your product. Very often, projects are omitted from the forecast in later sales stages because the technology doesn't fit or projects are lost because of "missing" functionality. During the potential lead stage and in the qualification stage, the PAM must make sure that your solution matches the requirements of the end customer. The chance of success factor is still 0% here, because there are still too many unknown parameters.

3. Qualification

The qualification phase probably reveals the biggest difference between dealing directly with an end customer and having a third party involved. Many leading vendors will put pressure on their partners to let them join in on the sales process to ensure that the end user learns about the value of their solution. Even if such close involvement requires a much bigger indirect sales force, the return on investment from it can be huge. Firstly, the channel partner can prove the commitment from the vendor and the special partnership they have. In addition, the channel partner can use the vendor's sales and technical resources to speed up the deal and see to it that the prospect receives the information they need at light speed. It can also increase the quality of the sales process, and as a result the chances of winning the deal, because the channel partner's vertical experience can be combined with the vendor's experience with different solutions involving their product.

The qualification stage results in a clear definition of the project requirements. You must ensure that the solution has the necessary functionality and that the partner has the capability to deliver it. This stage identifies the decision makers and their roles, the project owner and the main goals and also makes the decision process clear. The prospect needs to confirm that the decision will be made within a defined period and that a budget is already assigned.

It's crucial at this stage that the technical team understands your solution and agrees that it meets the requirements. The various competitors and alternative solutions should be made transparent (the channel partner needs to bring this information to the table). They should know what alternatives exist on the market and who their usual competitors are. It's critical that these competitors are the channel partner's and not yours!

The probability of success here is only 10% because at this stage, the prospect will normally still have various alternatives on offer and will be talking to different vendors and channel partners to make their selection. If you find out that there is a special relationship between the end customer and your channel partner (perhaps the channel partner has worked with the end customer for years), then the chance of success factor can be significantly higher. But if you forecast conservatively you'll never be wrong.

4. Discovery & Development

If you reach this stage and the relationship with the channel partner is good, your solution fits and you think you can close the deal this quarter, you should classify it as a "must win" deal. You must now focus your resources on winning this deal. It should be made transparent to your channel partner and your team that this project has a very high priority on your side. This means that your technical team will support the prospect proactively, solve any challenges in the shortest possible time and that good communication on all levels will take absolutely priority.

Use the "shark approach"; try to win this deal with your channel partner and assign the potential customer a higher priority than other existing customers for a short period of time. Everyone profits from winning new customers, including the existing customers, because this broadens the installed base and will make the product better over time.

On the other hand, if you still don't know the customer and you are dealing with a new channel partner, you should be careful with investing too many resources. One of the big challenges of taking on projects with channel partners is not knowing if the prospect accepts the channel partner as their solution provider. If the project seems to be large, then there is a good chance the prospect will be looking for a large solution provider. If the project requires a deep understanding of the business, then the prospect might be looking for a specialist. Make it clear to your channel partner that you will step back if there isn't enough transparency or if you don't see a chance of winning the deal.

Let's assume now, that the prospect is known and you have a good relationship with your channel partner. Now you need to identify the competitors, potential alternative solutions and what kind of advantages your solution provides in the eyes of the decision makers. An important aspect of your solution is the value the channel partner can provide. After you've identified the strengths and weaknesses of the competition you should agree with your channel partner on a proposed solution and presentation strategy. The proposed solution must deliver a clear RoI and must adhere to the known budget.

It's also important that you understand the compelling reason(s) why the prospect needs to start the project now. There are many potential reasons; very often it's just that their existing solution is outdated and requires a major remake (which is too expensive) or that the annual maintenance has come up or new legal requirements need to be met. Or the prospect is in an M&A (mergers & acquisition) situation with another company or has released a new product line or business model. If the existing solution is a homegrown solution, perhaps the lead developer will leave the company or they can't extend this solution with new necessary functionality. There are many reasons, so discuss the possibilities with your channel partner and if the prospect confirms a compelling reason, validate it. If you know the compelling reason, the requirements and the budget, then you can tailor the proposal to the prospect's need.

Work with your partner on a competitive pricing, implementation and resource plan that will convince the prospect. You as a vendor should have experience from comparable projects which means you should be able to provide frameworks for proposals and presentations that can be modified by your partner to fit the prospect's case.

The chance of success factor is now 20% as there is still a big possibility that the prospect will not make a decision and postpone the project or that your solution or your channel partner will not be accepted.

5. Proposal

Don't ever enter this phase if you haven't already resolved all questions and issues raised by the prospect and the channel partner. Some of the biggest concerns between a vendor and channel partner are who will take which risk, when the purchase of the solution will happen and when the vendor will be paid. Most projects are structured into stages with different milestones and when these milestones are reached payments are released.

The prospect, channel partner and vendor each have different interests and these all have to do with risk reduction and cash flow. Only the complete solution that the prospect has assigned the necessary budget for has a real value. Their goal is to pay as little upfront as possible and receive something valuable with every milestone. The channel partner has already invested in the sales process and wants to be paid for all additional work they carry out.

Very often, milestones are skipped because of changes to the project requirements by the customer. This could be in the form of project delays or even worse, when projects are halted or ended. The vendor, who normally delivers software or hardware and only some services, also has to invest in the sales process. Usually, they need to deliver software and hardware at the beginning of the project to ensure that the right infrastructure is in place to start the project.

I've seen many projects where the end customer was only willing to buy the software after the productive implementation of the solution and forced the channel partner to carry out the installation with a "test license". The ISV prefers to sell the software at the beginning of the project because then they will earn their margins in an early stage and don't have to wait for the successful completion of the project. The channel partner on the other hand is in a different position; they don't want the lion share of the first end user payments to go to the vendor. On a typical project, the investment into software AND hardware takes up approximately 40 - 50% of the total budget. If this payment has to be made in the beginning, then from the end customer's perspective, more than half of the budget is already spent without any tangible results. The vendor and the channel partner must solve this problem and put a proposal strategy together that clearly states who gets paid when and who is taking what risk.

There are some ways to avoid the aforementioned situation. The vendor and the channel partner can offer their parts of the solution separately, each in a different proposal. The software can be priced in such a way that there is a discount for buying upfront or that the end user rents the software instead of buying it.

Once the final proposal is completed and agreed upon between you and your channel partner, don't allow the partner to send it to the prospect without first having a meeting or telephone conference to walk the prospect through the cornerstones of the proposal. The prospect's project owner must understand the proposal and signal agreement. Even if that person can't make a decision regarding the offer or the budget, he or she will give a clear indication if they like it or not.

I've even seen many situations where the project owner either thought that the proposal was too low or that there would be more work involved or that some components were missing. Providing a good estimation of the actual workload creates another win-win-win situation; the project owner wants to ensure that the project will be delivered on time and on budget, the channel partner needs to make money with the project and you as the vendor want to generate revenues and create successful reference projects. If the project runs over budget, a whole list of bad things will happen. One, the project owner is put in a difficult situation because he or she will need to ask for additional money. The channel partner won't be able to invest more resources without getting paid. And you as the vendor face the risk of having the product returned or not getting paid.

Once you have the final buy-in from the project owner, your channel partner should complete the final proposal and submit it to the prospect. All associated legal contracts must be submitted to the prospect's financial or legal department. The next steps and the final decision date should be confirmed with the prospect. The chance of success factor has now only moved up to 25%, because there is still a high risk that a decision regarding the project will not be made within the defined time period. Don't be surprised if you don't hear from the end customer for a while after the official proposal has been submitted.

6. Short Listed

If the prospect has a real need for a solution and is in the decision process, the time between proposal and short listing shouldn't be too long. Sometimes, this phase can even be skipped. Being short listed means that the channel partner has been selected by the prospect as one of two preferred solution providers. One reason could be that the channel partner has already delivered value to the client in the past and has provided a convincing solution for the project. Most solution providers carry more than one vendor in their portfolio; this means at this stage, it's very important for the ISV to stay in close touch with the channel partner to make sure that their solution is the chosen one.

Normally, at this stage there should only be one alternative left in the game and there shouldn't be many obstacles left in the way of the prospect's decision making process. After the proof of concept is received by the prospect, the channel partner – with the help of the PAM - must push the project through the decision process. The chance of success factor now moves up to 40%. The biggest risks remaining are that the other short listed partner is chosen or that the project is postponed or canceled.

7. Selected

You've now reached the point where the prospect makes a commitment to your solution. But there may still be some detailed discussions necessary about resolving the remaining technical issues. Usually, the first project meetings will be held to streamline the proposal with input from the prospect's project team. The solution will be presented to the partner's decision makers and someone from the executive team will sponsor your solution.

The PAM must make sure that the channel partner works with the prospect's project team to finalize the proposal and the contracts. The channel partner should relay this information back to the vendor and push for the contracts to be finalized with the project team. The chance of success factor has now risen to 60% because the risk that the deal will be lost has been substantially reduced. The biggest risk now is that the final review of the contract and proposal takes too long. This could mean that you can't close the deal within the defined time period and then something unexpected happens, for example budget cuts.

8. Negotiation

During this phase, the solution itself is no longer being discussed. It's all about sorting out the terms and conditions. Following the verbal agreement of the prospect's executives, the vendor and the channel partner must focus on getting the contracts signed. The vendor's PAM and the channel partner's key account manager must work together to push the deal through. The chance of success factor is now 75% and nothing unexpected should happen.

9. Won

Congratulations! The final order was received and accepted. Now the implementation should start and the project managers take the lead. It's important that the PAM fills out a win/loss report and that this information is made available within your company. The channel team should use this information to communicate this success to other channel partners. It can be used to show them how to win similar deals. Make sure, however, that no confidential information is shared.

If the customer has agreed to be a reference client, then the PAM needs to introduce the ISV's marketing team to the channel partner's marketing team and ensure that the case study will be available right after the successful implementation.

10. Lost

This certainly isn't what you were working towards. But try and make the best of it. Sometimes a "no" can be a good answer. This is especially true if you are working together with a channel partner on a project. It doesn't matter when the "no" comes, just make sure you find out why and then share this knowledge within your channel network.

You can modify the different sales stages to fit your business model. If the project size tends to be smaller than US$10,000 or your typical sales cycle is less than 60 days, you should reduce the number of sales stages to 4 – 6 (max). In this case, I would also recommend to group together prospecting/potential lead, qualification/discovery and development, proposal/short listed and selected/negotiation. But this is up to you - the definition of the sales stages must reflect the typical sales cycle, match your business model and give you good confidence in the forecast.

Overview of the 10 sales stages

Sales Stage	Chance of Success	Typical information during this sales stage
1. Prospecting	0%	Target account criteria are met. Several conversations with the partner and the end customer/prospect have taken place.
2. Potential Lead	0%	Target end customer has a need or some need exists. Prospect indicated interest in doing "something" and the channel partner has scheduled a meeting with the prospect to get more details about the opportunity.

Sales Stage	Chance of Success	Typical information during this sales stage
3. Qualification	10%	First visits and product demonstrations are made. Prospect shows interest in the solutions and has a confirmed need. Project qualification profile is compiled and a confirmed budget is made available for the project. Prospect plans project within the next 6-9 months and a compelling reason is identified.
4. Discovery & Development	20%	Decision and approval process is known. Contact made to all decision makers. Budget is re-qualified and re-confirmed. Buying issues, competitive landscape and business case are transparent. Pricing, implementation plan and required resources are in range with prospect's expectations.
5. Proposal	25%	All prospect's issues and questions resolved. Proposal strategy defined and agreed by account team. Proposal is sent or presented to prospect and prospect confirms validity of proposal.
6. Short Listed	40%	Field of competitors narrowed down to few participants. Proof of concept meeting held with the channel partner and the prospect. Approval is in process and moving through decision path.
7. Selected	60%	All open requirements are identified and addressed. Competition is neutralized, channel partner and the value of the solution is accepted by prospect. All remaining technical or business issues resolved. Executive sponsors buying in. Anticipated project start and lead date is identified and reconfirmed.
8. Negotiation	75%	Verbal agreement on all terms and conditions. Finalization of contracts and all legal issues addressed. Executive sponsor agrees to deal.
9. Won	100 %	Contracts executed and delivered.
10. Lost	0 %	Prospect or channel partner stops the project. Reasons for ending the project need to be defined.

Lead Management

Does the following scenario seem familiar? Marketing provides lead information to the internal sales team and once the sales team starts making calls, they find out that the leads are already several weeks old and therefore not very valuable anymore. Or: Marketing distributed leads to a channel partner. These leads ended up on the channel partners general e-mail list and you as the vendor only hear about it when someone complains. Sometimes leads are given to the internal account manager and are never touched again. Or (another good one), leads generated through marketing activities are simply stored away and never touched because no one is appointed as responsible for them. There are tons of stories and everyone in the business will have a story to tell. You need to remember that in order to grow the business with partners, the pipeline must grow and therefore the number of prospects must grow.

Several studies have shown that lead management in most organizations is far from ideal and that only 20% of all leads are followed up.[64] Sales typically disqualify 70% of leads based on a lack of budget, timing or for other reasons. Can you believe that 80% of those "bad leads" buy a similar solution within 24 months? More than 70% of all companies have no process for re-qualifying leads even when it's industry wide knowledge that 80% of all sales take five contacts to close. 50% of all sales and marketing organizations don't nurture their leads properly and more than half of all sales execs are not happy with the quality of leads. These numbers apply to the direct channel, however, which means that the organization deals directly with the prospects. Working with a channel partner makes the process even more complex and reduces the closing rate of a lead even further.

Let's use an easy example to demonstrate how professional lead management can produce a significant investment return in a short time. To generate a sales ready lead for an enterprise product via web-based marketing (e.g. Google, ppc or banners) you have to go through several steps:

1. Get clicks on your advertisement/landing page. Let's say you pay US$10 for every click of a potential customer (of course you'll pay less than US$10 per click, but not all clicks will come from potential customers).

---

[64] Aberdeen Group, "Lead Nurturing: The Secret to Successful Lead Generation"; see http://www.aberdeen.com (2008) and Sirius Decisions: http://www.siriusdecisions.com (2010)

2. Make people take action (e.g. leave their address/call in). Hopefully you'll have a 10% conversion rate, which brings the cost of the potential lead up to US$100 (10 x US$10).
3. Screen the incoming requests before they enter the sales channel or are given to a channel partner as a real lead. If 20% can be considered as good leads then each "sales ready" lead costs you US$500.

If your channel team can close 20% of these leads with an average deal size of US$10,000, then the lead generation costs per closed sale are US$2,500 (5 x US$500) or 25% of the deal size. As a result, the total marketing return on investment is 300% and doesn't seem to be too bad. On the other hand, if you want to earn US$10 million in revenue, you'll need to spend US$2.5 million on lead generation, which is a lot of money! If the implementation of a lead management system can improve the process by 50%, you can save US$1.25 million just on marketing costs and, even more importantly, you can reduce the effort that is necessary from your channel team and your channel partners significantly. A higher quality of your leads will not only reduce your costs, it will improve the relationship with your channel partners. Make sure you calculate your marketing costs per closed lead by basing the numbers on how much you normally spend on a lead and then take into account what actually happened with it. If you can't do this, you really have to think about making improvements. To effectively manage the entire lead process, you'll need a system in place that allows marketing and the respective PAMs to check on the status of every lead from the beginning to the end.

Lead management objectives

- Invest your marketing dollars on the right leads.
- Work on all leads.
- Deliver the leads to the right channel partners.
- Make your channel partners match the leads (meaning the channel partner should also contribute some leads).
- Ensure transparency of the lead process.

- Don't waste marketing time and money.
- Review the results and use your learnings for further sales and marketing activities.

As I've said before, it'll be nearly impossible to build and grow an effective channel program without having the necessary systems in place. I strongly recommended a web-based, professional system. But even if you have to start "manually", put rules and processes in place to make sure that the lead management can be performed as described. Besides your existing customer base, leads are one of the most important assets of your company.

Here are ten steps for successful lead management with channel partners:

1. Define realistic and achievable goals

The first challenge is to define right goals when you start working on the lead process with channel partners. One of the biggest questions is: What's the best way to generate and nurture the leads? Is it better to generate leads on your own and then give them to your partner or is it better to share the costs of lead generation with your partner?

Since this book is meant to be a pragmatic guide, I recommend using a lead funnel that is very similar to the channel partner selection funnel I've described earlier in the book. The following example is based on the assumption that you're already made your partner selection and signed them on as revenue producing channel partners. The biggest difference is that now you have to generate end customer leads and work on these leads with your channel partners.

Your goal is to achieve US$1 million in revenues with your channel partners; the average revenue per deal is US$10,000 and the average sales cycle is 3 months from screening. To keep it simple, we'll assume that 50% of the residual leads always reach the next level.

There are 5 levels, resulting in a distillation factor of 16, which means that for every deal closed, we require 16 real prospects.

The result is that you need approximately 1,600 leads to close 100 deals and reach your US$1 million in revenue. Always keep in mind that US$10,000 of revenue on your side means that the average sale to the end customer is much bigger. Very often, these sales not only include the margin on your product, they also include additional services or other software or hardware products. Also remember, that during the first quarter, you'll invest in lead generation but won't generate any revenues yet.

Parameters	
Average Revenue	$10,000

Sales Funnel						
	Screening	Potential Lead	Qualification	Action Plan	Win	Distillation Factor
% in Next Stage		50%	50%	50%	50%	16
		Sales Cycle 3 Months from Screening				

Year One Period	Q1 / Y1	Q2 / Y1	Q3 / Y1	Q4 / Y1	Q1 / Y2	12 Months
Screening	400	400	400	400	0	1,600
Pot. Lead	200	200	200	200	0	800
Qualification	100	100	100	100	0	400
Action Plan	0	50	50	50	50	200
Win	0	25	25	25	25	100
Total Revenue	$0	$250,000	$250,000	$250,000	$250,000	$1,000,000

Ask yourself this: Is it realistic to expect your channel team to work together with your channel partners to create and work on around 1,600 leads within the next 12 months? US$1 million is an average sales quota for one channel manager who can realistically only work with 20 - 30 channel partners on these leads. This example also demonstrates why it's so important to invest some time in finding out where and how you are generating the leads. If you increase the lead quality, the time required for each step in the process can be reduced significantly. If your channel partner is already a well known company in a vertical or geographical area, create joint lead generation programs and share the costs. The leads will be of higher quality, which gives you a faster ROI on the money invested in lead generation.

You absolutely need to set realistic goals and make sure that your PAM has the capability to work on all the leads or can motivate a partner to work on them. I've seen situations where a lot of sales effort is involved just to win a small deal; intensive technical support, sales consulting and even face to face meetings. It'll be impossible to motivate your channel partners to work on these kinds of deals that don't deliver the revenue to cover their cost of sales. It also makes no sense for you to work on these deals directly. If this is happening in your company, you need to work on the sales process. Maybe you can raise the price or you can create some tools for automating some steps and reduce the effort.

Involve your channel team and your channel partner to optimize the lead generation and the sales process. Every goal is achievable as long as expectations are realistic, resources are available, and your channel team and the partners are motivated.

2. Generate the most qualified leads possible.

Increasing lead quality will help optimize the sales process. Your marketing department should be measured by the quality of leads they deliver and not only by the quantity. A lot of companies use generic web advertising and guide the leads to a website (landing page) where they have to fill out a form. Everyone who fills out the form is then considered a lead. The result is that these leads have an extremely broad range of interests and only a fraction is really suitable. This type of improper lead generation costs the sales team more time and only frustrates them if they have to follow up with a lot of people who have no interest in the solution. If you are going to use this method, make sure you have people on board who will carry out a prequalification before the sales team gets the lead.

If you want to generate more highly qualified leads, you should start by steering better traffic to your campaign. Always remember that directing the traffic to your landing or lead capture page is the easiest part. Converting this traffic into valuable leads is the hard part. How can you do this and make sure that not only you, but also your partners, are getting valuable leads?

Let's assume you are selling an enterprise solution which has to be implemented by a VAR. Then you should start by defining the right keywords (not too many and not too broad). Group your keywords tightly and write your ad according to the keyword you are bidding on. If you do it this way, the CTR (click through rate) will be much better and more qualified than with a more generic approach. For example, if you operate an Italian restaurant in Boston, your keywords should be "best Italian food in Boston" instead of "best restaurant in the US." You only want people clicking on your add who love Italian food and live in or are visiting Boston.

Another approach is to invest time in content marketing. This entails creating white papers, case studies, blogs with valuable content and becoming the expert in your area. If the content is marketed properly, which involves listings in other portals, newsletters and referencing in articles, this will guide more qualified traffic to your website.

The next step is creating landing pages with the relevant information about you and your channel partner's offering. They should include information about what specific benefits the solution offers and even the price range or the steps necessary for a successful implementation.

If you only have partners in specific areas and onsite implementation is necessary, then state this on the landing page. This way only the visitors who are looking for this exact solution and are in this area will fill out the form. This ensures that you are creating qualified leads that can be shared with your channel partners and relate to areas where the solution can be delivered. I've seen many situations where leads were followed up and time was even spent on technical support or creating a proposal, when it was totally unclear, however, how the solution could be delivered.

No matter how you generate your leads; through e-mail campaigns, outbound phone calls, advertisements, content marketing etc., always define your solution in detail, which industry you are targeting and what benefits the solutions will bring. And even more importantly, make sure that you and your channel partners can deliver the solution.

3. Don't send channel partners more leads than they can manage

Another critical factor is making sure that channel partners only receive the number of leads they can follow up on and give proper feedback about. This has a lot to do with lead ownership and the quality of the leads that get distributed. Regardless of who created the lead, the vendor or the channel partner, every PAM should always be aware of all leads and their status. Even if you can't expect the PAM to meet personally with each of the leads or even have detailed phone calls with them, you can expect that they understand the pipeline of every one of their assigned partners in detail – this is their job!

Determining the right quantity of leads is very difficult. It depends on your business, the type of solution and your channel partners. The first step is to group the partners and make sure that for each group, you have dedicated people who should get the leads. It's possible that you have different groups within one partner. A typical example of this is if your channel partner has both an SMB and an enterprise group. Then SMB leads should go to the dedicated person in the SMB department and enterprise leads to the dedicated person in the enterprise department. The same applies if your channel partner is divided into different sales regions. Make sure you reduce the number of people that "touch" the lead. Every time a lead is forwarded by someone it costs time. Remember, only "hot leads" are good leads.

Your PAM needs to structure their channel in such a way that they know where the leads are going and who is working on them. Then they must make sure that feedback on each lead is channeled back into your system. Standardize the feedback communication so that channel partners can do this quickly.

All leads generated by the vendor should first be distributed among the various PAMs, who then should divide these leads between their partners. The lead distribution should be as automated as possible, but under the control of the PAMs. Someone needs to control the process so that not only the best known partners (best friends), the biggest partners or the ones who are crying out the most will get the leads. The partners with the best conversion rate, from lead to sales, should get the most leads.

You might have large, successful partners who have almost no interest in your leads or no system in place to follow up on them. Or there might be smaller, more motivated partners who will follow up and qualify every lead but can't close them. In these situations, your PAM has to establish a link between these partners and get them to work together. Make sure that the smaller partners get rewarded for their work when a deal comes in. This is much harder in practice than in theory, but it is possible.

Only the PAM knows how many leads each channel partner can handle in which sales stage. They should also know about the effort each partner puts into the lead qualification, the team who can work on each sales stage and the closing rate. If a channel partner has more leads than they can handle at a certain sales stage, then it makes no sense to pass them more leads. It can even be a good sign if they can't handle more leads because it shows that they are investing the appropriate amount of time on each one. The channel partner might be putting the right amount of effort into each sales stage and achieving a good closing rate. If this is the case, then you have to convince them (or help them) to put more resources into the lead qualification.

Another situation arises if there is no movement in a partner's sales funnel or the closing rates are bad. This partner might not work on the channel or the people responsible have other priorities or they are just not educated enough about your products. The lead funnel is just like a water pipe - don't put more water in the pipe than it can handle, and if there's a knot in the pipe, you have to block the incoming water and repair the pipe.

The ultimate goal must be that you and your channel partners generate a steady flow of qualified leads that the channel partners can follow up on and implement if they are closed. This also shows why it makes almost no sense to create big marketing hype in too short of a timeframe; because a large number of the incoming leads can't be qualified and will fall off the radar.

4. Motivate your channel partners to follow up

You should spend some time thinking about what your channel partners really want and how you can motivate them to work hard for you and follow up on every lead. Show them that you value their work and that you believe in them, even if they've failed several times. If the channel partners see that you value their work and help them improve their processes, and even reward them from time to time, they will work harder to reach the goals.

Even though the people who work on the channel partner's side are not your employees, you can still reward them in different ways. You can see that they get an extra bonus, specific education, more qualified leads, something they really want (a gift) or simply praise (which very often helps the most). The key is to find out what people desire most. One thing that always works, and that you can control, is improving the quality and amount of leads every channel partner gets and helping them to close these leads. When given a higher quantity and quality of leads, each account manager on the channel partner's side can close more deals, make more money and secure their career. This is very motivating.

Another way to encourage the channel partners is to help them fight their competition. You can produce reference cases, competitive analyses or assist with creating presentations to demonstrate the benefits of the complete solution. Most importantly in this situation, you as the vendor must show your commitment to the channel partner and go on sales calls or presentations with them. This shows the potential customer that the channel partner is knowledgeable and is endorsed by the vendor.

5. Educate the marketing and sales force

I already mentioned that education is one important aspect for motivating your channel. Another key aspect is making sure that the marketing and sales force understands one another. A report by the CMO Council and Business Performance Management Forum found that only 7% of all mid level executives said their sales and marketing departments work together effectively.[65] Close to 50% of all leads that sales rejected as not interesting became sales ready opportunities within 12 months. If you combine this with the complexity that working with the channel creates, it's clear that there's lots of wasted potential. The main reason for this is that marketing is long-term oriented and sales focuses on short-term success. Even in small organizations, people from the different departments don't understand the role or goals of each other. This is why I highly recommend installing someone in the role of a sales controller or sales analyst who follows up the entire lead cycle and makes sure every lead is worked on properly.

Education starts with explaining to your channel partners how the entire lead generation process functions and how the teams must work together. When the sales team understands that marketing's job is the identification and targeting of the best possible audience, the creation of the respective material to deliver the key messages and the generation of a constant flow of leads, then an important goal has been reached. On the other hand, the marketing team has to understand that sales are measured by short-term goals (sales this

---

[65] CMO Council: www.cmocouncil.org (2010)

month or this quarter) and a lot of their income or commission is related to these short-term goals.

Provide your channel partner with follow-up techniques. You'll find that most of the people who are following up on the leads have never attended any training. Perhaps they've only received a "five minute" instruction from someone and then they had to start contacting prospects. Create sales guides that you can hand out to the channel partners which cover every step of the sales process and provide the right arguments showing why your product or solutions based on your product will deliver a lot of benefits.

Don't only train your channel partner's sales team, also help the channel partner's marketing department to improve lead generation and provide the relevant material to support sales in the sales process. You can help them with creating web marketing campaigns, building presentations, qualifying leads or sending follow-up emails. Show them what tools or platforms exist for automation of some processes. Don't forget to make the presales and support team aware of their importance in the sales process. The technical people shouldn't necessarily be involved in the sales process because some of them tend to cover every technical detail and make everything much more complex than necessary. But, on the other hand, there may be people in the support team who perform very well in front of the customer.

Help your channel partner define the roles of the technical team who support the sales and ensure that the technical team receives all the training and contacts they need to answer any request within a very short time.

Another important aspect is involving the management on both sides to support the effort to be successful. If the management shows commitment to the partnership, the teams will follow. You can educate the management about your market by giving them research and also providing them with success stories with other channel partners or within their own organization. Many vendors think that the partner's management is well informed about the market and is completely aware of previous successes with their solution. Don't make this mistake!

You may now be thinking "I'm an ISV not a training company", but if you want to work with the channel, this aspect is very important. Training and coaching partners and their employees for superior performance creates a win-win-win situation. The prospect will receive better assistance, your channel partner will close more deals and you will sell more products.

6. Win deals in collaboration with your partners.

You have the most experience in winning new customers with solutions based on your product. Most of the channel partners work with many different vendors at once and they only have incomplete knowledge about your product and the relevant arguments to win new customers. It's critical for long-term success with these partners that you include assistance on every deal as part of your channel strategy. In the beginning, you should also share those opportunities that are "ready to buy" in order to gain trust from the channel partners. If they see that you've worked on generating these opportunities and then hand them over for closing, they will ask your team to join them in the sales process with their customers. This allows for the unique opportunity to give the prospect a better understanding of the value of your company and your solutions.

Real partnership involves sharing opportunities with partners. Winning deals in collaboration with your partners will also help you gain mindshare. Your channel partners will always sell whatever is easiest and whatever they think will provide a good solution for their customers. If they know they can use not only your sales, but also your technical and management resources to close a deal, and that they can trust you, they will take this opportunity.

7. Put programs in place to address your total market

Very often a solution will be perfect for some market niches and bring great value to a specific type of customer or a vertical industry. Instead of trying to devalue your solution by entering other markets, you should put programs in place to address your total market. There are two different strategies for doing this; you can try to reach every potential prospect in the market that your existing channel partners still serve or you can increase your network of channel partners in other regions. Leveraging success is a very powerful tool in the channel business.

Imagine, for example, that you have channel partners who successfully sell and implement your solution for high schools in Washington DC, Boston and Chicago. Instead of trying to locate other customer groups (e.g. lawyers or doctors) in these areas, where your solution won't be as appropriate, you should try to address the same customer groups (high schools) with different partners in other metropolitan areas such as Los Angeles or New York. In this case you will need to put programs in place to find the right channel partners in these areas and to start generating end customer leads with them.

Another way is to address the entire market in the areas where you already have a committed and successful partner. Find out how your current channel partners sell the solution and how big the total market is in the areas they can reach. Very often, solutions will fit into customer groups that are similar to the existing ones - perhaps not only high schools can use the solution but it may also be suitable for elementary schools, kindergartens or universities.

Undertake these typical activities to address a larger market:

- Convince your channel partners to open new locations in other areas.
- Create success stories to find similar channel partners.

- Help existing channel partners open similar markets with market research.
- Visit vertical events to meet potential channel partners, multipliers and end customers.
- Create specific websites and landing pages.
- Modify your solution in such a way that it also fits other customers in a similar market (e.g. add another language or another operating system).

There are many more activities I could list, but the message should be clear: try to address your total market where you are already successful instead of generating unspecific leads that will probably not end up in a deal. Focus on existing channel partners with new but similar customer groups or roll out existing successful tools to find new channel partners who can build upon this success in new geographic locations.

8. Provide a web-based lead management tool

I've already discussed the need for web-based lead management tools. One of the main reasons why this is so important for effective pipeline management is that it gives you complete information about every lead generated in one central place. It should also be possible for channel partners to access this information.

A web-based lead management tool is a central repository for all opportunities in the pipeline. It makes it easy to manage leads, share them with partners and analyze the whole pipeline.

Using this tool, you can easily distribute the leads to partners, assign specific groups of leads to partners or give some partners direct access to the database so they can assign some opportunities to themselves. It's important to understand that a vendor should share opportunities with their channel partners because this way they can increase business or reach a certain market share faster than with the direct sales method. On the other hand, most channel partners resell products not only for the margin but also to reach new customer groups and sell them their total portfolio of products and services.

The system has to meet two critical requirements: it needs to be easy to use and generate real value if partners start working with it. One possible benefit for the partner is that they can instantly get help from the vendor when a lead has reached a critical stage or that working with the system is more comfortable than discussing every lead on the phone with the channel manager.

Systems such as Xeequa take the process of opportunity sharing one step further.[66] Everyone, even the channel partner you have distributed the lead to, can share every lead within their trusted network. This provides one important advantage; it motivates your channel partner to invite companies into their network if they are of value for closing a deal. This means that more and more independent companies will work together to close deals and build solutions based on the manufacturer's product.

Is the business world ready and willing to build and manage a global network of independent companies to increase sales? There definitely is a noticeable trend towards global networking. However, if you as the manufacturer do not believe in it or simply don't trust the technology, then at least start by using a web-based CRM or PRM system to manage and share your leads with channel partners.

9. Analyze and improve the lead process

Assuming you've done everything to generate a good quality of leads, helped your partners in every possible way to close deals and installed a web-based system for lead management, I now want to explain how to analyze and improve the lead process.

In theory, it sounds easy. Analyze the opportunities, take the information learned and channel it back into the process. In reality, this is actually very, very difficult. Even if you have all the necessary

---

[66] Xeequa: www.xeequa.com

information about every opportunity, there will always be some uncertainty about the reasons why certain things are happening. This is normal in this type of process. In any case, don't just talk about the process or listen to your gut feeling, base your analysis on clearly defined criteria.

For example, you could group the leads according to the method of lead generation, by solution, by PAM or by channel partner. You could further reduce complexity by removing all the cases where nothing "abnormal" is happening. Let the PAMs give you a summary of the lead situation regarding their respective channel partners. This analysis reveals just how well informed each PAM is about the deals their channel partners are working on and ensures that they take this information seriously. Ask the channel managers what their best partners do to win the deals and how they rate their lead quality and processes. Compare this with their answers about the channel partners who have the least success. Share this information and the pipeline analysis with your team and some selected channel partners. Make sure that this new information is channeled back into the lead generation process.

I don't want to go into too much detail here so I'll stop now. But keep in mind that analyzing the lead process is a very important part of lead management. Management has to stay on top of this.

10. Penalize the partners who don't do lead generation

There are different types of channel partners and each of them will present a different way of working with you. You'll have channel partners that don't care about lead generation because they use your product in a specific way (such as OEM) or in a market niche where your solution only complements their solution. These channel partners might have their own market and generate their own leads. If this is the case and they need some help, then you should make sure that they get this help as quickly as any other active partner.

The truly inactive partners make up a much larger share. They don't generate leads and don't actively participate in your partner program. The only motivation these partners have for becoming a channel partner of yours is when somebody asks for your product. In these cases, you must make sure that they don't undercut a more motivated channel partner who works on creating a real pipeline with you. You'll only have the ability to find this out if you have effective lead management in place.

One of the main reasons some channel partners won't work with you on creating a lead pipeline is because they want to stay independent and want to win the deals with the solution of their choice (either yours or that of a competitor). If they have the choice, they will always select the solution that gives them the best margin or allows them to make the most money on the project. A typical example is when the prospect is looking for a fixed price project and they rely on the reseller to deliver this solution. In this case, many system integrators will choose a solution that costs close to nothing and gives them the entire budget for professional services. It's important that you penalize these partners by giving them less discounts or a much lower level of support. To build a good pipeline, the commitment must come from both sides.

Pipeline Management

I've defined the various sales stages and identified some key factors for building and optimizing your lead management with channel partners. But I haven't talked about the "real" work you have to do on the pipeline yet, which involves dealing with different kinds of channel partners. I'll cover this on the pages where I look at how to work with project oriented and product oriented resellers.

Project oriented resellers

Project oriented resellers (e.g. system integrators) are interested in selling a complete solution. This normally includes different products (e.g. software and hardware) and the respective professional services to implement the solution. These resellers usually make most of their profit with professional services and see the respective products as enablers for selling these services. Many of them also carry several similar products from competing suppliers. From a reseller's perspective, this makes complete sense because they can offer different solutions to potential customers. The vendor needs to ensure that the right communication channels are in place and that the reseller is being effectively managed to make sure they prioritize the ISV's product. The PAM is in charge of managing communication with the reseller and working on opportunities to win the business.

To effectively manage a pipeline with your channel partners, you need to define the goals and objectives with each of the key channel partners (the peer group). This doesn't mean that a channel partner account plan has to be put in place with each of them - the goals can be defined very pragmatically. It should be transparent though, which goals need to be achieved, what the necessary steps are and who will do what in order to reach these goals.

Typical goals are:

- Generate 20 potential leads per month.
- Grow the pipeline by 20% per quarter.
- Close two projects per month.

Once the PAM has defined the goals with each of their channel partners, it's important to review these goals and make sure that they are achievable. The PAM should work closely with their channel partners during this process and understand how they can evaluate their partner's forecast in order to make their own forecast. The key here is that the PAM understands the business focus of their channel partners and that they can get in contact with them to discuss the pipeline in more detail. If possible, the channel partners should be categorized by region or by industry. Maybe you have PAMs who target the telecommunication industry or who are responsible for all channel partners in Southern California. If they don't understand the business of their respective channel partners, they cannot ensure that their forecasts are achievable.

After you have all the forecasts you can estimate the number of leads that are necessary for reaching the goals. A good rule of thumb is that the pipeline should be three times bigger than the anticipated result. If this is not the case then go back to the channel partners and make a plan for how you can achieve this. You will need to either increase the number of leads or the average value of each project.

I'll walk you through a typical sales process with a project oriented reseller. The different stages can be seen in the following illustration.

To reach the required number of leads, it's important that you initiate ongoing field marketing that will constantly generate new leads.

Using your information about the channel partners, you can determine each partner's ability to generate leads and what kind of help they will need to achieve the goals. Some channel partners may have a solid database of prospects but don't have the resources for following them up. If this is the case, you can help them with resources or even finance a funded head for a period of time.[67] You must always keep track of who makes how much money with every new deal. If the average project size is US$50,000 and the cost for your license is only US$10,000, then US$40,000 could be professional services. Even if the gross margin with professional services is only 30%, the channel partner will make more money than you. You should raise this issue with your partner and discuss who covers which costs for the lead generation.

You can help the channel partners with lead generation, but it'll be more difficult to help them in the next phases. The main reason for this is once the "real" interaction with the prospect starts, there must be someone in place who owns the communication with them and acts as the key point of contact for everyone. This person has to be from the channel partner. If the resellers also are responsible for the implementation, this is even more important because only the reseller knows all the components that are necessary to deliver the complete solution. Educate your partners, when necessary, to position the product and qualify the customers.

A joint sales approach should be used from the qualification phase onwards. Your involvement, however, depends on the knowledge of the channel partner. If they can carry out good product demonstrations, explain the value to the customers, set up web conferences and guide the technical team through your product, then your involvement may be quite small. But don't always stay in the background. Be aware that continued success comes from the end customer and it's only from them that you can learn how to improve your sales approach. You will also learn who influences the sale on the customer's and channel partner's side - if you are visible to the end customer, it makes it harder to replace your solution in the deal.

---

[67] You can download a "funded head" contract at www.channel-revolution.com.

From this phase on, only "real" projects should be in the pipeline. The PAM is not only responsible for the pipeline development, which means ensuring that there is movement, they must also work with the right channel partners. If there are partners that don't contribute to the pipeline development or who are not closing deals, then they shouldn't be given any more leads and should receive less attention. The PAM must make sure that they, and every resource involved from your side, are focused on the best producing partners and on the projects that can be closed within a short timeframe. To motivate the team and make the success visible within your organization (and the partner's) you should celebrate every win directly after the deal is closed. Promote the people who helped the most with closing the deal and ensure that management sends out thank you letters to the team and channel partners.

Project oriented resellers

Pipeline management with product oriented resellers such as distributors, e-tailers, or to a certain degree, SaaS providers is a different story. The main reason for this is that most product oriented resellers don't sell additional services with the solution; their main revenue stream comes from reselling products. So they focus on selling the products with the highest margins and the shortest sales cycles (wherever the highest demand from the end customer comes from).

It's important to understand that product oriented resellers will NOT create demand for their vendors without getting paid for it. Assuming they will create demand for free is one of the biggest mistakes manufacturers make! Where project oriented resellers see products from different manufacturers only as enablers for their core business, reselling products is the core business of product oriented resellers and so their mindset is totally different.

The main question is: How can manufacturers motivate product oriented resellers to sell their products and how can they use this channel successfully?

There are many types of distributors, e-tailers and SaaS providers with many different business models. They each have their specialties; some are very channel oriented and sell to resellers only, some also sell to end customers and others will only resell your solution under their own brand. In this chapter, I'd like to focus on the success factors for building and managing a pipeline with these types of partners. I'll concentrate on channel partners who have a distribution model in place, and therefore focus on selling products. On the next pages, I'll use the term "distributor" as a general term for product oriented resellers.

Here's a situation everyone wants to avoid: Your products are listed in a distributer's product catalog, you finance various marketing campaigns and begin to reroute your reseller channel to buy from them. Then, after nothing much happens for a certain amount of time, the distributer asks for more marketing money. Once this money is used up, your products are delisted. This scenario is frustrating for everyone; for you because you wasted time and money, for your resellers because the direct lines between you and them were cut and for the distributor because they made some investments on training their internal staff and promoting your product that didn't pay off.

You can apply the selection funnel for product oriented resellers if you want to avoid such disastrous situations. The funnel looks quite different from the one for project oriented resellers. This is because with project oriented resellers, you work from project to project, and with product oriented resellers it's important to reach a critical size of recurring business in order to be successful. Recurring business, in this case, either means that there is a steady market demand for your product from end users or that the customer base has grown to a certain size and this generates monthly recurring revenues.

If you want to build business with the distribution channel, you should think about the following questions:

- What are the main reasons for entering the distribution channel with your product?
- What kind of distribution model is better: "Two tier", which means the distributors, sell to resellers, or "one tier", working with distributors who sell to end users also?
- Is the actual market demand for the product high enough or are there ways to create this market demand?
- Do the product and your organization meet the requirements of the distribution channel (are you channel ready)?
- What size marketing budget is necessary and are you willing to invest the required resources?

In order to answer these questions, your pipeline management with product oriented resellers should start with market research. You'll have to evaluate the following points:

1. Which markets do you want to address?

If you decide to go to market with a distribution channel partner, it means that you'll have to invest a lot of time and money with this partner. You'll also need to give additional margins, which can be significant in the beginning. The decision between two tier and one tier distribution is especially important as this has dramatic consequences for how you will have to work with resellers. It's only when markets already exist that can't be reached directly or with a one tier distribution model that an investment in two tier distribution makes sense.

Typical reasons for making the decision to use two tier distribution include the building of a reseller network or entering a new international, vertical market or channel that can't be served directly (e.g. retail). Don't use the two tier distribution model without first identifying clear advantages. It's the most costly way of selling products but can also create huge market coverage for the right products.

2. What are the most important success factors in this market?

There are many advantages a distributor can offer. They are the best when it comes to logistics and financial services and their two tier distribution will definitely cover most of the resellers in the areas they operate. If your product already is somewhat well-known (has brand) or has already created market demand and doesn't require extensive explanation or technical support, then order fulfillment might be the most important success factor. If the product is more complex and your goal is to leverage success from other markets, then support, training and other services become more important.

The manufacturer needs to build a plan and define realistic assumptions about what their market position is today and what the most important factors are for taking the product to market. Also don't forget country specific factors such as language or legal requirements and regulations.

3. Which type of distribution channel do you need?

Based on your plan, you should create a prioritized list that details what you expect from a new distributor and what the advantages will be for you and them.

Typical questions for the evaluation list are:

- Which important geographical area does the distributor cover?
- What are the terms and conditions that are expected?
- How many resellers does the distributor work with?
- What is their motivation for working with you?
- Will there be a product manager who can focus on your product?
- What additional services does the distributor offer to you and the resellers?
- Which competitors do they represent and what are the reasons for including your product.
- Will they promote the product and what kind of market development funding (MDF) is expected?
- How is their sales team organized?
- How many products will the sales team represent?
- Do you have access to the sales team?
- Can you incentivize the sales team?

The next step is evaluating the "potential distributors." Here you take a closer look at a group of potential distributors that seem to suit your needs. But keep in mind that there are always two perspectives; what kind of distributors do you need and is your product interesting to these distributors?

When contemplating the kind of distributors you need, it's necessary to consider if your products are of value to the target group of distributors. Large, volume based distributors require a minimum of US$1 million in revenue during the first year of operation. Do you think the market potential is there? If they sell your product for US$25, then they'll need to move around 40,000 units!

In general, you need to make a decision about what types of distributors will be the best for reselling your products. Please make this decision before you search for specific names or begin to work with a distributor just because you already have a contact within them. Sooner or later, every personal relationship will be overruled by the amount of business you create together. If you're not successful together then either you or the distributor will terminate the relationship, which means you will have lost time and money.

The following pages will describe the advantages and disadvantages of working with the different types of distributors and which approach to take.

International Broadliners

International broadliners such as Ingram Micro or TechData could be the right partners if your goal is to sell a huge number of products to thousands of smaller resellers, and if the main challenges are logistics and reaching out to these smaller resellers in a short time span.[68]

For some years now, the market has progressively been shifting from a need for physical logistics and financing towards getting the best price and support. As a result, the broadliners face increasing competition from e-tailers and value added distributors. The broadliner's answer to this has been to start their own e-commerce portals and to add value to their software distribution, but in most cases they're still following the rules of a traditional broadline distributor.

These types of broadliners can help you with increasing your market share if you already have a fairly strong brand or if there is market demand and you have the resources to support the partners. It's important that you have a dedicated budget and a dedicated team to support these broadliners. If your budget is limited however, and

---

[68] Ingram Micro: www.ingrammicro.com; TechData: www.techdata.com

you can't invest a minimum of US$200,000 p.a. for MDF in order to gain visibility in the distributor's organization, or if you can't afford to run additional campaigns to the reseller base about the broadliner, it will be extremely difficult to become successful.

How can a smaller vendor gain mindshare among the hundreds of internal sales people employed by these huge broadliners? It's impossible, and therefore you need to make the resellers ask for your product and create the demand. This is because if a reseller calls in and asks for a specific vendor's product, they will get exactly that product from the vendor. The distributor's sales team will not argue with the reseller, even if another (your) product provides the sales team with a little more margin or fits the reseller's need better, and not even if you run an incentive program. The distributor's sales team will sell whatever is the easiest product to sell. It's most likely that this will be the product with the best known brand. Creating market demand is therefore the only way to make this channel work for you.

Specialized or National Broadline Distributors

Specialized or national broadline distributors like Navarre, SFC or Hexacom are smaller than the international broadliners.[69] They focus on a national market or a specific market segment but use the same broadline business model. I list them separately here, because working with them is quite different from working with international broadliners.

Even if they're not a multibillion dollar company with thousands of employees, their business model will basically be the same as that of an international broadliner. This means that they will have systems in use for attaining a high degree of efficiency and that they'll work for low margins. There's no room for manufacturers who can't deliver the product and the required information in the proper format. Be aware that they often require special price lists, special marketing

---

[69] Navarre: www.navarre.com; SFC: www.sfc-software.de; Hexacom: www.hexacom.com

material, and have strict requirements about product upgrades and handling of returns. These are all points which have to be negotiated before beginning to work with them.

Smaller national distributors can help represent your company in a specific territory and will help you build a network of resellers, as long as you provide them with the necessary amount of funding or give them higher margins. However, they cannot deliver technical support or any additional services and they can't focus on your products alone. Nevertheless, together with your help, they can create some product demand for you.

Many manufacturers don't differentiate between larger and smaller broadliners. But you have to understand that smaller ISVs without strong brands won't be very successful when working with the large broadliners. So you should start working with smaller broadliners first if you are a small manufacturer. Don't ignore this advice. Large broadliners will take the time to talk to smaller ISVs through, especially when the discussions are driven by marketing people. They'll just try to get the highest marketing budget possible from the vendors. In many cases, the vendor's marketing budget is where most of the broadliner's margins come from.

Value added distributors (VAD)

There are many differences between broadliners and VADs such as Infinigate or Foreseeson.[70] Many distributors call themselves "value added", but often this only means that they can deliver a product on time. Real value is only created if the VAD offers a full range of services from marketing to license management to training and support.

You should expect a genuine VAD to be a specialist in a specific technology area (e.g. storage, security or network management) and possess specific knowledge about this area. Within their specific area, the VAD should have a wide network of committed resellers

---

[70] Infinigate: www.infinigate.com; Foreseeson: www.foreseeson.com

that buy on a regular basis. Normally, a VAD serves between 1,000 - 3,000 VARs. This is a large number and can be especially interesting for a manufacturer just entering a market.

The business model for most VADs is significantly different from that of broadliners. VADs differentiate themselves so that they can work with smaller manufactures; helping them to build a reseller network, adding value to the product and supporting these products. If the manufacturer is ready to invest in marketing and supply the VAD with additional margins, then they will help to develop a market with the manufacturer. The main reason for this is that the end customers will buy what the resellers are promoting and the resellers will only promote what they feel comfortable with. The VAD can make sure that the resellers reach this level of comfort. But always keep in mind that a VAD will not create market demand or build a network of VARs without commitment and help from the manufacturer.

Working with a VAD can be a good option for those smaller manufacturers who are successful in specific market segments. Or for those who have the budget and resources to support a VAD and want to enter a new market where they will need to recruit new resellers and provide them with sales, marketing and technical support. These smaller manufacturers shouldn't begin working with too many VADs at the same time though - I highly recommend working with just one at a time. Only once you've achieved success with one VAD in one market is it the right time to enter the next market or increase the market share by adding another VAD.

Direct market reseller (DMR)

The main difference between a DMR and a distributor is that DMRs such as TigerDirect or CDW sell to resellers and also to end users directly.[71] They operate in a very aggressive market environment which is driven mainly by price. They compete with the distri-

---

[71] TigerDirect: www.tigerdirect.com; CDW: www.cdw.com

bution channel and with the retailers, but they also very often buy the products from the distributors and sell to smaller retailers.

These companies are mostly marketing driven, but often also supply basic support and education services. At most DMRs you'll find specialists for specific technologies or products who can help install the product. This service is mostly offered to larger vendors who sell products with a high market demand. The DMRS buy the products in large quantities with large discounts but normally don't ask for a return policy if they can't sell them.
If you are entering a new market or trying to build a reseller network, it may seem inappropriate to work with DMRs.

Working with a DMR makes sense if the manufacturer and product have a brand and want to take intensify their contact with the end user market. Another reason for selecting a DMR can be that the product is already widely distributed via downloads or another OEM cooperation. In this case, the manufacturer should look for as many channels to the market as possible.

E-tailer (B2C)

E-tailers like Amazon, NewEgg and ZipZoomFly target the end user market and usually take orders only via the internet.[72] They have perfect logistics and purchasing support but in most cases they can't explain the products and don't offer any technical support.

Working with e-tailers is a perfect scenario when selling highly standardized products where no explanation is necessary and end customers can access all technical help either via a website or directly from the manufacturer. Most e-tailers don't sell maintenance along with the product and they only list who they have sold the product to for their finance (billing) systems. If a manufacturer wants follow up business, they should make sure that the end user registers the product with them.

---

[72] Amazon: www.amazon.com ; Newegg: www.newegg.com ; ZipZoomFly: www.zipzoomfly.com

Like the DMRs, e-tailers are also very price sensitive and always want to be the cheapest on the market. Working with e-tailers can be a very good solution for manufacturers who have a specific consumer product line or already have an existing brand name and want to increase their branding or market reach.

Manufacturers need to be aware that working with DMRs or e-tailers means aggressive pricing. They often offer products at a discount of 30% - 50% to the recommended retail price - meaning they're selling the products to the end customer for less than the VAR has to pay to buy them. Even distributors who receive a 40% discount (and offer the product to the resellers at a 25% discount) can't compete with the aggressive pricing of the DMRs. Manufacturers have to be cautious and consider the consequences before they start working with DMRs and e-tailers.

SaaS Resellers

SaaS resellers like SaaS distributors represent a new breed of channel partner.[73] Whilst in the beginning there was discussion surrounding SaaS and whether there was a place in the channel for SaaS solutions, it's now clear that there is. As already stated previously, in my opinion most resellers will use a hybrid model – selling software and offering hosted SaaS solutions – for the next few years. These are the types of SaaS resellers I will focus on here.

If you are trying to figure out which type of distributor to work with, you may want to use the following table as a decision making tool. It lists key decision criteria for you as the ISV and will help you evaluate how well each type of partner matches your company's needs. I recommend that you use a score where 1 is the lowest match and 5 is the highest match. Then add up the points. I prefer this methodological approach, as it forces you to analyze the situation more carefully.

---

[73] www.saas-distribution.com

Let's look at a simple example: A midsize ISV wants to start selling their SMB product line in a market where they only have a small presence. The product requires some technical support during the implementation and has to be installed by the partner. In this example, the VAD emerges as the best choice. This makes sense, because we are not dealing with a SaaS solution or a low priced "boxed" standard product.

Channel Partner Decision Criteria	Intl. Broad-liner	Natl. Broad-liner	VAD	DMR	E-tailer	SaaS Re-seller
I can work with the potential partner on equal terms, management is involved	1	4	3	2	2	4
My brand is well enough known in the market to fit the partner's business model	2	2	4	2	1	1
The channel partner has a reseller network which can sell our products	5	4	4	3	1	1
The partner can provide the necessary technical support	1	3	4	3	0	0
The required marketing budget fits our budget and is in line with the expected revenues	3	4	3	3	3	1
We can get the necessary access to sales & support resources	1	4	4	2	1	2
The channel partner can offer the necessary professional services	0	1	3	2	0	0
...						
Sum	13	22	25	17	11	9

Working with Value Added Distributors (VAD)

If you've decided that you want to work with a VAD, you'll have to identify the one that best suits your needs. If you've already identified a number of VADs as potential partners, you need to research them more carefully and start the qualification process. Many of the things I list also apply to other types of distribution partners.

Qualification

I recommend that you look at the following typical parameters:

VAD's reasoning: Every VAD that wants to work with a new manufacturer should explain in detail why this will be beneficial for both parties. Typical reasons are that the VAD needs to replace an existing vendor (perhaps due to low margins, slow sales, customer complaints or simply because the vendor has terminated the contract), or they want to enter a new market segment, or they need an additional vendor to offer an alternative solution, or they've received many requests from their customer base (e.g. the VARs) - which is usually the best reason.

If the VAD can't provide a specific reason why you as a vendor are important to them, then it will be difficult to make this partnership successful. It's therefore essential during the initial discussions that the vendor "listens" to the VAD and doesn't just present their company, their products and what value they can bring to the VAD and resellers. Smaller vendors particularly tend to take this approach. Even by the time the contracts are signed, they often know next to nothing about the VAD's interests, needs and strengths.

VAD business model: Try to understand the VAD's business model and how they position their company. Does the VAD focus on reselling the solution with the main objective of making margins on the products or do they try to sell more services (implementation, consulting, training, support)? If the VAD is focused on reselling, then they'll want to have standardized, well known products with short sales cycles that allow many units to be moved in a very short time. In this case, the resellers need to know the product because they will have to cover all the sales and support work. Most VADs who follow this business model are very marketing driven, have predominantly inside sales people and only a few people with deep technical knowledge.

If the approach is more consultative and the VAD wants to make their margin on services, then more complex solutions in an early lifecycle with a need for education and implementation services will be their focus. These VADs often have account managers and pre-sales consultants on board who can help their resellers throughout long and complex sales cycles. These VADs expect the manufacturers to provide education material, guidelines for implementation and support.

As a manufacturer you have to decide which business model fits your solution best. Very often, manufacturers don't understand their VAD's business model and then wonder why the results don't match their expectations.

Competitive solutions represented by the VAD: Find out which competitive solutions the VAD has in their portfolio and why? Analyze how they offer these solutions and what their market position is compared to yours.

I've already listed some reasons explaining why a VAD might want to replace solutions from other vendors. On the other hand, many VADs want to represent a whole product range within one market segment and therefore they need to carry all the important vendors. Another reason might be that the existing manufacturer has grown too large and the VAD foresees problems in the long term, but can't replace the leading solution due to high market demand. Often, existing solutions will start to develop into new directions or won't support special technologies anymore (e.g. operating systems or storage devices). It's also not unusual for the pressure to come from the reseller's side. Some resellers may not be able to fulfill their quotas to reach a specific partner level, especially with larger manufacturers (e.g. in terms of revenue or making the necessary investment in education). The resellers will therefore push for the product offered by a smaller ISV to be included in the VAD's product range. This will allow them to sell the product and reach a high status with the smaller ISV.

Internal sponsor: Do you have an internal sponsor? This means, does somebody in the VAD's organization support your business? What is this sponsor's role and how big is their influence on your business? It's especially useful in the beginning of a relationship that someone in the VAD headquarter supports the manufacturer and that this person has an influence on the business. It can help if you know someone on the VAD's board, but this person must show their commitment to the joint success.

Very often, the product managers or technical support people are the most helpful. They can convince and motivate the sales team to sell your product. It's even better if the sponsor has a personal goal connected to the success with the product. This can, for example, be a revenue oriented goal; perhaps winning 20 new resellers within 3 months or generating 3 reference cases. If there are personal goals connected to your success, this really shows commitment from the VAD and it represents the first win in your business relationship.

Access to VAD sales team: One of the most important aspects is your access to the VAD sales team. Many VADs make sure that the manufacturers receive limited or no access to the sales team. There are different reasons for this. Most VADs carry a large number of products and if every manufacturer was able to talk to the sales team, there wouldn't be enough time for them to sell. Another reason is that the VAD prefers to control the relationship between the manufacturers and the sales team. What is good for the manufacturer and the sales team isn't necessarily so great for the VAD. A typical example of this is when a VAD only gets a small margin from the manufacturer and wants to sell other products with a higher margin. In this case, the VAD's sales team has a specific compensation model and the VAD wants to avoid a situation where the sales get spiffed aggressively.

The challenge for every manufacturer is that, in the end, it's the sales team that sells the products to the resellers. If they don't promote your product, it will be nearly impossible to leverage the VAD's reseller network. So as a manufacturer, you need to make sure that you are given access to the sales team.

Costs of working together: It's necessary to be aware of the costs and have the budget in place when you start working with a new VAD. Within the last couple of years, distributors have become very creative and have developed programs in which the manufacturers can participate. This participation always costs money which comes from the manufacturer's marketing budget and is called "market development funding" (MDF). I'll come back to MDF later. Apart from the costs for MDF, there are other costs associated when working with a VAD. The manufacturer must be aware of these costs and assign a value them.

VADs normally get a bigger discount than resellers. Smaller vendors are even asked to give the VAD an additional 20% - 30% on top of the discount the reseller would receive. In the software business, this can be 40% or more (instead of 25%).

Other costs are additional discounts for reaching specific goals or for special deals. Very often, goals are defined and if the VAD reaches these goals, they get an additional 2% - 5% discount. These will be used for targeted promotions, like competitive upgrades or a discount that is given only to a special customer group such as the public sector or for limited offers such as "end of month" discounts. Even if the manufacturer agrees to these additional discounts, they have to be careful not to pay twice; firstly for advertising the promotion and then again when giving the discount.

Stock rotation is the next cost category worth mentioning. Even if it's understandable from the VAD's point of view, it's often not necessary and unacceptable from an ISV's point of view. If the VAD buys a certain quantity of the product in order to get better discounts and make more margin, then the consequence should be a "no return" policy. Free upgrades for the next version or the newest product should be included, but if there are costs involved, the manufacturer has to be clear who covers these costs.

Many distributors argue that they should get a funded head, which is someone dedicated to promoting the manufacturer's product. In many cases, this makes a lot of sense and if the VAD doesn't treat the funded head as a profit centre, then this is something a manufacturer should consider. If there is a dedicated person with access to the VAD's database and to the sales and marketing team, then funded heads can bring good value. I'll look at the pros and cons of a funded head in more detail later. By the way, you can download a draft funded head contract at www.channel-revolution.com.

Another service that many VADs like getting paid for is reporting. This often includes basic reporting showing what products were sold to which resellers (sell out report) or some form of analysis such as which products were sold along with the manufacturer's product. From my point of view, it's totally unacceptable to pay for these basic reports. It's understandable, however, that additional analyses which can be used in other channels are not provided free of charge.

When the manufacturer develops their business plan, they must take every possible cost into consideration and look at what they will receive in return.

Necessary MDF: Many VADs will not start working with an ISV without an MDF (market development funding) commitment. It's simple, you have to "pay to play". Typical services included within the MDF are mailings, banners and advertisements. Every MDF activity needs to be controlled by the manufacturer and assigned resources. Remember, doing something once is not enough. You have to achieve frequency. So be prepared to undertake multiple activities and don't expect a huge ramp up after the first activity. If you've just begun working with a new VAD and have started educating their sales people or started approaching their resellers, you'll notice that everyone is waiting for the first success story. Most sales / resellers will have seen quite a few vendors come and go. There's a lot of skepticism that the manufacturer needs to overcome. So plan conservatively and make sure you don't run out of steam. Don't invest all the money in a big bang and expect huge returns. It won't happen.

Very often, the VADs offer to do newsletters or joint advertisements. This means that the manufacturer can promote their products in the VAD's newsletter or magazine or carry out a joint advertisement in another magazine. Before a manufacturer spends money on these activities, they should analyze the potential (and realistic) results. The truth is that these "indirect" activities help the VAD build their own brand. For larger, well known manufacturers this can be worthwhile because if the VAD strengthens their brand and increases their revenue, the manufacturer will be the one who profits the most. A newer, unknown manufacturer, however, will not benefit from these activities.

There is something, which I really recommend doing though, namely sending target emails to a specific group of resellers. This makes total sense if you want to win new resellers in a specific territory. Most VADs have a well maintained reseller database and can target them by region, product group, size etc. Before you email these resellers, create a clear message, a landing page and make sure that someone follows up on these resellers. If they sign in on your website, you should be prepared to supply "not for resale" (NFR) keys, product demos and support. You won't believe how many manufacturers pay for e-mailings but don't install a follow-up process. What a waste of time and money! Actually, this can even have a negative effect, because the resellers (the "innovators" as you might remember) who have contacted the manufacturer and don't receive a reply will be annoyed (to put it mildly).

Many VADs have an internal order system (intranet), where manufacturers can create landing pages. This means everyone from the VAD (sales, marketing, support) and their resellers can get more information about the manufacturer, their product, success stories, support etc. Having an information base such as this is extremely helpful and all manufacturers should consider doing it. It's also usually not very costly.

Access to the sales team is one of the most important success factors from the manufacturer's point of view. As I already mentioned, most distributors want to limit access to their sales team. But they have also become creative and will offer packages to the manufacturers which give them access to the sales team. Table tops, internal presentations or participation in in-house events are some of these activities. However, it makes almost no sense for a new manufacturer to present their product to the entire sales team in just a few minutes. It's much smarter to focus instead on a specific group of sales people. For example, focus on the enterprise software sales team in a particular region, find a sponsor and make them successful. Once a few sales have been generated, you'll have reference cases and the word will spread. Next thing, other sales people will approach you to learn more about the product.

Incentives are another helpful tool. These are often termed spiff programs. Again, usually VADs won't allow incentives or they will charge for setting up a spiff program in their system. Before you set up a program to incentivize someone, you have to define the targets of the program; are they technical, sales or marketing people. Very often, technical people are driven by learning new technologies or receiving easy access to the manufacturers support staff, while sales people are mostly money driven.

Always keep in mind that technical people will recommend what they know and what they can support, and sales people will always look for the easiest sale and making the most money (if this becomes a tradeoff they will go for the money). Marketing people can be motivated with education (sponsored training) or other incentives such as travel, gift cards etc. In the beginning especially, the manufacturer should push for giving some special incentives to a dedicated group of people. These incentives should be very motivational, even if it means the manufacturer hardly makes money on the first product sales. But this shouldn't be the goal; the goal must be that everyone realizes the products are saleable. The worst case scenario is, if there are no sales for a long time.

Whatever marketing program a manufacturer uses, one thing is pretty clear: without a marketing budget, it'll be very difficult to become successful with a new VAD. I recommend using an easy rule: the newer the relationship and the weaker the brand of the manufacturer is, the more direct each marketing activity should be. If the relationship is more mature, some success stories already exist or the manufacturer has a strong brand, then a broader target group can be addressed.

Investments from the VAD: Investments from the VAD are also necessary for a successful partnership. Typical investments from the VAD can be listing the manufacturer's products, letting the manufacturer educate their team, conducting training workshops for a peer group of resellers and working with the manufacturer on a viable business plan. I would not expect that the VAD actually invests money, but even not charging for something or cutting their margins on the first deals to make special offers is a good sign.

The definition of goals is extremely important for every partnership. I've already described how to develop a channel partner account plan. This can also be used when working with a new VAD (with slight modifications). It's absolutely essential that the manufacturer and the VAD are clear about their goals and both show a 100% commitment to reaching these goals. Then the next step is putting an action plan into place. Simply agreeing on the goals is not enough, you need to define milestones and be specific about activities and responsible individuals.

VAD Action Plan

Before I get into the action plan, I want to say again that I believe a manufacturer shouldn't work with too many VADs at once. Often, one is enough. If a manufacturer doesn't have the resources to make these VADs successful or increase the market demand fast enough, then the market becomes over distributed. This means that everyone selling the product starts competing on price, which is not a healthy market development. So if you've gone through the qualification, please select one or two VADs to work with. This means coming up with an action plan. A typical action plan should describe the action and objective (what are the goals for this action), have a dedicated direct responsible person (DRI – this person should be from the manufacturer's side) and someone who is responsible for the implementation. There should be defined milestones and a status update. The action plan should be shared between the partners (the manufacturer and the VAD) and should be part of the contract. Very often, market development fails due to a lack of resources. Within the quarterly review it will become clear if both partners are contributing the described resources.

Example for an action plan

VAD Action Plan						
Action	Objective	DRI	Implementation by	Next Milestone Date / Milestone		Status Update / Comments
Create mailers to target re-sellers from the VAD - build landing pages for each group of resellers.	Start attracting new resellers, position the solution and make them sign in for the channel program.	CMM	VAD eMarketing Manager	15-Mar	Send Mailers.	Commitment from VAD that they will send out emails.
3 new, "solid" resellers each week (two contacts minimum within each of them).	Increase number of resellers who can buy on a regular Basis. Focus on small system builders/VAR with larger customer base.	PAM	PAM	12-Mar	Get information about new sign-ins.	Marketing has started research on potential resellers.

VAD Action Plan						
Action	Objective	DRI	Implementation by	Next Milestone Date / Milestone		Status Update / Comments
Every POS (Point of Sale) reseller contacted and given basic information about company products (two contacts minimum from each).	Qualify new resellers who have bought from the VAD, make sure talking to the right person - increase address base and make sure they understand the solution.	PAM	PAM	18-Mar	Build Presentation.	Still waiting on the report from the VAD.
Try to educate and certify all partners (past and future) who have bought from this VAD.	Technical and sales training to the channel partners - certify them to next partner level.	PAM	Training & Support	22-Mar	Set up and offer training for the resellers.	Offering will be ready on time.

PAM = Partner Account Manager

CMM = Channel Marketing Manager

Monitoring

Goals must be defined, action plans must be worked out and marketing initiatives must be started. Money and resources must be invested. Monitoring doesn't only mean checking if the goals have been reached but evaluating the use of resources as well as channeling new information back into the channel. Nobody can perfectly forecast the market's reaction to a new offer. Typically, new competitors will appear, new products will be released or market trends will differ from the forecast. It's important that you adjust your plans to the actual situation. If things go well, you might have to adjust your forecast upwards because more resellers than expected started selling your product.

Continue/Terminate

The last stage continue/terminate should really be executed by both partners. There are no guarantees when you start working with a new VAD, but there is a guarantee that if you don't terminate unhealthy partnerships and don't start working with someone different, the competition will overtake you. On the other hand, if a relationship works out very well, think about what you can do to leverage this relationship and increase sales with this VAD. During this stage, you'll need to analyze the business in detail. Why did it fail? Or, hopefully: Why was it successful? Do the analysis together with the VAD - everyone can learn a lot from this discussion.

If the business failed, then it's worthwhile to find out why. Wrong partner? Wrong channel? Was the competition too strong or big? Were there not enough resources or simply no teamwork? This analysis is decisive for what you do next. Are you going to continue approaching this market or will you try the approach using another VAD or another channel? Maybe you'll find out that the product is not "localized" enough, more local support is required or that strong local competitors exist. If you don't know the reasons for the failure in the first phase, you shouldn't start the same game again with another player.

Hopefully though, the partnership was successful and you reached your goals. What's next? Find answers to the following questions: Can you improve your market share in this market or should you enter new markets? What were the reasons for your success? Perhaps the VAD sold a similar solution in the past and the resellers replaced this solution with yours. Another reason could be that you won some very reputable clients and you were able to generate a lot of noise in the market with these reference cases. Based on your analysis, you can decide what your next steps should be; maybe you have to take on another VAD to increase your market reach or you could grow with the same VAD, maybe you've only worked with their team responsible for the Midwest and now you can spread the results from this reference story to other teams.

In any case, adjust your goals and action plan each quarter. If you don't see the trend moving in your direction, then don't wait too long - change your strategy quickly.

In the channel business, it's all about analytical forecasting after a short ramp up period. If you planned to grow by 50 new channel partners each quarter, but you only got five, then something is wrong - either your strategy or your execution.

Deal Registration

Another way to increase sales is deal registration. So definitely pursue this topic. It's particularly relevant when dealing with project oriented resellers but can also be effective with product oriented resellers.

If a manufacturer provides products that have a longer sales cycle and they work with channel partners that add their own professional services or products to offer a total solution, then sooner or later, questions about deal registration or deal protection will come up. The same situation arises when product oriented resellers work on large tenders - especially with VAD tenders for the government.

Most channel partners will only register deals if they need additional help from the manufacturer or a direct interaction between the ISV and the end customer is required. If no help is needed or the channel partner can "hide" the end customer's name, most of them will do so. Some manufacturers offer additional discounts for registered deals, free training or other benefits. My experience with deal registration is that channel partners will do it to make sure that they receive exclusive support from the manufacturer so that they can demonstrate to the end customer how great their relationship with the manufacturer is.

When it comes to deal registration, there are some important criteria to address. Good deal registration programs must be easy to use, protect the channel partner's information and must show the benefits for the channel partners. A deal registration program can have huge benefits for manufacturers; they find out which partners work on bigger deals and they can help when the deal reaches the critical stages. As a result, registered deals will be closed with a much higher probability. I recommend installing a web-based system (as part of the partner portal), where channel partners can register all deals that have a minimum deal size and will be closed within 90 days. This is good practice.

There will always be some channel partners who want to make sure they don't waste money in a presales phase. These channel partners will talk to the PAM and try to find out if they can get exclusive support from the ISV. Before agreeing to this, the PAM has to carefully evaluate if the channel partner has a realistic chance of winning the deal. If this is the case, the partner should register the deal.

A situation that typically occurs is that an end customer already knows which product they want and asks different system integrators to submit proposals for a solution based on this product. This inspires system integrators to want to become a reseller and register the deal. But be careful. If you as the manufacturer support this new system integrator over an already existing channel partner, you may lose your existing channel partner.

If a conflict arises in an incident where two or more channel partners are working on the same deal (a situation most manufactures enjoy because their chance of winning is higher), clear rules must be put in place. I suggest giving equal support to all channel partners who register a deal within a certain period before closing. If this is not possible because a lot of customer interaction is called for or the manufacturer doesn't have the resources, you need rules that stipulate who will be supported. I always advise to support the first partner that registers a deal. But this recommendation can backfire if it's obvious that the faster partner is less likely to win.

Key Performance Indicators (KPI)

I already addressed some key trends in the channel business. A common saying (especially in the investment industry) is "the trend is your friend." Closely watching trends is one of the most significant factors for increasing sales. This means you need to have a reporting system in place that gives you the necessary information for analyzing these trends.

You can't manage what you can't measure! If you don't have access to some key numbers, it will be difficult to define actions for improvement. Management by "gut feeling" alone will always fail in the channel business. If you're in discussions with your channel team or channel partners and want to see them make changes, you'll have to base your arguments on hard facts (= numbers).

Following is a brief explanation of the KPIs I recommend using.

Time from lead distribution to action and to feedback

How long does it take for a channel partner to follow up on a lead and how is the quality of their feedback? If the follow up and feedback take too long, leads become "cold" and it's only the "hot" leads that have a high conversion rate. Channel partners that take too long and have a poor success rate with leads shouldn't be given any more leads. But don't do this silently - communicate with the channel partner and with your team and find out where the problem is. I'm a believer in putting your cards on the table - meaning that you shouldn't hold back information if you think things aren't going well with a partner.

Leads to sale conversion

Another insightful indicator is the "lead to sale" conversion rate. The following questions need to be answered:

- Are direct sales people closing more leads than the channel partners?
- Which channel partners are converting the most leads to sales?
- How many leads are still open after 30, 60, 90 days?
- Which sources produce the best leads?

It seems strange to be comparing direct sales people with channel partners; but in fact, in many organizations a direct sales force exists that operates in a specific area, on a defined account or simply competes with the channel partners in some areas. In this case, it's obviously necessary to have defined rules regarding who gets the leads. It's also important to compare the closing rates of these leads. This is particularly useful if the manufacturer has just started to work with a channel partner and wants to switch from a direct to an indirect business model. Only the channel partners who achieve good closing rates should continue getting leads.

In order to control the sales funnel, the manufacturer should analyze which leads are still open after a certain amount of time and why. Where are these leads coming from? Which lead source produces the best / worst quality? You can define the lead quality using many factors; closing rate, average sales cycle, revenue per sales, costs of lead generation. Continue activities that meet the following requirements: (1) they generate leads that can be converted to revenues; (2) the revenues significantly exceed the costs of lead generation /sales.

Revenue by geography or market segment

The revenue generated per geographic region or market segment reveals where a manufacturer has presence and where they don't. In the US there are approximately 50 metropolitan regions. If a major portion of the deals come from the Northeast, but there are almost no deals in the Midwest, then it's important to analyze the reasons for this situation. One of the most successful activities for growing the channel is to leverage success.

Compare channel partners' sales cycles and average deal sizes

Each partner has a distinct business model and sells different products and solutions. Therefore, their sales approaches will vary. This means that there can be significant variations between the channel partners in terms of sales cycles, closing rates and revenue per sale.

It's important to compare the average sales cycles and the average deal sizes - not only concerning your product, but also in terms of what the channel partner is selling along with your products. It makes a difference if your product is 10% of the whole deal or 50% and if the total deal size is US$100,000 or US$ 10,000. The bigger the deal, the longer the sales cycle. But a long sales cycle isn't necessarily a bad thing. If your closing rate with partners with long sales cycles is superior, then it's worth working with these partners. On the other hand, if your closing rate for long sales cycle leads is poor, you should give your leads to product oriented resellers and avoid the pre-sales costs.

I really have to emphasize the impact of analyzing these indicators. My experience is that many smaller vendors don't actually have a functioning reporting system and therefore are managing their channel blindly. As a result, they undertake activities with the wrong partners, have unnecessarily long discussions and hardly ever make any real improvements. Proper reporting systems are often one of the major differences between larger and smaller manufacturers.

Revenue and Deal Forecasts

The channel forecast meeting is the counterpart of the sales forecast meeting. Creating an accurate forecast is actually one of the most challenging aspects of channel business. It's definitely more difficult than in direct sales. A key account manager handling direct sales talks to the end user and can make a fairly predictable forecast. The PAM on the other hand has to work very closely with the channel partners and rely on their input.

Revenue forecast - project oriented resellers

Every PAM should make sure that the actual status of each sizable opportunity from their project based channel partners is included in the forecast list. What you consider sizeable depends on your business but I would recommend listing every opportunity with a license volume of US$10,000 or more. All other smaller partners, product based resellers or distributors should be listed as described in the next section

Many PAMs complain that they don't know the exact status of the leads because of missing information from their channel partners. If this is the case, their total forecast, which is the volume of all projects they assume will close within a particular timeframe, can't be accurate. However, there are many reasons why you shouldn't accept this excuse. One is that a PAM can work with many channel partners and these channel partners can each work on many deals. This means that they can work with more channel partners and leverage the forecast - something you basically can't do in direct account management. A direct account manager can only work on a certain number of deals. They also need to have a higher closing rate to reach their quota because of the time invested in every deal. The channel provides another advantage; usually channel partners have better relationships to the prospects and better vertical knowledge. This makes the chance of closing the deal much higher.

As described earlier in the book, the pipeline is made up of prospects at various stages in the sales process. In order to get viable information from your PAM, you need to define milestones for the pipeline which are to be regularly assessed throughout each project. You should at least make sure the following information is included:

- Prospect name (account name).
- Partner involved (name of the channel partner).
- Opportunity (what is this opportunity about?).
- Action items for winning this opportunity - are there issues that need to be resolved before moving forward?
- Sales stage - make sure that you can see the movement over the last couple of weeks.
- Closing date (when the opportunity is expected to close).
- Total revenue in US$ (or whatever your currency is) - this should be the revenue related to your business (especially li-

censes, professional services and education), but you should also know the total deal size. Either make a separate column or include this in the description of the opportunity.

- Chance of success - this should be related to the sales stage (this has been described earlier in the book).
- Weighted revenue in US$ (total revenue multiplied by the chance of success factor).

If you have an ERP/CRM system, then a forecast should be created automatically from the system. If the sales team enter their data in a spreadsheet, then it's important to make sure that they all work on the same spreadsheet and that there is an easy way to enter the data. If they have to enter too much data or it's difficult to get access to then the data will never be accurate.

A sales forecast report (see the example below) gives you a good overview of your current sales projects. It's easy to filter by channel manager or by channel partner or by sales stage and closure date. If there is other information that is important to you such as the product or region then you should add this to the report.

Pipeline report for project oriented resellers

Based on the entry for each project in the pipeline report, it should be possible to understand where the projects sit in the pipeline, to assess each project's status and if necessary to define further steps for closing the gap between the goals defined in the business plan and the sales forecast.

While you're analyzing the pipeline, your focus should be on the partners' deals that have a high closure rate and the fast moving opportunities (these are the most likely to close quickly). Opportunities with partners who are either new or have a low closure rate should be separated and weighted lower.

Major Bids/Must Wins (sorted first by Partner, then Close Date, Revenue and Chance of Success)
Closing Period: Q2 2010
Region: US
Date: 31-Mar-10

Account	Partner Involved	Opportunity	Action/ Issue (next Step)	Sales Stage			Today	Close Date	Total Rev. in US$	Chance of Success	Weighted Rev. in US$
				8 Weeks before	4 Weeks before	2 Weeks before					
American Best-Fly	NetDevelopment, MA	Replace existing Storage Solution	Proof of Concept with R&D Executives 5th April 10	2	4	4	8	31-May-10	$230,000	75%	$173
Business Air	NetDevelopment, MA	Add. licenses for new location	Getting official RFP 12th April 10	2	3	3	4	15-Jun-10	$80,000	20%	$16
Retail4All	Best World Consulting, CA	Add Online Backup to their Offering	Joint Meeting with Buying Center 10th April 10	4	4	4	6	30-Jun-10	$450,000	40%	$180
LuckyStar Casinos	Best World Consulting, CA	50 Server Lic. for new site	Presentation of Prototype 18th April 10	4	4	4	7	31-Jul-10	$150,000	60%	$90
Worldtire Corp.	TechGuys, TX	Replace existing Storage Infrastructure	Final Contract Disc. with Partner&Customer 21st April 10	1	2	2	8	28-Aug-10	$200,000	75%	$150
ChinaTrade	Oasis Group, RI	DataProtection for their salesforce	Development of Specifications 30th April 10	2	3	3	3	15-Sep-10	$240,000	10%	$24
								Total	$1,350,000		$632,500

This might seem like a lot of work, and it can be. But it's a vital part of every channel manager's job. Channel managers must put pressure on their PAMs to ensure that the forecasts are in line with the business plans. Don't accept inaccurate forecasts - these simply reveal that something is wrong in your channel organization.

Revenue forecast - product oriented resellers

The forecast structure should be different, if you are forecasting revenue with product based resellers. Product oriented resellers such as distributors, DMRs or e-tailers aren't usually aware of every single opportunity - they are driven by demand. This demand comes from new product releases, marketing pushes or it might be a business trend of a particular distributor. The role of the PAM is also different when working with product oriented resellers; they have to make sure they have the information in order to steer demand and they must really push your product.

For this type of pipeline report, I suggest including the following columns as a minimum requirement:

- Channel partner (name of the channel partner).
- Forecast comment/special opportunities - all additional information that is needed for the actual forecast. If special business opportunities exist they should be entered here also.

- Action to reach forecast - which activities are planned for reaching the forecast (special marketing events, trainings, new products etc.)?
- Last 12 months/average month - the average revenue over the last 12 months.
- Last quarter/average month - the average revenue over the last 3 months.
- Last month - last month's revenue.
- Forecast - the forecast for the current month.

The table[74] below provides an example forecast. I'll explain how to analyze the information a little later. I recommend listing each of the larger product oriented resellers separately and grouping the smaller ones together. It's important to define the activities that are planned for reaching the forecast and to analyze if the forecast is in line with the general trend over the last 12 months.

Your PAM will enter this information based on their communication with the reseller, the trend over the last months and their knowledge about the market. This will lead to a more solid overview rather than a forecast that is just based on gut feeling. You're probably thinking: "Hey, everybody uses numbers for their forecasts", but deep down you know that a lot of people actually don't or don't base them on any hard facts at all!

Pipeline report for product oriented resellers

If you look at the below example, you'll see a positive revenue trend, which is what we all want to see. If this isn't the case, however, then dig deeper and analyze what's happening. Make sure your channel team has the right contacts at the resellers and that there is commitment from the reseller's side also. Conduct periodical, face-to-face meetings and show these resellers that the channel team is backed by management.

---

[74] The table is available for download at www.channel-revolution.com.

Pipeline Product Oriented Resellers
Closing Period: Q2 2010
Region: US
Date: 31-Mar-10

Channel Partner	Forecast Comment / Special Opportunities	Action to Reach Forecast	Last 12 Months/ avg. Month in US$	Last Quarter/ avg. Month in US$	Last Month in US$	Forecast in US$
EastCost Distribution, MA	Business consistently growing because more resellers signing up	Reseller Certification Newsletter	$180,000	$210,000	$230,000	$250,000
Best Software Deals, NY	Not a focus product, but steady promotions	Web advertisements Product Specials	$75,000	$80,000	$85,000	$80,000
Value Deals Inc, CA	No special deal this month - Gov. has budget freeze	Follow up existing customers	$150,000	$75,000	$250,000	$120,000
New World Comp., TX	Focus product - replacing comp. solution	Competitive Upgrade Offer - Push Mailers	$50,000	$150,000	$180,000	$250,000
Other Resellers	Based on their forecast and general trend	Whitelabel Marketing New Release	$450,000	$500,000	$550,000	$75,0000
		Total	$905,000	$1,015,000	$1,295,000	$1,450,000

Pipeline Analysis

Once the information about the project and product oriented resellers has been entered, you should have a good overview of the forthcoming month. But this is only the beginning of pipeline analysis. Real pipeline analysis goes much deeper and will provide you with information that can help you manage and optimize your channel business.

Real pipeline analysis is one of the most underestimated instruments in channel business (probably for all other business areas as well) and many companies avoid conducting these meetings because of a lack of knowledge, availability of numbers or simply a lack of time. In this chapter, I'll focus on what real pipeline analysis entails and why it's vital for reaching the objectives in your business plans and growing your channel. I'll also explain how to automate the weekly creation of a pipeline report and how you can save time when analyzing the information.

The goals of pipeline analysis are forecasting revenue, comparing the forecast with your objectives and defining actions to close the gap if necessary.

The different elements of pipeline analysis

In order to analyze a channel pipeline efficiently, you need to break down the numbers in at least two different ways, one by review period (e.g. calendar year) and the other by PAM.

The "Pipeline Development 2010" table below shows the development of the total pipeline within the reviewed period.

Pipeline Development 2010

Project Oriented Resellers Pipeline I Stages		CW 03 2010		CW 07 2010		CW 09 2010		CW 10 2010	
		US $	#Opps	US $	#Opps	US $	#Opps	US $	#Opps
Prospecting (0%)		1059	28	1144	30	1078	27	1104	31
Potential Lead (0%)		693	30	599	27	565	25	565	25
Qualification (10%)		513	23	453	22	438	21	342	19
Cover the Buying Centre (20%)		555	6	345	7	338	5	279	5
Proposal (25%)		227	10	173	6	138	5	200	7
Short Listed (40%)		130	13	168	13	190	14	165	12
Selected (60%)		171	25	153	24	128	21	114	22
Negotiation (75%)		282	24	275	23	358	24	382	21
Won (100%)		442	67	483	73	480	72	479	72
Lost (0%)		30	2	60	3	60	3	65	4
Pipeline I Total		4,102	228	3,853	228	3,773	217	3,695	218
Pipeline I Weighted	avg opps#	1,026	18	1,005	17	1,049	17	1,040	17
Product Oriented Resellers Pipeline II Weighted		1,200	5	1,250	5	1,295	5	1,450	5
Total Pipeline Weighted		2,226	23	2,255	22	2,344	22	2,490	22
Results 01.01.2010-30.06.2010	%Obj	420	14%	470		510		550	
Objective 01.01.2010-30.06.2010		3,000		3,000		3,000		3,000	
To Be Done	%Pipe	2,580	116%	2,530	112%	2,490	106%	2,450	98%
Estimate (MD/VP Sales)		3,500		3,200		3,000		2,500	
GAP Objective	%Obj	-500	-14%	-200	-6%	0	0%	500	20%

(Left margin labels: License & Services; Pipeline; Revenue)

I recommend that the reviewed period starts either with a calendar year or with a new quarter. The chart shows the total pipeline, which is a summary of all deals your channel team is working on and also includes the prospected revenue from the product oriented resellers (distributors, e-tailers etc.). The overview should be built in such a way that it includes the development over the last couple of months. I advise that it shows how the pipeline looked 3 months ago, 6 weeks ago, last month, two weeks ago and within the current week. Using this information, it's easy to get an overview of the total development.

The second table is the "Pipeline Development by PAM". This shows you the actual pipeline of each PAM and gives you an overview of who has the most valid opportunities, the actual results of each PAM and who has the best chance to reach their quota or who has the biggest gap to close.

Pipeline I Stages		CW 010 2010		PAM 1		PAM 2		PAM 3		PAM 4	
		US $	#Opps	US $	#Opps	US $	#Opps	US $	#Opps	US $	#Opps
Prospecting (0%)		1104	31	164	7	0	0	668	15	272	9
Potential Lead (0%)		565	25	52	2	31	3	60	2	0	0
Qualification (10%)		342	19	85	4	8	1	72	4	50	1
Cover the Buying Centre (20%)		279	5	0	0	135	5	254	3	0	0
Proposal (25%)		200	7	40	1	8	1	0	0	6	2
Short Listed (40%)		165	12	35	1	15	1	0	0	0	0
Selected (60%)		114	22	0	0	58	8	0	0	11	2
Negotiation (75%)		382	21	0	0	8	1	84	9	70	6
Won (100%)		479	72	0	0	49	12	0	0	0	0
Lost (0%)		65	4	0	0	0	0	0	0	0	0
Pipeline I Total		3,695	218	306	12	312	32	1,055	26	259	15
Pipeline I Weighted	avg opps#	1,040	17	33	26	126	10	138	41	65	17
Results 01.01.2010-30.06.2010	%Obj	44		0	0	18	18	18	18	8	8
To Be Done	%Pipe	800	32%	0	0%	192	58%	282	26%	212	69%
Estimate (MD/VP Sales)	%1	800		0		210		300		220	
GAP Objective	%Obj	700		0		140		300		230	
Objective 01.01.2010-30.06.2010	%Obj	1,500		0		350		600		450	

(Left axis labels: License & Services — Pipeline; Revenue)

This chart is an instrument for analyzing the situation of every single PAM. Sales managers, who are familiar with this type of pipeline analysis, can see with just a glance who provided the updated information for the pipeline, which of the PAMs has the most serious forecast and who has the most deals in a critical sales stage.

Even if your forecast system is built on spreadsheets, it's possible to generate different perspectives and analyze the information for every deal in further detail. This enables a sales manager to supply accurate forecasts to their management. Even if the forecast isn't as good as management expects, it's much better than supplying an inaccurate forecast and ending up with surprises. Instead of managing the channel blindly, the status is transparent and decisions can be made for how to reach the goals.

Of course, every pipeline needs to be constructed differently. You can download my examples at www.channel-revolution.com and modify them to suit your needs.

How to read a pipeline report

The tables contain a lot of information and I think it may be useful to explain the different fields in a little more detail.

Pipeline: By definition, a pipeline is an aggregation of all opportunities with a scheduled end date given in the report. An opportunity is defined as the expected revenue within a deal and normally includes product and service revenue.

Weighted pipeline: The weighted pipeline is the opportunity revenue weighted against the win probability (sales stage) assigned to each opportunity. For example, if the opportunity has a total volume of US$100k and it's in the short listing phase which has a 25% win probability, then the weighted value of this opportunity is US$25k.

#opps is the total number of opportunities in this stage or in the total pipeline.

avg. opps#: The average opportunity number is the value of the total pipeline divided by the number of opportunities. The average opportunity value is the total weighted pipeline divided by the number of opportunities. This represents the average size of an opportunity.

Pipeline II Weighted: In the channel business, a pipeline report often needs to be broken down according to different parameters. In my example (Pipeline Development 2010), the pipeline represents the forecast for project oriented resellers and for product oriented resellers. To enable an individual assessment of each group, I've created an additional category within the report called Pipeline II Weighted which summarizes the forecast for the product oriented resellers.

Results: The second component of any pipeline report is the revenue section (show me the money!). This section begins with the category "Results" which is the current revenue on signed orders and issued invoices. This revenue shows what has already been reached.

%Obj: The percentage %Obj shows how much of the objective has already been achieved.

Objective: The next line is Objective which shows the revenue target (your goal!). This should reflect the business plan and the budget.

Pending Revenue ("To be done") is the estimate minus today's results and shows how much revenue needs to be generated in order to reach the estimate of the manager (sales manager or managing director).

% Pipe shows the revenue that has to be achieved in relation to the existing weighted pipeline. If this percentage is higher than 100% then it shows that the objective can't be reached with the existing pipeline.

Estimate: This estimate is the estimation by sales management or another senior manager regarding the revenue that will be achieved based on today's pipeline. The estimate is based on the sales managers' experience and should reflect their forecast based on the results achieved and the existing pipeline. Even though this estimate should be very close to the result plus the weighted number, it can be significantly lower if sales management doesn't trust the pipeline or higher if sales management believes the forecast is too conservative.

Gap Objective is the variance between estimate and objective and shows the revenue that needs to be achieved based on the sales manager's prediction. In this context %Obj shows the percentage difference between the estimate and the objective. It's important to show a percentage here, because a number is always absolute. If the objective is US$500 million, then a difference of US$1 million is close to nothing. But if the objective is US$2 million, then this represents 50%. If the objective is negative, then the estimate is higher than the objective - meaning that management is confident about reaching the goals. A positive value means that a real gap exists and you need to do something to increase the pipeline.

A real-world example

Now let me use the table I've provided to walk you through an analysis and explain how you can manage a channel and a channel team. For ease of use, I'll include the table shown earlier again.

Project Oriented Resellers / Pipeline I Stages		CW 03 2010 US $	CW 03 2010 #Opps	CW 07 2010 US $	CW 07 2010 #Opps	CW 09 2010 US $	CW 09 2010 #Opps	CW 10 2010 US $	CW 10 2010 #Opps
Prospecting (0%)		1059	28	1144	30	1078	27	1104	31
Potential Lead (0%)		693	30	599	27	565	25	565	25
Qualification (10%)		513	23	453	22	438	21	342	19
Cover the Buying Centre (20%)		555	6	345	7	338	5	279	5
Proposal (25%)		227	10	173	6	138	5	200	7
Short Listed (40%)		130	13	168	13	190	14	165	12
Selected (60%)		171	25	153	24	128	21	114	22
Negotiation (75%)		282	24	275	23	358	24	382	21
Won (100%)		442	67	483	73	480	72	479	72
Lost (0%)		30	2	60	3	60	3	65	4
Pipeline I Total		**4,102**	**228**	**3,853**	**228**	**3,773**	**217**	**3,695**	**218**
Pipeline I Weighted	avg opps#	**1,026**	**18**	**1,005**	**17**	**1,049**	**17**	**1,040**	**17**
Product Oriented Resellers Pipeline II Weighted		**1,200**	**5**	**1,250**	**5**	**1,295**	**5**	**1,450**	**5**
Total Pipeline Weighted		**2,226**	**23**	**2,255**	**22**	**2,344**	**22**	**2,490**	**22**
Results 01.01.2010-30.06.2010	%Obj	420	14%	470		510		550	
Objective 01.01.2010-30.06.2010		3,000		3,000		3,000		3,000	
To Be Done	%Pipe	**2,580**	**116%**	**2,530**	**112%**	**2,490**	**106%**	**2,450**	**98%**
Estimate (MD/VP Sales)		**3,500**		**3,200**		**3,000**		**2,500**	
GAP Objective	%Obj	**-500**	**-14%**	**-200**	**-6%**	**0**	**0%**	**500**	**20%**

The example uses a time span from calendar week 3 (CW03 mid/end of January) to calendar week 10 (CW10 beginning/mid of March). It's the end of the first quarter and the first three months of the year are already over.

In my example, the goal is to reach US$3 million in the first 6 months (Objective 01.01.2010 - 30.06.2010). In CW03, the total pipeline I (project oriented) is US$4,102k and the weighted pipeline I is US$1,026k with an average opportunity (avg opps#) size of US$18k. Together with the pipeline II (product oriented), the total weighted pipeline is US$2,226k. The results until now are US$420k, which is only 14% of the objective. In order to reach the objective, US$2,580k has to be generated, which represents a challenging 116% of the weighted pipeline. Management is still optimistic and estimates the results for the first six months at US$3.5 million. This means, the gap objective is negative because the forecast is higher than the objective.

A closer look into the pipeline shows that there are more than 200 opportunities and that most of them are either in the first three phases (from prospecting to qualification) or won. Another point of interest is that the average deal size of all won opportunities is only US$6.5k (US$479k / 72 deals). The average deal size in the first stages is close to US$30k. This shows that either the deals have become smaller with each sales stage or that the lead generation process is now able to attract customers with larger average deal sizes. I won't discuss every single figure, but I want to demonstrate what can be learned from a pipeline report like this and show how the channel can be used to improve the situation.

A look at the pipeline in CW07 shows us that the number of opportunities is the same - meaning that there weren't many new opportunities (leads) generated. Within 4 weeks, only 6 new deals were closed, with an average deal volume of around US$7k. This confirms the trend that opportunities become smaller with every step in the sales pipe. If you look even further ahead at CW09 or CW10, there still aren't more deals being closed. In fact, the pipeline is shrinking and movement in the pipeline is generally bad. From CW07 to CW10, only 34 leads move to the next sales stage (565 remain in the sales stage of a "potential lead"). The product oriented pipeline on the other hand has good movement, which makes the total pipeline grow.

The total result is still very bad, since the figures only increase from US$420k in CW03 to US$550k in CW10. Be careful to compare the closed opportunities (Won) with the result. The Results are always booked revenue, while Won only represents the closed opportunities. You might have a situation where channel management is forecasting good results until late into the quarter. However, suddenly at the end of the quarter, they start to reduce the expected project sizes. Your company forecast should therefore take this tendency into account in order to make realistic estimations.

What does this pipeline report show us and what can management do to create more sales? In general, the pipeline shows that there is almost no movement and it's obvious quite early on that it will be very hard to reach the targeted result. If you are serious about reaching the result, the pipeline should be, at minimum, three times bigger than the objective and the deals must continually move from sales stage to sales stage. Another fact that needs to catch your attention is that the average deal size of won opportunities is significantly smaller than the average opportunity in the pipeline.

In a summary, this pipeline reveals the following challenges:

1. The pipeline is not big enough

As soon as channel management identifies the problem that a pipeline is not big enough, they need to react. Increasing the pipeline is a time consuming process and it's important to start the following activities as soon as possible:

- Start lead generation activities.
- Check if an increase of the average opportunity size is possible.
- Work with channel partners if they have other opportunities (maybe they haven't revealed all existing opportunities).

2. There's no movement in the pipeline

If the deals within a pipeline don't move, there's a real problem with the pipeline. This is the case for direct sales, but it's even more relevant to the channel business. A static (nonmoving) pipeline reveals that there is a communication issue between your PAMs and their key partners. In this case, you should take immediate action:

- Analyze the opportunities for each key channel partner.
- Identify the channel partners with the most important deals and verify them.
- Discuss the leads by sales stage in the channel meetings and focus on the PAMs with the most static pipeline.

If movement stops at certain stages, then find out if there are certain points where your sales process is either too complex or if this is the stage where evaluation takes longer because of testing.

3. Opportunities are shrinking

If the opportunities are shrinking with each sales stage, this can reveal some other challenges. Maybe one or all of the following is happening:

- The channel partners don't have enough experience with the service (the channel partner may have never worked with your product or on a similar project) and their estimates are too high in the beginning. If you're working with a distributor, this can also show that the distributor's account manager doesn't know the projects and the channel partners well enough.
- Sometimes, during the test phases, the customers find out that a smaller solution will also fit their needs or they decide to begin with a limited number of users.
- Maybe your channel partner is reducing your portion of the revenue in the project by decreasing the budget dedicated to software and increasing the total paid for their services. This often happens when the end customer will only accept a fixed price budget. In this case, the channel partner either asks the manufacturer for better margins or, if it's possible, they simply reduce the number of licenses in the deal.
- Very often opportunities shrink because of huge discounts (month-end, quarter-end or year-end) applied to close a deal due to time pressure. If channel partners or customers know that you accept their requests for these bigger discounts, they'll wait until the last minute.

Perhaps it's a mixture of the points listed above or there's a totally different reason for the shrinkage. In any case, it's critical to analyze why the size of opportunities is shrinking in the later sales stages. Keep in mind, this is money you could have earned if the aforementioned problems had not arisen and you and your channel partner had still won the deal. If the standard deal size of the "won" opportunities is too small, you should also consider trying to reduce the effort in the total sales process.

4. PAMs are not performing

When a pipeline looks similar to this example, a break down by PAM and deeper analysis is necessary. Typical findings and solutions are:

- Often, when a pipeline contains low numbers, most of the PAMs have similar problems. This indicates there is either a problem with your channel concept, pricing, the market, competition or the products. It should be your top priority to find out where the problem is coming from and solve it.
- If there are some PAMs that are on track, it's important to find out what they are doing differently to the ones who report bad numbers. It could be the quality of the PAM but it can also be that the successful PAMs are serving specific types of resellers. Find out if they are moving specific products, serving dedicated verticals, bundling your product or working in a specific geographic area. On the other hand, if you think it's the quality of the PAM, replace the PAM.
- If some PAMs are successful, it should be possible to solve the channel problem within a relatively short amount of time. If all PAMs are unsuccessful, then you probably have a more general problem and it'll be necessary to conduct deeper analysis.
- Many companies start using a channel when their direct sales are unsuccessful - but in reality, if the vendor can't sell the product nobody can. The same is true the other way around. If the channel can't move a product successfully, a direct sales model can't either.

Dealing with a Static Pipeline

If you're suffering from a static pipeline, you should – together with your channel team – produce a detailed forecast of the current month and quarter based on the pipeline report. You should discuss the most important deals and the wins and losses in detail. Look at the success factors of the partners with the highest closure rate and the challenges facing the partners with the lowest closure rate.

If the main revenue stream is coming from project oriented re-sellers, then another important topic for discussion are the "must win" projects. These are the projects with the highest revenue potential. Make sure that your PAM is on top of these projects and can report detailed information such as sales stage, customer value, next steps, challenges and competition etc.

The analysis of your existing partners should be another topic for discussion. Group your partners into the most important (perhaps the "gold partners" who deliver more than US$5,000 per month) and the "rest", who represent the long tail business. Whilst the first group needs to be managed by the PAMs, the second group should be mostly supported by your standard marketing activities. The PAMs should report which regions the existing successful key partners cover, what kind of business models they have and which verticals they are targeting. They should also present their strategy for farming these existing key partners, demonstrating their annual revenue potential and their action plans.

Channel marketing should report which activities are planned for supporting the PAMs and how they will manage the long tail partners (perhaps with marketing campaigns) and motivate them to buy online. They should show how they will win new key partners by mapping the geographic areas, analyzing the verticals or working on target partner lists. It's important to separate the tasks between the PAMs and channel marketing. I recommend that the PAMs should be 100% sales driven and work on the existing key partners only. Channel marketing should take care of the other partners, creating marketing campaigns and trying to locate new partners. It's only with this kind of separation of roles that you can make sure the PAMs are investing their full effort into getting the pipeline to move.

I could go on here, but want to focus on the key message. Strictly monitoring your sales processes and managing your pipeline is as important for you and your channel partners as developing the right products, targeting the right market and having the right team in place.

Conclusion

Experience is not what happens to a man -
it is what a man does with what happens to him.

Aldous Huxley

Every reader of this book, ISVs in particular, should now be convinced that growth is impossible without the channel. But before you dive into the channel, you need to develop a clear strategy. This not only needs to be realistic and well researched, it also has to be innovative and creative. To put it simply, you need to take a revolutionary approach.

In the good old days, the structure of the channel was far simpler; the ISV sold to the distributor, the distributor sold to the reseller and the reseller sold to the end user. Nowadays, you have to understand the wide range of channel partners that are available to you and how they can be used creatively to expand your business.

In addition, there are many new and exciting trends emerging in the IT world, such as SaaS, that are strongly impacting how products are sold. If you want to build a channel strategy that stands the test of time, you'll have to opt for a multi-channel strategy.

The process of selecting your channel partners requires very close attention. If you don't put good procedures in place for this important phase, you're sure to encounter problems further down the road. Once you've chosen your partners, you can't just list your products and then sit back and wait for the sales to come in. You have to manage, support and push your partners to success. Motivating them and providing incentives is a key success factor. Always remember that the channel is not a one way street. You need to build solid and lasting relationships with your partners and show them that your success will be their success too.

Consistent monitoring and analysis is an essential aspect of any sound channel strategy. You have to put processes and tools in place right from the start that let you measure and assess progress in the channel. How can you improve your revenue if you don't understand how it is being generated? Keep a close eye on the figures at all times.

It was my aim to provide readers with a pragmatic guide to building and maintaining a profitable channel. That's why I included many examples and calculations in the book. Feel free to download them from www.channel-revolution.com and use them to plan your own strategy. Let me know how things go ...

Stefan Utzinger
December 2010

Appendix

The ideas I stand for are not mine. I borrowed them from Socrates. I swiped them from Chesterfield. I stole them from Jesus. And I put them in a book. If you don't like their rules, whose would you use?

Dale Carnegie

Glossary

B2B
Business to Business; a transaction conducted between a business and another business. For example, a software vendor may sell a solution to another company instead of a home user. As these transactions are generally defined by higher demands and often lead to long-term business relations and partnerships, B2B sales are viewed as fundamentally different from B2C sales (see "B2C").

B2C
Business to Customer; a sale between a business and a home user of the product that is sold. For example, a software company may sell a license to a home user who installs the product in a home environment. Home users do not use the product for a professional purpose, which excludes reselling the product as well as implementing it in enterprise infrastructures.

BPO
Business Process Outsourcing; the increasing trend of relocating entire business functions to either self owned or third party service providers, typically in low cost locations.

CAM
Channel Account Manager; a person responsible for making sure certain partners are enabled to achieve optimum results.

Cloud, the

The internet is sometimes referred to as "the cloud", based on how it is depicted in network diagrams.

Cloud computing

Cloud computing is internet-based computing, whereby shared resources, software, and information are provided to computers and other devices on demand (like the electricity grid). Most cloud computing infrastructures consist of services delivered through common centers and built on servers. In general, cloud computing customers do not own the physical infrastructure and avoid capital expenditure by renting usage from a third party provider.

CMM

Channel Marketing Manager; a person who supports partners in their marketing activities, e.g. by creating marketing plans and providing basic material such as data sheets to partners.

COGS

Costs of Goods Sold; the direct costs attributable to the production of the products a company has sold. These costs include the expenses for the materials used in creating the product as well as the direct labor costs associated with the product. Excluded are indirect expenses such as costs for distribution and sales force.

Complementor

A term used to describe businesses that directly sell a product (or products) or service (or services) that turn a product into a complete solution. Complementors complement one product or service of another company by adding other products or services to add value to mutual customers.

CRM

Customer Relationship Management defines in what way a company interacts with customers. Typically, companies use software products to support and document the process for each individual customer.

Deal Registration
Deal registration is a feature of some vendors' channel programs in which a channel partner, often a VAR (value added reseller) or SI (systems integrator), informs the vendor about a lead and is given priority for it. Once a lead is registered with a vendor, the partner usually has a set period of time to close the deal. During this time, other channel members, or even the vendor's own sales team, are not allowed to negotiate a similar deal with that lead.

De-facto standard
A de-facto standard is a technical or other standard that is so dominant that everybody seems to follow it like an authorized standard.

DMR
Direct Market Reseller, an umbrella expression for companies that sell directly to consumers online without running storefront operations of any kind (see "e-tailer").

DRI
Directly Responsible Individual. This person is held responsible for the completion of certain tasks, even if a whole team has to do the work.

End user
The end user is a popular concept in software engineering, referring to an abstraction of the *group* of persons who will ultimately operate a piece of software (i.e. the expected user or target-user).

ERP
Enterprise Resource Planning; a system that is used to manage and coordinate all the resources, information, and functions of a business.

e-tailer
An e-tailer is a retailer that primarily uses the internet as a medium for customers to shop for the goods or services provided.

Field marketing

Field marketing is a traditional discipline in marketing; it involves people distributing, auditing, selling or sampling promotions on the "field". Field marketing can be differentiated from all other direct marketing activities because it is face-to-face personal marketing. Field marketing includes highly targeted direct selling promotions, merchandising, auditing, sampling and demonstration, experiential marketing, organizing road shows and events.

Flag partner

A flag partner is another business or company that represents your business in a distant geographical area.

Funded head

A "funded head" is a distributor employee (at least in part) paid for by an ISV. Here's how it works: The distributor hires a new person and focuses their attention on the ISV's product line. While employed and managed by the distributor, a certain amount of direction comes from the ISV.

Horizontal market

A horizontal market is a market which meets a given need of a wide variety of industries, rather than a specific one. In technology, horizontal markets consist of customers that share a common need that exists in many or all industries.

KAM

A Key Account Manager is a person who takes responsibility for the development of the sales and general business relationship with certain key customers or partners (see "PAM").

Kick back

A reward given for good performance.

KPI

Key Performance Indicators; a set of quantifiable criteria that a company or industry measures in order to gauge, qualify or compare performance in terms of meeting strategic and operational goals.

Lead
An individual person or company that has been identified as potential customer and has to some extent been qualified with respect to individual needs and requirements

Lead pipeline
In correspondence to a sales pipeline (see "sales pipeline") the lead pipeline defines a systematic approach to processing an interested individual, termed a lead, through different steps of the sales cycle.

Lead management
The process of attempting to move a particular lead from one stage of the lead pipeline to the next.

Legacy solutions
An IT solution that is in place when a new solution is implemented. Often, the term legacy solution denotes a system that continues to be used because it works, even though newer technology would be available.

Letter of Intent (LoI)
A Letter of Intent is an agreement that describes in detail a corporation's intention to execute a corporate action. The management and legal counsel create the letter of intent to outline the details of the action.

Man day
An industrial unit of production equal to the work one person can produce in a day.

Market Development Funding (MDF)
Market Development Funding; funding of activities that may be executed by another company, but serve the purpose to improve the general sales opportunities of a company.

NFR
Not For Resale; a copy of the product that may not be sold, but only be used for testing or presentations.

PAM
Partner Account Manager; a person who assists and supports partners in achieving optimum results.

Peer group
A peer group, within the context of this book, represents a selected group of partners who share roughly the same characteristics such as size, business type or capability to serve a particular market.

Pipeline see "sales pipeline"

PPC
Pay per click (PPC) is an internet advertising model used on websites, where advertisers pay their host only when their ad is clicked. With search engines, advertisers typically bid on keyword phrases relevant to their target market.

PRM
A Partner Relationship Manager or Management is an individual employee or a unit who focuses on improving and exploiting the business relationship with business partners in order to increase the mutual benefit of the relation.

PS
Professional Services are technical services related to the implementation, individual configuration and operation of an IT solution.

QA
Quality Assurance is a crucial step in software development involving the testing of a product and reporting of the test results to the developing engineers in order to assure a certain level of quality of the product upon market entry.

R&D
Research and Development is the core unit in software development.

RFP
Request for Proposal; official request for a calculation of time and money that need to be invested in a defined project.

ROI
Return on Investment; earning power of assets measured as the ratio of the net income (profit less depreciation) to the average capital employed (or equity capital) in a firm or project.

SaaS
Software as a Service, often provided on fee-basis, in contrast to selling software as a license.

Sales pipeline
A sales pipeline, also known as a sales tunnel or a sales funnel is a systematic approach to selling a product or service.

SEO
Search Engine Optimization refers to the attempt to improve the ranking of a website when entering core business fields into search engines.

SI
System Integrator

SLA
Service Level Agreements define in what way a service will be made available to customers.

SMB
Small and medium-sized business; SMB denotes a market segment that groups companies from different branches as a homogeneous

group of potential customers with similar requirements due to the size of the enterprise

Spiff
Slang term for the sum paid by a vendor's salesperson to a retailer's salesperson to motivate him or her to push the vendor's goods.

TCO
Total Cost of Ownership; estimate of all direct and indirect costs associated with an asset or its acquisition over its entire life cycle.

VAD
Value Added Distributor. A distributor who combines a product and/or a service with another product in order to create a complete solution with greater value for the customer, e.g. in order to address a particular market segment.

VAR
Value Added Reseller. A reseller who combines a product and/or a service with another product in order to create a complete solution with greater value for the customer, e.g. in order to address a particular market segment.

Vertical market
A vertical market (often referred to simply as a "vertical") is a group of similar businesses e.g. lawyers, healthcare, and education.

Viral marketing
Viral marketing refers to marketing techniques that use social networks to increase brand awareness or to achieve other marketing objectives through self-replicating viral processes, analogous to the spread of virus or computer viruses. It can be word-of-mouth delivered or enhanced by the network effects of the internet.

Documents Available for Download

If you would like to use some of my calculation examples or need help getting started with your business plan, please go to www.channel-revolution.com to download the following list of helpful tools:

- Channel Strategy Plan

- Channel Partner Business Plan

- Distribution Agreement

- Funded Head Agreement

- Channel Partner Program: ValueCREATE!

- Pipeline Management Report

- White Papers

- Collection of Useful Links

- And more …

Made in the USA
Middletown, DE
10 November 2014